TERROR, COU

To the women who fight for peace
in times of terror and war

Acknowledgements

We would like to acknowledge the interest and help of several friends who helped us locate and access some of the essays in this anthology. Among them are Srilatha Batliwala, Lynette Dumble, Mary Fillmore, Ruth Frankenberg, Sarah A. John, Lata Mani, Ritu Menon, Bharati Sadasivam and Meredith Tax.

We are also grateful to the following newspapers, magazines and periodicals for generously allowing us to reproduce material originally published by them: *The Guardian Newspapers*, *The Hindu*, *the little magazine*, *Meridiens*, the Laura Susjin Agency, *The Nation*, *Pravada*, *The Progressive*, *The San Francisco Chronicle*, *Salon*, *Socialist Worker*; and Henry Holt and Company.

Contents

SECTION 5—THE WAR ON WOMEN

SECTION 6—DISPLACED/DISPOSSESSED

SECTION 7—WOMEN AGAINST WAR

Publisher's note

Terrorism is a matter of fact. Globally.

Peace is mostly a matter of faith; but both peace and terror are ultimately about power.

War, peace, terrorism, most fundamentalisms and fascisms are contracts between men—men make the rules, decide when and how wars are to be waged and for what; when to cease firing; when—and how and at what cost—peace is to be negotiated, or not. The history of peace-making around the world has demonstrated quite clearly that it is also about redistributing power—perhaps this is one reason why women, traditionally, have been part of neither war nor peace, except as ancillaries.

Feminists, who have been analysing relations of power between men and women for at least the last 30 years, have often been accused of waging a war between the sexes, disturbing the status quo, and of being "power-hungry"—simply wanting what men have. But, as all revolutions, and any amount of experiential, empirical and analytical writing has shown, a redistribution of power, including the power to make change, lies at the heart of any progressive, democratic politics. The struggle of the women's movement, world-wide, has been to alter the asymmetrical relations of power between men and women by uncovering their structural, systemic and social underpinnings.

The use of violence—against women, but also as a strategy for maintaining dominance—has been a critical rallying point for women's movements all over the world, and a crucial input in theorising women's subordinate status. Put simply, feminist analysis has identified violence, and the threat of violence against women, as an important weapon in patriarchy's arsenal. But violence also lies at the heart of war and terrorism and, over the years, women have documented and unravelled its workings with particular reference to women, in every recent major conflict in the world. Palestine, Argentina, Chile, Bosnia, Rwanda, Sri Lanka, Kosovo, Ireland, India and Pakistan... Afghanistan. Especially Afghanistan.

The UN Special Rapporteur on Violence Against Women has reported specifically on armed and ethnic conflict, and on violence under fundamentalism.

Much before the attack on the World Trade Center on September 11, 2001, women activists and academics drew the world's attention to the correspondence between rising levels of violence and violence against women, children and the dispossessed, especially in the countries of the South, and East Europe. As a feminist press that has grown out of the women's movement, as well as the women's studies movement, Kali has taken the initiative to bring together some of this important earlier writing, and women's responses to 9/11 and the events thereafter, as an expression of an old and consistent concern with the growing use of violence to resolve conflicts, north or south, east or west. As part of a movement that has, both, understood the use of violence at first hand and repudiated it as a valid means for changing power relations—whether of gender, class, caste, community or race—we hope this anthology will offer a perspective on peace and terror that has been ignored for too long.

Introduction

There is no doubt that the events of 9/11 were in themselves shocking and tragic. They resulted in the deaths of at least 3000 human beings from about 115 countries, not only in the buildings hit by aircraft turned into missiles but in the four hijacked planes used in the attacks. They caused widespread sorrow and suffering, fear and panic. They also led to considerable economic loss to individuals, families, companies and, indeed, economies across the globe.

They have had political repercussions, too, with an appreciable erosion of human rights, civil liberties and democratic values within many nations, including the US and India (the world's largest democracies), and the virtual suspension of established norms for the settlement of international disputes through peaceful, bilateral or multilateral negotiation and action. They have fuelled the ideology of militarism and the process of militarisation across the world, with even normally sensible and peaceable persons succumbing to the bizarre notion that violence is the only solution to violence.

It is not for nothing that 9/11 has come to be widely regarded as a turning point in global politics. In today's unipolar world there is a growing and disquieting tendency to assume, and even accept, that when the US sneezes the rest of the world must perforce catch a cold. However, the significance of 9/11 goes beyond such a response; indeed, it goes beyond the events of that day to encompass the reaction and response to them, especially by the American government. The fact is that a 9/11 syndrome has come into being that is, and will continue to be, invoked across the world, by governments as much as by militants, to justify violent means to achieve questionable ends.

Women are well placed to question this emerging syndrome and to expose both its shaky foundations and its precarious outcomes. Feminists have had a long history of engagement with the potent forces that promote such dangerous diagnoses and cataclysmic cures for the ills of the world, and with the powerful ideologies that underpin them. Women are in a position to challenge the renewed faith in violence that is an integral part of the 9/11 syndrome because they have long dealt with it at the experiential, practical and theoretical levels. They have faced violence in various forms and in different spheres of life from time immemorial. In times of peace, as well as war, their right to physical security is routinely violated through a range of violent acts, including rape, sexual harassment and sexual exploitation. During periods of social upheaval or political discord they experience heightened levels of violence and trauma, both physical and psychological, both within the home and outside it. Tension and strife are often used to curtail women's human rights in the name of culture and tradition, nationalism and patriotism. In times of conflict, they bear additional social and economic burdens as they often find themselves solely responsible for their families (including the very old, the very young, and the sick) under circumstances where even food and shelter are not always available. Yet their political right to participate in decision-making and governance is generally ignored, with their views seldom taken into account when wars are waged or when peace is negotiated.

Women's movements across the world have historically been involved in struggles to highlight and counter violence in different aspects of life, ranging from the domestic to the social and political. Building on women's direct experience and intimate knowledge of violence, they have redefined peace as not just the absence of war, as commonly understood, but the absence of violence in both public and private life.

Feminist scholars have made significant contributions to contemporary theories on violence in its multiple manifestations. For instance, they have examined the links between violence, militarism and patriarchy, and between different categories of violence, oppression and threats to security, pointing out that all these are mediated by factors like race, caste, class and gender. Some have argued that militarism and patriarchy are interdependent, while militarisation and conventional notions of masculinity are intertwined. They cite parallels between sexism and militarism, with the former propounding the notion that men are aggressive by nature and the latter proposing that the social order must be maintained through force. If patriarchal structures are reinforced by militarisation, they argue, the latter props up gender-based differences, affecting men and women in dissimilar ways. They point out that the sexual violence women often endure in situations of armed conflict is but one example of such gender-specific experiences of violence.

Few feminist scholars hold on to the illusion that all women are peaceful by nature; many now highlight the need for more analyses of women's material and ideological contribution to the militarisation process, and their own propensity to violence in certain circumstances. However, most acknowledge that women as a group have a special stake in peace, as demonstrated by the fact that women's movements have long been involved in struggles against violence of all kinds, at all levels of society.

Another significant feature of the 9/11 syndrome is a resurgence of narrow definitions of nationalism, national interest and national security. Again, women are particularly well-placed to question these concepts. Feminists have routinely challenged the traditional assumptions on which nationalism and national security doctrines, not to mention patriotism, are based. For example, most do not accept that the nation-state is the only or most significant source of political identification or allegiance. They propose that real security has to be less state-centric and more society-centred, and that there can be no security without social and economic justice, political liberty and egalitarian democratisation. They do not differentiate or discriminate between domestic, social and public violence, viewing all of them as equally violative of human rights. They perceive peace as the absence of violence in both the private and the public spheres, and believe that real security includes security within the home.

Women are also well-placed to challenge the 9/11 syndrome in terms of the legitimacy and respectability it has afforded to the "clash of civilizations" theory that divides the world into "us," symbolising all that is good and civilised, and "them," representing all that is evil and barbarous. If there is an intimate relationship between violence, militarism and patriarchy, there is an equally strong bond between that unholy trinity and what has come to be known, somewhat inaccurately, as "fundamentalism". Women's rights are among the first to be diminished by reactionary forces within society, including religious fundamentalists cutting across creeds and nations, rich and poor. It is no accident that women's movements have had a history of struggle against fundamentalisms of various kinds in different parts of the world. Feminists have critiqued the politics of identity promoted by diverse forms of fundamentalism and based on strategies of divide and rule, pointing out that women have more to lose than gain from associating with such regressive ideologies.

Likewise, women are in a position to understand and reveal the economic implications of the 9/11 syndrome. As human beings who wield little economic power but who bear the brunt of unjust economic structures and systems, as well as ill-conceived economic policies, women have an intimate knowledge of the links between economic and political power in various forms and at different levels. They are aware that their lack of economic clout has much to do with the fact that their productive and reproductive contributions to economies generally go unrecognised and unaccounted. Women's movements have initiated and participated in efforts to highlight and correct the resulting economic imbalances at the micro and macro levels. Feminist economists have made signal contributions to economic theory and analysis, providing alternative perspectives on major economic issues and developments. Women are, therefore, able to see the connections between economic globalisation and deprivation, militarism and terrorism.

The 9/11 syndrome also involves a revival of racial, ethnic and religious prejudice. Thanks to their experience of gender as a socially constructed system dividing human beings into two groups characterised by unequal status, rights and privileges, women know only too well how discriminatory, inequitable and oppressive other such systems can be, whether they are based on race, ethnicity, caste, religion or any other distinguishing factor. Although they do not constitute a numerical minority in most societies, women experience many of the disadvantages typically faced by minorities. Over the years women's movements across the world have learnt (the hard way) to be inclusive, to recognise that gender is one among many unjust social systems, to take on board the issues facing underprivileged minorities in various societies, and to provide time and space for women from such communities to define their own agendas. Feminist scholars have established the linkages between gender and other forms of unfair social stratification. Women are, therefore, in a unique position to expose the stereotypes and biases based on religion, race and ethnicity that underlie the 9/11 syndrome.

And, finally, women are well-placed to interrogate the divisive geo-political worldview promoted by the 9/11 syndrome. The women's movement is among the oldest of global movements. Over the years, through learning processes that have at times been hard and painful, they have begun to demonstrate the positive potential of a globalisation process based on equality, justice and mutual respect. Feminists know for a fact that patriarchy has no nationality and that gender cuts across geographical and other boundaries. They recognise that gender-based discrimination and oppression vary only in form and degree across societies and cultures. This awareness has helped them build bridges across social, cultural, economic and political difference. It has enabled them to construct an alternative worldview that seeks to unite people against all forms of oppression instead of creating demeaning, disruptive, destructive divisions among them. As the celebrated writer, Virginia Woolf, put it, "As a woman I have no country. As a woman I want no country. As a woman my country is the whole world."

Thanks to their long engagement with many of the problematic issues that underlie the 9/11 syndrome, women in general, and feminists in particular, are in a unique position to shed light on issues relating to war and terror. They have been writing on these issues for years. And, after September 11, women from different parts of the world responded to the events themselves and the processes they triggered off, drawing on the strength of women's experience, activism and knowledge over several decades. Many of these writings were scattered across publications, most of them inaccessible to people across the globe except via the Internet, which is still not widely available in many countries, including India.

As editors, we had a wide variety of material from which to choose. There were essays, trenchant journalistic comment, poetry and statements. Those that are included in this anthology represent but a sliver of the range of writing and thinking that have, over time, emerged from the pens and keyboards of women—writers, activists, academics, journalists—reflecting on war and conflict.

Several of the essays in this collection look at the overlap between militarism and terrorism—terms that seems interchangeable depending upon which side is using it. If acts of terrorism are deeds or threats of violence against ordinary, unarmed civilians, carried out in the pursuit of a political objective, as suggested by Rohini Hensman in her essay, then what is the difference between the actions of national armies and armed brigades of militants? For instance, are the terror tactics used by the military in the name of fighting "terrorism" any more justified than the suicide bombings which have come to be recognised as a signature strategy of "terrorists"?

Nowhere is this contradiction more apparent than in the political stand-off between Palestine and Israel, where one side's terrorist is the other side's soldier. Thus, when the Israeli army razes homes of Palestinians and strikes terror in their hearts or an Israeli missile attack on a building in a crowded area of the Gaza strip kills the leader of the Hamas but also 14 civilians, it is not regarded as terrorism. Yet the desperate response of young Palestinians turned suicide bombers — for whom death is more of a presence than life, and respite comes only when it is accompanied by flight, as Anisa Darwish writes in her "letters" in *Tinatol Waja* (Diary of the Al-Aqsa Intifada)—is automatically condemned as criminal and unacceptable.

Militarism and so-called terrorism are similar in their indifference to human life and the killing of innocents. Civilian deaths during war are written off as inevitable "collateral damage" while the loss of life in terrorist attacks is also considered a regrettable but unavoidable consequence of the battle for a cause. Furthermore, modern methods of warfare and the use of overwhelming force, as witnessed in the US military campaign against Afghanistan in 2001, have removed the "people" from "war". Carpet bombing of supposed military targets from an unreachable height was considered a safe option for the US military even as it devastated the countryside and killed innocent civilians. When the figures of civilian casualties were exposed in the press, US Defence Secretary Donald H. Rumsfeld was quoted as saying, "It's an unfortunate fact of war that, inevitably, innocent civilians are killed. This has been true, true throughout the history of warfare, and it remains true even in this age of advanced technology and precision-guided munitions." (*The New York Times*, July 23, 2002.) Such disregard for the loss of life during wars or in terrorist attacks has gone a long way in endorsing the use of force to settle political disputes, national and international. It has undercut the value of dialogue and negotiation. The Afghanistan campaign, in particular, has sent out one message: that dialogue can only follow the subjugation of "the enemy" by force.

It is this attitude towards warfare that has been questioned by many women. Even before the shock of the 9/11 events had worn off, women writers in the US presented a radically different perspective on these issues. Susan Sontag, for instance, asked why the term "cowardly" was used to describe the men who rammed commercial aircraft into the Twin Towers, while military bombing from an unreachable and safe height (as in Kosovo) was regarded as brave. Barbara and Rosa Ehrenreich argued that terrorists could be motivated by the same sense of duty, honour and sacrifice as soldiers in a war. After all, both sets of men are moved by a love of country or a cause that pushes them to kill others, or to die.

Women outside the United States also raised compelling questions about American foreign policy and its "war against terror". But, like Sontag, who was attacked for her statement and termed an "America hater", "moral idiot" and "traitor", they were also pilloried for being critical. Canadian academic Sunera Thobani, for example, was called morally bankrupt, an academic imposter and a hate-monger. On the other side of the Atlantic Ocean, Madeleine Bunting, a columnist for *The Guardian* experienced similar censure. She writes, "A stream of emails arrived from American readers with plenty of advice (get laid, get pregnant, shut your fat legs, shut up) and prognostications for my future (you'll be fired). One told me that I made them feel sick: 'untouched by our tragedy, yet [you] feel the right to criticize our country's actions'."

In India, we are familiar with the illiberalism with which any form of dissent or questioning on a range of issues is now met. Those who have argued against India's nuclear programme, its policy on Kashmir, its attitude towards Pakistan and towards other neighbours in the region are routinely attacked as unpatriotic and "anti-national." Such intolerance of even "thoughtful hesitation," as Barbara Kingsolver puts it, is particularly acute during times of war or conflict.

In an interview given after her controversial statement, Sontag asks why "debate equals dissent, and dissent equals lack of patriotism now." This raises an important question about the place and role of dissent at times when governments try and silence all criticism for what they project as "the greater good" of the nation. As experiences in the US and India, both democracies, have amply demonstrated, the governments' only concern is "the greater good" of the party in power. "National security" is a convenient peg on which to hang long-term agendas of managing, controlling and even silencing dissent, and "patriotism" is used to justify the isolation and persecution of inconvenient individuals, or communities.

What then is real "patriotism"? Does it always need to have a negative connotation? Does loving your country mean you have to hate others? In America, patriotism was reduced to flag-waving in the months immediately after September 11. Women were urged to do their patriotic duty by going out and shopping and thus contributing to economic revival. And if you were an Arab-American, or even someone who could be mistaken for an Arab, you had to literally wear the American flag on your sleeve to exhibit your loyalty to the country, and also to protect yourself from being attacked.

In other countries, such as India, patriotism has taken on a distinctly religious hue; majoritarianism and patriotism have been merged. Those who belong to a minority community, and more specifically the Muslims, are expected to go out of their way to "prove" their loyalty to the country by deferring to and endorsing the demands of the majority, in this case Hindu. Once India and Hindu are collapsed into one identity, anyone who falls outside this definition must necessarily establish his or her "patriotic" credentials.

Women writers have asked whether patriotism must necessarily be exclusionary, uncritical and aggressive. Does love of a nation mean that you care less for the rest of the world? Or is there a compassionate version of patriotism that is inclusive? Martha Nussbaum suggests that people cannot be asked to renounce patriotism any more than parents can give up their love for their children. But at the same time, love for our children, or our nation, does not mean we thwart the desires or abilities of other children, or other nations. The trouble arises when patriotism is reduced to shouting loudest and expressing your hate for other nations, "the enemy", or other people: then there is no room left for tolerance.

While concepts of what constitutes "patriotism" are politically determined, it is interesting to note how notions of honour and valour seem to carry the same resonance today as they did in times when war meant that men physically grappled with one another. They are essentially part of a masculinised culture, one that glorifies manhood and links it to conquest and victory in war. Dubravka Ugrešić, who writes about the war in the former Yugoslavia, describes the intertwining of the imagery of war and sex. War was projected, she writes, as an "attractive, exciting male adventure, less often as a holy, ascetic struggle for the homeland." And women, she says, were "post-boxes" who were used to send messages to other men, the enemy. Thus rape was justified as "quite a normal thing, it's part of the male psychology, it's irrational.... but it's a kind of negative complement to a woman, an ugly sexual blunder". The fact that even in the 21st century men can speak of rape, which has finally been recognised as a war crime, as no more than a "sexual blunder" emphasises the gendered aspect of war. Nelofer Pazira from Afghanistan also writes of the irony of honouring "war heroes" and thereby obscuring the destruction of human life that is the inevitable consequence of every war. From her personal experience, she says,

"War is a committed act of violence. It reproduces violence and cultural amnesia, not its opposite."

Women usually feature in the war landscape as victims in whose name wars must be fought. The most recent example is the bombing of Afghanistan. But this is an excuse that has been used from time immemorial. In the Afghanistan context, the cynicism attached to using the oppression of women as a reason to "free" the nation and its people is apparent. The Taliban were a creation of the very country that then decided to rid Afghanistan of them. Osama bin Laden's base in Afghanistan was the reason the country was bombed. Yet Osama, too, was a creation of the US, and his family had strong business links with the country he considered his prime enemy. Furthermore, few international leaders, including those in power in the US, cared about the fate of women under the Taliban despite the explicit information provided to them by Afghan women's groups like the Revolutionary Association of the Women of Afghanistan (RAWA) over several years. Yet, come September 11, suddenly the US and its allies found that they had to "save" Afghan women by bombing their tragically poor and devastated nation.

Ironically, at the end of this violent and destructive exercise, women's voices were barely heard. The negotiations for a new Afghanistan have remained firmly in the hands of Afghan men, many of whom have a record not much better than that of the Taliban when it comes to respect for women's rights. And at the Loya Jirga in June 2002, even the token women who had been included in the transition government were left out.

Displacement and flight are another aspect of war that impact women most. The burden of recreating home and life for their families in their new locations falls primarily on their shoulders. The over one million Afghan families who have lived for two decades in Pakistan, for instance, have developed their own tools of survival. Ayesha Khan narrates the first person account of Hafeeza, an Afghan refugee, whose experiences echo those of Kashmiri Hindu women displaced when Kashmir became the theatre of a shadow war between India and Pakistan. Sonia Jabbar describes their attempts to recreate the feel of their homeland in a refugee camp which has become their permanent address. And no one knows better the meaning of displacement and flight than the Palestinians. How, asks Anisa Darwish, "could one transport laughter or anguish or all the words one has said, the history of a place, as it were, that you know lingers unseen, like scent."

Yet, despite all this, women also constitute the largest constituency for peace. Within countries, and between countries at war, women have been in the forefront of movements to bring about peace and reconciliation. Even in that old and complicated arena of strife that has straddled many decades, West Asia, women on both sides of the divide have continued to strive for peace. When war and strife are constantly presented as the only option, the only way to resolve intractable situations, it is women who have consistently argued for dialogue as a viable alternative. In Palestine and Israel, even as women deal with the internal contradictions in their own societies, they have held on to the belief that there can be a solution without violence. Thus, they have joined hands to form the Jerusalem Link, a connection that has not been severed despite the growing violence which affects ordinary people on both sides. Gila Svirsky writes of the support this network provides to Palestinian families facing the trauma of seeing their homes demolished by Israeli bulldozers. And the reassertion of women's belief in a world where disputes need not be settled by war is echoed in the statements from women's groups from around the world included in this book.

The world after September 11 has been polarised once again, not into communist and capitalist as in the days of the Cold War but, as Rosalind Petchesky suggests, between "the permanent war machine (or permanent security state) and the regime of holy terror." Without implying equivalence between these two polarities, Petchesky points out the disturbing parallels, which she pictures as "phantom Twin Towers arising in the smoke clouds of the old—fraternal twins, not identical, locked in a battle over wealth, imperial aggrandizement and the meanings of masculinity."

War today is justified in the name of building a "safer" world but instead the world is being pushed into a higher state of insecurity. Thus, the US administration is pushing for a war against Iraq. But will this rid the world of terror? And, on the subcontinent, both India and Pakistan have justified their development of nuclear weapons in the name of "national security". But after the nuclear tests of 1998 both countries have faced more insecurity and been closer to war than at any other time in the last 30 years.

This polarisation has also enhanced divisions within many nations. Governments have used it to justify repression and discrimination. Oppressive laws have been enacted in the name of national security. In the US, the Patriot Act has been followed by the Terrorism Information and Prevention System where ordinary people are supposed to spy on their neighbours. Racial profiling has been accepted as a necessary evil. In Pakistan, an older Anti-Terrorist Act has been revived, while in India the Prevention of Terrorism Act has given law-enforcers increased powers to detain suspects without trial.

Worse, the consequence of the "war against terror" has manifested itself through greater insecurity and heightened divisions within nations as identity politics constructs a permanent atmosphere of hostility and fear, with a majority backed by the state and a minority forced to defend itself by any means. Rohini Hensman writes of "communalist terrorism" in this context. She defines communalism to mean "an adoption of identity based overwhelmingly on membership of a community, with corresponding isolation from or hostility to others." In practice, when this type of communalism is also backed by state force, atrocities like the systematic targetting and killing of Muslims by supporters of Hindu right-wing political groups that took place in the western Indian state of Gujarat in 2002, become possible.

And, as in war of the more conventional type, women are the worst victims of such terrorism. In Gujarat, we witnessed crimes against women of a kind rarely seen before in India despite its legacy of violent conflict between religious groups and castes. In that sense, it was a "gendered pogrom," as described by Anuradha Chenoy, because as in Bosnia, Rwanda or Afghanistan, aggression, violence and rape were seen as "proof of manhood". What happened in Gujarat, however, has a wider significance in the context of the new power formations in the world, for it demonstrates the inevitable consequences of a politics that demonises nations and people. In India, the relentless campaign by the Hindu Right to link Pakistan, a state formed in response to a demand by a section of Indian Muslims, to Muslims who stayed behind in India, laid the ground for what happened. The Hindu Right has harped on the fact that Indian Muslims had the option to choose to live in a Muslim state. According to them, if Muslims chose to remain in a predominantly Hindu India, they must bend to the will of the Hindu majority. This demand has arisen despite the fact that the Indian Constitution is secular and that the country has no official state religion.

The massacre of Muslims in Gujarat was preceded by a decades long campaign to inject suspicion and hatred of Muslims in the minds of ordinary Hindus. The politics of hate and sectarianism installed a Hindu nationalist party in power at the Centre for the first time in 50 years; this party also ruled the state of Gujarat. And in the months immediately preceding the killings, the Indian Parliament had been the target of a terrorist attack which brought India and Pakistan close to an all-out war. It is in this kind of situation that the Hindu Right linked the death of 60 Hindus in a train that was set on fire with a larger plan by "Muslim" Pakistan to attack "Hindu" India, and used the alleged link to virtually justify the brutal killings.

In such an atmosphere of virulent hatred, the shared histories of people are forgotten under the weight of hate, suspicion and a permanent state of conflict. We read this in Sonia Jabbar's moving essay on Kashmir, a land where Muslim and Hindu tradition sat comfortably together for centuries until divisive and communal politics created a permanent schism. Yet, even today some of these traditions survive. But for how long?

As the world hurtles towards greater conflict, fragmentation, poverty and deprivation, where are the voices of sanity, of hope, of conciliation, of healing? As this anthology will demonstrate, many of these voices are of women, in many different parts of the world. What they say has relevance over time, even if their words were prompted by particular moments in time.

AMMU JOSEPH
KALPANA SHARMA
October 2002

1
Personal/Political

Suheir Hammad

First writing since

1.
There have been no words.
I have not written one word.
no poetry in the ashes south of Canal Street.
no prose in the refrigerated trucks driving debris and DNA.
not one word.

Today is a week, and seven is of heavens, gods, science.
evident out my kitchen window is an abstract reality.
sky where once was steel.
smoke where once was flesh.

Fire in the city air, and I feared for my sister's life
in a way never before.
And then, and now, I fear for the rest of us.

First, please God, let it be a mistake, the pilot's heart
faiied, the plane's engine died.
then, please God, let it be a nightmare, wake me now.
please God, after the second plane, please, don't let it
be anyone who
looks like my brothers.

I do not know how bad a life has to break in order to kill.
I have never been so hungry that I willed hunger
I have never been so angry as to want to control a gun over a pen
not really. Even as a woman, as a Palestinian, as a
broken human being.
never this broken.

More than ever, I believe there is no difference.
The most privileged nation, most Americans do not know
the difference between Indians, Afghans, Syrians, Muslims,
Sikhs, Hindus.
more than ever, there is no difference.

2.
Thank you Korea for kimchi and bibim bob, and corn tea
and the genteel smiles of the wait staff at Wonjo—
The smiles never revealing the heat of the food
or how tired they must be working long midtown shifts.
Thank you Korea, for the belly craving that brought me
into the city late the night before
and diverted my daily train ride into the World Trade Center.

There are plenty of thank yous in NY right now.
Thank you for my lazy procrastinating late ass.
thank you to the germs that had me call in sick.
thank you, my attitude, you had me fired
the week before.
thank you for the train that never came,
the rude NYer who stole my cab going downtown.
thank you for the sense my mama gave me to run.
thank you for my legs,
my eyes, my life.

3.
The dead are called lost and their families hold up
shaky printouts in front of us through screens smoked up.
We are looking for Iris, mother of three.
Please call with any information.
we are searching for Priti, last seen on the 103rd floor.
She was talking to her husband on the phone and the line went.
please help us find George, also known as Adel.
his family is waiting for him with his favourite meal.
i am looking for my son, who was delivering coffee.
i am looking for my sister girl, she started her job on monday.

I am looking for peace.
I am looking for mercy.
I am looking for evidence of compassion.
any evidence of life.
I am looking for life.

4

Ricardo on the radio said in his accent thick as yuca,
"I will feel so much better when the first bombs drop over there, and my friends feel the same way."

On my block, a woman was crying in a car parked and stranded in hurt.
I offered comfort, extended a hand she did not see before she said,
"We're gonna burn them so bad, I swear, so bad."
My hand went to my head and my head went to the numbers within it of the dead Iraqi children, the dead in Nicaragua.
the dead in Rwanda who had to vie with fake sport wrestling for America's attention.

Yet when people sent emails saying, this was bound to happen, lets not forget US transgressions,
for half a second I felt resentful.
hold up with that, cause I live here, these are my friends and family,
and it could have been me in those buildings, and we're not bad people,
do not support america's bullying.
can I just have half a second to feel bad?

If I can find through this exhaust people who were left behind to mourn and to resist mass murder, I might be alright.

Thank you to the woman who saw me brinking my cool and blinking back tears.
She opened her arms before she asked, "Do you want a hug?"
A big white woman, and her embrace was the kind only

people with the warmth of flesh can offer.
I wasn't about to say no to any comfort.
"My brother's in the navy," I said. "and we're Arabs."
"Wow, you got double trouble."

5.

If one more person asks me if I knew the hijackers,
one more motherfucker asks me what navy my brother is in.
one more person assumes no Arabs or Muslims were killed.
one more person assumes they know me, or that I represent a people,
or that a people represent an evil,
or that evil is as simple as a flag and words on a page.

We did not vilify all white men when McVeigh bombed Oklahoma.
America did not give out his family's addresses or where he went to church.
or blame the Bible or Pat Robertson.
When the networks air footage of Palestinians dancing in the street,
there is no apology that these images are over a decade old.
that hungry children are bribed with sweets that
turn their teeth brown.
that correspondents edit images.
that archives are there to facilitate lazy and inaccurate journalism.

When we talk about holy books and hooded men and death,
why do we never mention the KKK?

If there are any people on earth who understand how New York is feeling right now,
they are in the West Bank and the Gaza Strip.

6.

Today it is ten days.
Last night Bush waged war on a man once openly funded by the CIA.
I do not know who is responsible

I read too many books, know too many people to believe what
I am told.
I don't give a fuck about bin Laden.
His vision of the world does not include me or those I love,
and petitions have been going around for years trying to
get the US sponsored Taliban out of power.
Shit is complicated and I don't know what to think,
but I know for sure who will pay in the world.
It will be women, mostly coloured and poor.
Women will have to bury children, and support themselves
through grief.

"Either you are with us, or with the terrorists"
—meaning, keep your people under control
and your resistance censored.
Meaning we got the loot and the nukes.

In America, it will be those amongst us who refuse blanket
attacks on the shivering,
those of us who work toward social justice, in support of
civil liberties, in opposition to hateful foreign policies.

I have never felt less American and more New Yorker—
particularly Brooklyn, than these past days.
The stars and stripes on all these cars and apartment windows
represent the dead as citizens first
—not family members, not lovers.
I feel like my skin is real thin,
and that my eyes are only going to get darker.
The future holds little light.

My baby brother is a man now, and on alert,
and praying five times a day that the orders that he will
take in a few days' time are righteous
and will not weigh his soul down from the afterlife
he deserves.

Both my brothers—my heart stops when I try to pray—
not a beat to disturb my fear.
One a rock god, the other a sergeant, and both
Palestinian, practising
Muslims, gentle men.
Both born in Brooklyn and their faces are of the
archetypal Arab man
all eyelashes and nose and beautiful color and stubborn hair.

What will their lives be like now?

Over there is over here

7.
All day, across the river, the smell of burning
rubber and limbs
floats through.
The sirens have stopped now.
The advertisers are back on the air.
The rescue workers are traumatized.
The skyline is brought back to human size,
no longer taunting the gods with its height.

I have not cried at all while writing this.
I cried when I saw those buildings collapse on themselves
like a broken heart.
I have never owned pain that needs to spread like that.
And I cry daily that my brothers return to our mother
safe and whole.

There is no poetry in this.
There are causes and effects.
There are symbols and ideologies.
Mad conspiracy here, and information we will never know.

There is death here and there are promises of more.

There is life here.
Anyone reading this is breathing, maybe hurting, but
breathing for sure.

And if there is any light to come
it will shine from the eyes of those who look for peace
and justice
after the rubble and rhetoric are cleared and the phoenix
has risen.

Affirm life.
Affirm life.
We've got to carry each other now.
You are either with life, or against it.
Affirm life.

Suheir Hammad, "Poet Laureate of the People's Republic of Brooklyn", is of Palestinian heritage. She edits the journal, Butter Phoenix, *is the author of the poetry collection, Born Palestinian, Born Black* (1996), *and is featured in* Listen Up! An Anthology of Spoken Word Poetry (1999). *A film producer, she is working on a film based on her memoirs.*

Robin Morgan

New York City
September 18, 2001

Ghosts and echoes

Dear Friends,

Your response to the email I sent on Day 2 of this calamity has been overwhelming. In addition to friends and colleagues, absolute strangers—in Serbia, Korea, Fiji, Zambia, all across North America—have replied, as have women's networks in places ranging from Senegal and Japan to Chile, Hong Kong, Saudi Arabia, even Iran. You've offered moving emotional support and asked for continued updates. I can't send regular reports/alerts as I did during the elections last November or the cabinet confirmation battles last year. But here's another try. Share this letter as you wish.

I'll focus on New York—my firsthand experience—but this doesn't mean any less anguish for the victims of the Washington or Pennsylvania calamities. Today was Day 8. Incredibly, a week has passed. Abnormal normalcy has settled in. Our usually contentious mayor (previously bad news for New Yorkers of color and for artists) has risen to this moment with efficiency, compassion, real leadership. The city is alive and dynamic. Below 14th Street, traffic is flowing again, mail is being delivered, newspapers are back. But very early this morning I walked east, then south almost to the tip of Manhattan Island. The 16-acre site itself is closed off, of course, as is a perimeter surrounding it controlled by the National Guard, used as a command post and staging area for rescue workers. Still, one is able to approach nearer to the area than was possible last weekend, since the law-court district and parts of the financial district are now open and (shakily) working. The closer one gets the more one sees—and smells—what no TV report, and very few print reports, have communicated. I find myself giving way to tears again and again, even as I write this.

If the first sights of last Tuesday seemed bizarrely like a George Lucas special-effects movie, now the directorial eye has changed: it's the grim lens of Agnes Varda, juxtaposed with images so surreal they could have been framed by Bunuel or Kurosawa. This was a bright, cloudless, early autumnal day. But as one draws near the site, the area looms out of a dense haze: one enters an atmosphere of dust, concrete powder, and plumes of smoke from fires still raging deep beneath the rubble (an estimated 2 million cubic yards of debris). Along lower 2nd Avenue, 10 refrigerator tractor-trailer trucks are parked, waiting; if you stand there a while, an NYC Medical Examiner van arrives—with a sagging body bag. Thick white ash, shards of broken glass, pebbles, and chunks of concrete cover street after street of parked cars for blocks outside the perimeter. Handprints on car windows and doors—handprints sliding downward—have been left like frantic graffiti. Sometimes there are messages finger-written in the ash: "U R Alive." You can look into closed shops, many with cracked or broken windows, and peer into another dimension: a wall-clock stopped at 9:10, restaurant tables meticulously set but now covered with two inches of ash, grocery shelves stacked with cans and produce bins piled high with apples and melons—all now powdered chalk-white. A moonscape of plenty. People walk unsteadily along these streets, wearing nosemasks against the still particle-full air, the stench of burning wire and plastic, erupted sewage; the smell of death, of decomposing flesh. Probably your TV coverage shows the chain-link fences aflutter with yellow ribbons, the makeshift shrines of candles, flowers, scribbled notes of mourning or of praise for the rescue workers that have sprung up everywhere—especially in front of firehouses, police stations, hospitals. What TV doesn't show you is that near Ground Zero the streets for blocks around are still, a week later, adrift in bits of paper—singed, torn, sodden pages: stock reports, trading printouts, shreds of appointment calendars, half of a "To-Do" list. What TV doesn't show you are scores of tiny charred corpses now swept into the gutters. Sparrows. Finches. They fly higher than pigeons, so they would have exploded outward, caught midair in a rush of flame, wings on fire as they fell. Who could have imagined it: the birds were burning.

From a distance, you can see the lattices of one of the Towers, its skeletal bones the sole remains, eerily beautiful in asymmetry, as if a new work of abstract art had been erected in a public space. Elsewhere, you see the transformation of institutions: The New School and New York University are missing persons' centers. A movie house is now a rest shelter, a Burger King a first-aid center, a Brooks Brothers' clothing store a body parts morgue, a record shop a haven for lost animals. Libraries are counseling centers. Ice-rinks are morgues. A bank is now a supply depot: in the first four days, it distributed 11,000 respirators and 25,000 pairs of protective gloves and suits. Nearby, a mobile medical unit housed in a Macdonald's has administered 70,000 tetanus shots. The brain tries to process the numbers: "only" 50,000 tons of debris had been cleared by yesterday, out of 1.2 million tons. The medical examiner's office has readied up to 20,000 DNA tests for unidentifiable cadaver parts. At all times, night and day, a minimum of 1000 people live and work on the site.

Such numbers daze the mind. It's the details—fragile, individual—that melt numbness into grief. An anklet with "Joyleen" engraved on it—found on an ankle. Just that: an ankle. A pair of hands—one brown, one white—clasped together. Just that. No wrists. A burly welder who drove from Ohio to help, saying softly, "We're working in a cemetery. I'm standing in—not on, in—a graveyard." Each lamppost, storefront, scaffolding, mailbox, is plastered with homemade photocopied posters, a racial/ethnic rainbow of faces and names: death the great leveler, not only of the financial CEOs—their images usually formal, white, male, older, with suit-and-tie—but the mailroom workers, receptionists, waiters. You pass enough of the MISSING posters and the faces, names, descriptions become familiar. The Albanian window-cleaner guy with the bushy eyebrows. The teenage Mexican dishwasher who had an American flag tattoo. The janitor's assistant who'd emigrated from Ethiopia. The Italian-American grandfather who was a doughnut-cart tender. The 23-year-old Chinese American junior pastry chef at the Windows on the World restaurant who'd gone in early that day so she could prep a business breakfast for 500. The firefighter who'd posed jauntily wearing his green shamrock necktie. The dapper African-American midlevel manager with a small gold ring in his ear who handled "minority affairs" for one of the companies. The middle-aged secretary laughing up at the camera from her wheelchair. The maintenance worker with a Polish name, holding his newborn baby. Most of the faces are smiling; most of the shots are family photos; many are recent wedding pictures. . .

I have little national patriotism, but I do have a passion for New York, partly for our gritty, secular energy of endurance, and because the world does come here: 80 countries had offices in the Twin Towers; 62 countries lost citizens in the catastrophe; an estimated 300 of our British cousins died, either in the planes or the buildings. My personal comfort is found not in ceremonies or prayer services but in watching the plain, truly heroic (a word usually misused) work of ordinary New Yorkers we take for granted every day, who have risen to this moment unpretentiously, too busy even to notice they're expressing the splendor of the human spirit: firefighters, medical aides, nurses, ER doctors, police officers, sanitation workers, construction-workers, ambulance drivers, structural engineers, crane operators, rescue worker "tunnel rats". . .

Meanwhile, across the US, the rhetoric of retaliation is in full-throated roar. Flag sales are up. Gun sales are up. Some radio stations have banned playing John Lennon's song, "Imagine." Despite appeals from all officials (even Bush), mosques are being attacked, firebombed; Arab Americans are hiding their children indoors; two murders in Arizona have already been categorized as hate crimes—one victim a Lebanese-American man and one a Sikh man who died merely for wearing a turban. (Need I say that there were not nationwide attacks against white Christian males after Timothy McVeigh was apprehended for the Oklahoma City bombing?) Last Thursday, right-wing televangelists Jerry Falwell and Pat Robertson (our home-grown American Taliban leaders) appeared on Robertson's TV show "The 700 Club," where Falwell blamed "the pagans, and the abortionists, and the feminists and the gays and lesbians. . . the American Civil Liberties Union, People for the American Way" and groups "who have tried to secularize America" for what occurred in New York. Robertson replied, "I totally concur." After even the Bush White House called the remarks "inappropriate," Falwell apologized (though he did not take back his sentiments); Robertson hasn't even apologized. (The program is carried by the Fox Family Channel, recently purchased by the Walt Disney Company—in case you'd like to register a protest.)

The sirens have lessened. But the drums have started. Funeral drums. War drums. A State of Emergency, with a call-up of 50,000 reservists to active duty. The Justice Department is seeking increased authority for wider surveillance, broader detention powers, wiretapping of persons (not, as previously, just phone numbers), and stringent press restrictions on military reporting.

And the petitions have begun. For justice but not vengeance. For a reasoned response but against escalating retaliatory violence. For vigilance about civil liberties. For the rights of innocent Muslim Americans. For "bombing" Afghanistan with food and medical parcels, NOT firepower. There will be the expectable peace marches, vigils, rallies. . . . One member of the House of Representatives—Barbara Lee, Democrat of California, an African-American woman—lodged the sole vote in both houses of Congress against giving Bush broadened powers for a war response, saying she didn't believe a massive military campaign would stop terrorism. (She could use letters of support: email her, if you wish, at barbara.lee@mail.house.gov.)

Those of us who have access to the media have been trying to get a different voice out. But ours are complex messages with long-term solutions-and this is a moment when people yearn for simplicity and short-term, facile answers. Still, I urge all of you to write letters to the editors of newspapers, call in to talk radio shows, and, for those of you who have media access—as activists, community leaders, elected or appointed officials, academic experts, whatever—to do as many interviews and TV programs as you can. Use the tool of the Internet. Talk about the root causes of terrorism, about the need to diminish this daily climate of patriarchal violence surrounding us in its state-sanctioned normalcy; the need to recognize people's despair over ever being heard, short of committing such dramatic, murderous acts; the need to address a desperation that becomes chronic after generations of suffering; the need to arouse that most subversive of emotions—empathy—for "the other", the need to eliminate hideous economic and political injustices, to reject all tribal/ethnic hatreds and fears, to repudiate religious fundamentalisms of every kind. Especially talk about the need to understand that we must expose the mystique of violence, separate it from how we conceive of excitement, eroticism, and "manhood"; the need to comprehend that violence differs in degree but is related in kind, that it thrives along a spectrum, as do its effects—from the battered child and raped woman who live in fear to an entire populace living in fear. Meanwhile, we cry and cry and cry. I don't even know who my tears are for anymore, because I keep seeing ghosts, I keep hearing echoes. The world's sympathy moves me deeply. Yet I hear echoes dying into silence: the world averting its attention from Rwanda's screams . . . Ground Zero is a huge mass grave. And I think: Bosnia. Uganda.

More than 5,400 people are missing and presumed dead (not even counting the Washington and Pennsylvania deaths). The TV anchors choke up: civilians, they say, my god, civilians. And I see ghosts. Hiroshima. Nagasaki. Dresden. Vietnam.

I watch the mask-covered mouths and noses on the street turn into the faces of Tokyo citizens who wear such masks every day against toxic pollution. I watch the scared eyes become the fearful eyes of women forced to wear the hejab or chador or burqa against their will . . .

I stare at the missing posters' photos and think of the Mothers of the Disappeared. And I see the ghosts of other faces. In photographs on the walls of Holocaust museums. In newspaper clippings from Haiti. In chronicles from Cambodia . . .

I worry for people who've lost their homes near the site, though I see how superbly social-service agencies are trying to meet their immediate and longer-term needs. But I see ghosts: the perpetually homeless who sleep on city streets, whose needs are never addressed. . . I watch normally unflappable New Yorkers flinch at loud noises, parents panic when their kids are late from school. And I see my Israeli feminist friends like Yvonne, who've lived with this dread for decades and still (even yesterday) stubbornly issue petitions insisting on peace. . . .

I watch sophisticates sob openly in the street, people who've lost workplaces, who don't know where their next paycheck will come from, who fear a contaminated water or food supply, who are afraid for their sons in the army, who are unnerved by security checkpoints, who are in mourning, who feel wounded, humiliated, outraged. And I see my friends like Zuhira in the refugee camps of Gaza or West Bank, Palestinian women who have lived in precisely that emotional condition—for four generations.

Last weekend, many Manhattanites left town to visit concerned families,try to normalize, get away for a break. As they streamed out of the city, I saw ghosts of other travelers: hundreds of thousands of Afghan refugees streaming toward their country's borders in what is to them habitual terror, trying to escape a drought-sucked country so war-devastated there's nothing left to bomb, a country with 50,000 disabled orphans and two million widows whose sole livelihood is begging; where the life expectancy of men is 42 and women 40; where women hunch in secret whispering lessons to girl children forbidden to go to school, women who risk death by beheading—for teaching a child to read.

The ghosts stretch out their hands. Now you know, they weep, gesturing at the carefree, insulated, indifferent, golden innocence that was my country's safety, arrogance, and pride. Why should it take such horror to make you see? the echoes sigh. Oh please, do you finally see? This is calamity. And opportunity. The United States—what so many of you call America—could choose now to begin to understand the world. And join it. Or not.

For now my window still displays no flag, my lapel sports no red-white and-blue ribbon. Instead, I weep for a city and a world. Instead, I cling to a different loyalty, affirming my un-flag, my un-anthem, my un-prayer—the defiant un-pledge of a madwoman who also had mere words as her only tools in a time of ignorance and carnage, Virginia Woolf: "As a woman I have no country. As a woman I want no country. As a woman my country is the whole world."

If this is treason, may I be worthy of it.

In mourning—and absurd, tenacious hope.

Robin Morgan is an award-winning writer, feminist leader, political theorist, journalist and editor, and has published seventeen books, including six of poetry, two of fiction, and the now-classic anthologies Sisterhood is Powerful *(1970) and* Sisterhood is Global *(1984). A founder of contemporary US feminism, she has also been a leader in the international women's movement for twenty-five years. Her latest books include* A Hot January: Poems, 1996–1999 *(2001),* Saturday's Child: A Memoir *(2000) and (reissued and updated)* The Demon Lover: The Roots of Terrorism *(1989, 2001).*

Nelofer Pazira

War: violation of human Life

Experience of war is something that no human being should ever go through. It is not like a nightmare, simply agonizing, frustrating and irritating. It is a traumatizing and not easily fogettable experience.

Spring 1989, I was still living inside Afghanistan. It was already ten years since the invasion of the country by the former Soviet Union. It was already a decade that the country was plunged into a war—involving Russia and the "freedom fighters" or "holy warriors" known as Mujahideen.

In that spring, no tree was blossoming, no grass was green, the air was thick and filthy with smoke, smelling of burning rubber and gas. Mujahideen were firing Katosha rockets from their base outside the city. The aim was to force people to flee and to show the communist government that it had lost its grip over the country

At night the Kabul sky lit up with fire. Katosha rockets, sounding like a long annoying scratching noise of a train wheel on the metal track, often landed with a horrifying explosion. There was sporadic shooting. One could follow the thin red line of the tracer bullets through the sky. A military depot—not far from our house—was on fire. The sound of explosion from the blazing depot was terrifying as it got louder and louder.

We were all in one room. My parents, my sister, two aunts, my grandmother and I were sitting on the floor, against the wall, holding our knees. Scared and lost, we were staring at each others' faces, in utter silence. No one had the strength to comfort the other.

As the early morning light broke, we were the living dead. We had no desire to move or speak. We were astonished that we could still sense the harsh ground underneath us. I did not want to see the night ever again.

I relived that horrible night on September 11 as I watched on television the smoke coming out of the World Trade Centre towers, the images of the desperate need-to-survive faces of the victims. Since then the same nightmare has been repeated over and over with the American attack on Afghanistan, the continuation of war, and the death of more Afghan civilians in "America's war on terror". The images are all too familiar; the war is all too real for me.

I wonder if those of my generation who have been born and raised in the West could relate to the war in the same way. Shortly after September 11, a Canadian friend told me that he cannot fully comprehend the North American media's comparision of the scene in New York to a "war zone". "It is irrelevant. I don't understand this description," he said.

Lucky for him, he has never known what it is like to be in a war. Unfortunately, thousands of people around the world can only wish that war was as alien to them as to my friend.

I do wonder if we actually realize the impact of war and its destructive nature. Especially since the understanding of war, at least for my generation in the West, begins and ends in Hollywood. War heroes are Hollywood's creation. War for those of us who have experienced it, does not have heroes. It only has victims. And women and children are almost always its least talked about victims.

What is astonishing is that in the West we have laws to protect human rights and civil liberties. We condemn human rights violations, but we have not come to regard war as one of the greatest violators of human rights. It is usually the outcome of the war that is percieved as a crime, not the act of war itself.

Those who die in battle are honoured. They are made into national heroes, respected and followed. The myth of "war heroes" justifies the brutality of war. It covers the ugly face of its havoc to the point that even mothers—the gentle graceful souls of the planet—accept the death of their sons in battle. The grotesque irony is that mourning the destruction of human life is celebrated as part of national pride and honour. The same standard is never applied to other forms of death. For instance, the death of civilians is a matter of mathematical uncertainty, a "disputed" number or a casualty, "collateral damage" as the North American media phrase it.

War is a committed act of violence. It reproduces violence and cultural amnesia, not its opposite. Afghanistan, the country of my origin, is its living example. The Mujahideen, who were funded by America and its allies during the 1980s, were the victims of the Cold War, not its heroes as most of us are persuaded to believe. It was then that an entire generation of Afghans grew up with war and in the war. After the collapse of the Soviet empire in the early 1990s, Mujahideen went on fighting. America and the West had lost interest in Afghanistan. Another generation of Afghans grew up in despair and torment produced by the violence of war. The Taliban became one of its by-products.

In Afghanistan, every day in the past 23 years, human rights have been abused. Innocent people have been imprisoned, tortured and killed. Defenceless Afghans, particularly women and children, have been made targets by all parties and groups involved. For two generations of Afghans fighting has become an occupation and the continuation of violence has brought about a pathology of warfare.

In the "civilized", technologically advanced western world war is not condemned as a form of violence. Perhaps it is because what we actually have come to oppose is the form of violence, not violence itself? What is the difference between killing someone with a lethal injection, slitting someone's throat with a knife, and blowing up people with bombs and rockets? The act—which is killing—is the same; it is only the form of the killing that we oppose. For example a calculated surgical death, such as the use of lethal injections, does not seem as appalling to us as slaughtering with a knife. Is the killing of human beings just a matter of relativity, differing by degrees and type—who we kill and how we come to kill them? Or, is it the act of violence—through military or non-military means—that we ought to despise?

I walked for ten days from Kabul to Pakistan with my family about a month after that horrific night in Kabul. We were lucky to survive. Many others did not. I hope for a day when we will not have any violations of civilians' rights, and war will only be an obsolete vocabulary in the dictionary of human history.

Nelofer Pazira, the Afghan-Canadian star of Kandahar, *is a journalist who has written widely on the treatment of women in Afghanistan.* Kandahar, *by the Iranian director Mohsen Makhmalbaf, is an attack on the corrupt ideology of the Taliban. Set in 1999, it describes the journey of Nafas, a journalist played by Pazira, who travels from the Iranian border with a series of guides toward Kandahar, Afghanistan's first capital and the centre of Taliban power. The film is based on Pazira's own story and is very much her film. She acted as interpreter and negotiator with the Afghan refugees in the border village where the film was made, and as script advisor on the fictional treatment of her story.*

2
The War on Terror?

Rohini Hensman

The only alternative to global terror

Father, son and holy war

My apologies to Anand Patwardhan, but I can't resist the temptation to borrow the title of his film as an apt description of what is happening in the world right now (i.e., October 2001, the month after the terrorist attacks in the US). Whether the father is Saudi billionaire Mohammed bin Laden, with his close ties to the Saudi royal family, the son is his estranged offspring Osama, who is enraged every time he thinks of infidel American troops stationed on the holy soil of Saudi Arabia, and the holy war is the *jihad* which the latter has declared against America and Americans; or the father is George Bush, Sr. who started it all with his war to defeat Saddam Hussein by gradually exterminating the people of Iraq, the son is George Jr., who has trouble opening his mouth without putting his foot in it, and the holy war is the crusade the latter has declared against—well, let us say vaguely specified enemies who happen to be Muslims—in both cases, the themes of religious communalism, militarism and machismo are inextricably intertwined.

There is even an uncanny similarity in the ways that the two sons think, if we ignore the cowboy rhetoric of one ("wanted—dead or alive," "smoke 'em outa their holes," etc.) and the pious expressions of the other ("may God mete them the punishment they deserve," etc.). Bush tells us, "either you are with us, or you are with the terrorists" Osama tells us the entire world is divided into "two regions—one of faith...and another of infidelity" (statement of 7/10/01). In other words, they both want us to believe that the population of the world is divided into two camps, one headed by Bush, the other by bin Laden.

If this is true, then we are heading into an epoch of unlimited violence and terror. South Asia is right at the centre of the conflict, and could suffer the most from it. For example, if the war goes on much longer, General Musharraf could be overthrown by even more extremist communal forces in Pakistan, who would then have nuclear weapons in their hands. On the other side of the border, there could well be a hidden agenda behind the BJP-led government's enthusiastic support for the US war. What do they hope to gain from it? Not US mediation in Kashmir to put pressure on Pakistan to stop cross-border terrorism—Foreign Minister Jaswant Singh made it very clear that mediation would not be welcome. Belligerent speeches by Kashmir's Chief Minister Farooq Abdullah and Home Minister L.K. Advani, as well as aggressive firing across the border the same day that corruption-tainted Defence Minister George Fernandes regained his ministry, suggest that what they want is the US go-ahead to do exactly what Big Brother is doing: i.e. to bomb Pakistan as the US is bombing Afghanistan, on the same pretext of "a war against those who harbour terrorists". That could be the prelude to a nuclear war.

For those of us who are opposed to both camps, the only way to avert such a catastrophe is to build a viable third alternative—a new non-aligned movement for human rights and democracy—at top speed. This will become obvious when we take a closer look at the two camps which have already constituted themselves. But first we need to be clear what we are talking about when we refer to "terrorism".

What do we mean by "terrorism"?

The first kind of definition of terrorism is lack of definition. Eqbal Ahmad, after going through at least twenty US documents on terrorism, came up with a surprising (or perhaps not so surprising) discovery: not once was terrorism defined, and he concluded that this was quite deliberate: "If you're not going to be consistent, you're not going to define" ("Terrorism: Theirs and Ours", Alternative Radio programme). Since September 11, we find the definition chopping and changing, according to expediency. First it is made clear that only acts of violence against US citizens are acts of terrorism; the same acts against citizens of other countries don't count. When some governments whose support the US wishes to retain question this, the definition is expanded slightly. At no point are similar acts of violence committed or supported by the US defined as terrorist.

Ranged against this are counter-definitions by anti-globalisers like Vandana Shiva, who classify hunger, poverty, unemployment and environmental degradation as terrorism; we can call this an economic reductionist type of definition. One problem is that it is so wide that it becomes impossible to define a strategy to fight it; it is a bit like trying to make tables, chairs, beds, windows and doors with a tool-kit consisting entirely and solely of a hammer: you end up unable to make any of them. Another problem is that terrorism as political violence is nowhere acknowledged, so that it becomes possible to join hands, as Vandana Shiva has done, with terrorists of the Sangh Parivar in the struggle against globalisation. I would say that even disasters like Bhopal and Chernobyl, which kill and injure tens of thousands of victims, should not be classified as terrorism, because they occur in the pursuit of economic gain and therefore require different remedies (e.g., health and safety and environmental legislation which makes them impossible). The US is not the only state whose definition of terrorism shifts according to who is the perpetrator and who is the victim. In Sri Lanka, the UNP and its supporters defined the JVP and Tamil militant groups as "terrorist" when these groups committed admittedly horrific acts of indiscriminate violence, but even more violent responses by the state and state-sponsored paramilitaries were, supposedly, not terrorism. The militants, on the other hand, denounce state terrorism, but would not call their own actions terrorist. In Kashmir, violence against civilians by militants from Pakistan are called terrorism by the Indian state, which does not, however, give the same name to its own violence against Kashmiri civilians; conversely, the Pakistani state refers to the militants as "freedom fighters" and denounces Indian state terrorism. It is not possible to fight something without knowing what it is.

Against this miasma of rhetoric, and taking off from dictionary definitions of "terrorism", I would say that acts of terrorism are acts or threats of violence against ordinary, unarmed civilians carried out in the pursuit of a political objective. It should be irrelevant whether the perpetrators are state parties or non-state parties, and other characteristics (like skin colour, ethnicity, gender, religion, nationality, sexual orientation, disability, social origin or anything else) of the perpetrators and victims should likewise be irrelevant. Further, the stated political objective should not come into the picture either, whether it is a religion, nationalism, national interest, national security, national liberation, democracy, socialism, communism, infinite justice or enduring freedom. A murderer's claimed motive does not change the fact of a murder.

In this connection, we need to dispense with another term: "collateral damage". In the context of terrorism as defined above, it makes no sense, because the purpose of terrorism is not to kill or injure people, that is merely a means to some political end. For example, in the case of the September 11 attacks, we cannot know for sure the motives of the hijackers because they are all dead, but if we assume for the sake of argument that they were in some way connected to Osama bin Laden, then the demands are very clear: the US must stop supporting Israeli aggression against the Palestinians; stop the bombing of Iraq and lift the sanctions against that country; stop supporting corrupt regimes in the Middle East; and move their armed forces out of Saudi Arabia. The purpose was not to kill all those people in the aeroplanes, the World Trade Center and the Pentagon; they were merely collateral damage.

Does that sound outrageous? Of course it does. Because we are not used to hearing dead Americans referred to as "collateral damage". But shouldn't it sound equally outrageous when Bush, Blair and their cohorts justify the killing of Afghan civilians in the bombing as "collateral damage"? According to Michael Tonry, Professor of Law at the University of Minnesota,

> In the criminal law, purpose and knowledge are equally culpable states of mind. An action taken with a purpose to kill is no more culpable than an action taken with some other purpose in mind but with knowledge that a death will probably result. Blowing up an airplane to kill a passenger is equivalent to blowing up an airplane

to destroy a fake painting and thereby to defraud an insurance company, knowing that the passenger will be killed. Both are murder. Most people would find the latter killing more despicable ("Malign Neglect", A.J. Chien, *The Civilian Toll*, Institute for Health and Social Justice, October 11, p. 32).

So let us forget about collateral damage. Murder is murder, and mass murder is mass murder. Terrorist acts which result in mass murder can additionally be defined as crimes against humanity.

It seems to me that this could be a functional definition of terrorism or acts of terrorism, which can be agreed upon by pacifists as well as those who believe that armed resistance to armed aggression is justified. Fighting between combatants would not count as terrorism. Only minimal grey areas are left; for example, those cases where settlers on land seized from others by acts of terrorism either defend their gains with arms or are defended by armed forces, as in the case of the Israeli settlers in the occupied territories of Palestine, whom Nigel Harris graphically describes as "Jewish Taliban and Zionist Red Necks"("Collapse of the Peace Process", *Economic and Political Weekly*, 15/9/01). In such cases, I would say that adult settlers cannot be regarded as innocent unarmed civilians, whereas children can. Another problematic case would be that of a politician who advocates and promotes the transfer of populations (a crime against humanity according to the Nuremburg Principles articulated to prosecute Nazi war criminals), such as Israeli Minister Rehavam Ze'evi, who is assassinated. All one can say is that if that is terrorism, so was the attempted assassination of Hitler.

The bin Laden-Taliban camp: communalist terrorism

I prefer the term "communalism", as used in South Asia, to the more commonly-used "fundamentalism", for two reasons. One: communalism, meaning an adoption of identity based overwhelmingly on membership of a community, with corresponding isolation from or hostility to others—ranging from opposition to intermarriage to genocidal massacres—is a much broader term. It can encompass identities based not only on different religions, but on different ethnic groups, and on sects within the same religion (Shia and Sunni, Protestant and Catholic, etc.) Two: claims of fundamentalists that they are defending the "fundamentals" of their religion have convincingly been contested by theologians of those same religions; it is therefore a misleading term, suggesting that more humane interpretations are somehow less authentic.

Attacks like those of September 11 were unprecedented in the US, but not in our countries. Indeed, almost nine years earlier we felt the same horror and fear when a terrorist attack brought down the Babri mosque, accompanied and followed by anti-Muslim riots which took a death toll similar to that of the US attacks. So, unlike several consecutive US administrations which have supported and still continue to support communal forces in our countries (more about this later) many of us, especially women, have long recognised the dire danger posed to women's rights in particular, and human rights and democracy in general, by communal terrorism, and have been battling against it for decades.

The hell that women have gone through under the Taliban—girls and women denied education, women not allowed to earn a living, even if the only alternative for them and their children is death by starvation, not allowed to go out except covered from head to foot by a burqa and accompanied by a male relative, brutal punishments including stoning to death or being buried alive if they break any of the draconian rules imposed on them—these are only the most extreme examples of the violation of women's rights, which is much more widespread. And while patriarchal authority in its Islamic form receives the widest publicity, let us remember that other forms—like the common practice of female infanticide in India, bride-burning, ill-treatment of widows, and the lynching of young people who have out-of-caste relationships—can be just as barbaric. Other forms of communal terrorism may provide more space for women, and the LTTE even encourages them to become suicide bombers, but all this is premised on blind support for the supreme leader. The penalty for independent thought, expression or action, as Rajani Thiranagama and Sarojini Yogeswaran found to their cost, is death.

The suppression of women's rights goes along with a more general authoritarian control over what members of the religious or ethnic community may or may not say and do. Depending on the degree of power the communal group enjoys, punishments for those who refuse to abandon the struggle for human rights and democracy can vary from social boycott, to beatings (e.g., Asghar Ali Engineer), to death (notably Neelan Thiruchelvam). But the greatest violence is directed outward, towards other ethnic/religious communities. Massacres of the type that the Taliban inflicted on non-Pashtun tribes in Afghanistan (which warlords of those tribes also carried out when they were in a position to do so) are familiar in India, Pakistan, Sri Lanka, Bangladesh. They have been carried out in the name of Islam, Hinduism, Buddhism, Sinhala, Tamil and a whole range of other ethnic nationalisms. The victims, starting from the Partition riots, add up to millions dead, apart from massive displacement and destruction of livelihoods.

Nor is this kind of terrorism confined to South Asia. Rwanda, East Timor and the Balkans have recently seen horrific communal killings. They can even be seen as genocidal, if genocide is seen not as an attempt to exterminate a people from the whole face of the earth but, rather, to clear them out of the territory controlled by a particular ethnic or religious group. How can we explain such terrorism? This is important if we wish to combat it. One popular explanation is that terrorism is a response to oppression, but I am not happy with this. If this is true, why is it that millions of exploited and oppressed people throughout the world never become terrorists? Why is it that women, who are the most oppressed of the oppressed, rarely go down this path, since it is not biologically impossible, as the female fighters of the LTTE show?

Secondly, there is a fine line between explanation and justification, and I fear that this explanation slips over the line into justification. Thus, for example, Steve Cohen, who correctly makes a clear distinction between Jews and Zionists, actually blurs the distinction when he goes on to explain Zionism as a response to anti-semitism ("That's Funny, You Don't Look Anti-Semitic"). That, I feel, is an insult to all those Jewish people who suffer anti-semitism without endorsing ethnic cleansing. It is entirely legitimate and understandable for people who suffer constant persecution and regular pogroms to wish for a place where they can live in security and dignity. It is quite something else to create this place by clearing out the majority of the indigenous population by murderous terror. The same goes for Sri Lanka Tamils: the craving for a homeland where one can be safe and enjoy equal rights is absolutely justified; trying to create it by driving out and killing ordinary Sinhalese and Muslims is not justifiable, as all my research suggests that the majority of Tamil people would agree.

Thirdly, this explanation ignores terrorist movements within Europe and the US, like those who were responsible for the Oklahoma bombing and are now suspected of spreading anthrax. This newspaper report is highly revealing:

> The FBI's domestic terrorism unit is investigating the possible role of illegal militia groups in the spate of anthrax outbreaks in Florida and New York. Timothy McVeigh, the Oklahoma bomber who killed 168 people when he blew up a federal building in 1995, was a supporter of one such group, the National Alliance.
>
> Others have threatened to use biological weapons, including anthrax, botulism, and ricin in their struggle against what they see as a global conspiracy between the US administration and the United Nations to disarm and enslave them. Every state has its own "patriot" group of disaffected right-wing Christian radicals opposed to central government and federal regulations. Most are organised along paramilitary lines. The FBI estimates their numbers at up to 40,000, with the larger militias in backwoods country areas. They claim they are mobilising to fight the "New World Order".
>
> In places like Idaho, Texas, Montana and West Virginia, they wear army surplus camouflage uniforms and train with assault rifles and explosives against the day when they might have to defend themselves against direct interference from the federal authorities. They range in outlook from Pat Robertson, a failed 1988 presidential candidate, with his vision of a "Christian America" to the sinister Posse Comitatus, Aryan Nations and Minnesota Patriots' Council, who favour armed insurrection. . .
>
> Most of the militias' philosophy is based on white-supremacist principles, looking down on blacks as "mud people" and Jews as instigators of the global plot against them and manipulators of the

world economy for their own benefit. Despite their redneck reputation, they have developed a sophisticated communications network using computer e-mail, shortwave radio, and fax. The North American Patriots, a group with members from California to Kansas, publish a newsletter entitled *Firearms and Freedom*. . . In January 1999, police and security forces responded to 30 anthrax hoaxes in southern California alone. Since then there have been thousands of false alarms across the country. Many aimed at government buildings, including deliveries of envelopes containing suspicious white powder, were militia inspired. (Ian Bruce, *The Herald*, 16/10/2001.)

These people, who bomb Black churches, synagogues, abortion clinics and gay bars, are clearly not reacting to oppression to what they see as unwarranted restrictions on their "right" to oppress.

When capitalism develops, it produces broadly speaking, three types of social forces: the old dominant elites, the bourgeoisie, and the working classes. In colonies, the bourgeoisie is further split into the imperialist ruling class and the nascent local capitalist class. Each of these forces is pitched against all the others, but in specific conjunctures, depending on who is perceived as the greatest enemy, they may make pragmatic alliances. My own feeling is that communal terrorism represents a resistance to social change from traditional dominant groups, whose power is undermined by the development of what has been called bourgeois democracy or modernity. Patriarchy, clerical power, monarchy in some countries, hierarchical caste domination in India: these are the values they uphold. But they are internally divided into those who seek an accommodation with modernity while preserving traditional values, and those who represent an all-out rejection of modernity and everything that goes with it. The governments of India, Pakistan and Saudi Arabia are examples of the former variant, hence their ability—even obscene eagerness in the case of India—to join the US-led alliance. The RSS, VHP, jihadi groups in Pakistan, Osama bin Laden and the Taliban are examples of the latter. They are certainly not seeking to put an end to oppression: far from it. The whole basis of the way of life they seek to perpetuate is that all human beings are not born equal, are not entitled to equal respect as persons.

And yet, their resistance to a certain type of oppression, usually associated with foreigners and especially the West, provides them with an appeal for oppressed people who do not see effective resistance to their oppression coming from anywhere else. This is clearly the reason why Osama bin Laden has become an icon to so many. What does he protest against in public? US support for Israel's murderous occupation of Palestine, where Palestinians who were driven out decades ago are barred from returning while more land is occupied (in clear violation of several UN resolutions) and more Palestinians are being killed every day; the bombing of Iraq, which killed around 200,000 at the time of the war, many of them conscripts massacred while retreating from Kuwait; and sanctions against Iraq which have killed 1.5 million civilians, including some 540,000 children; support for corrupt and undemocratic regimes in West Asia; and now the bombing of Afghanistan. Don't these causes strike a chord with us? They certainly do with me. I don't have to be the mother of the Palestinian child shot dead while he crouched terrified by his father, the young man conscripted to fight for Saddam Hussein and killed by the US in cold blood, the Iraqi child dying of leukemia from exposure to depleted uranium; I don't even have to be an Arab or a Muslim to feel grief and fury at the cruelty and injustice of it all, at the apparent failure of all legal and democratic attempts to enforce respect for human rights. So is it surprising that people who are not necessarily aware of Osama bin Laden's real agenda regard him as a hero for highlighting these iniquities? Is it surprising if boys and men burning to wipe out the humiliation, and in some cases bereavement they have been subjected to, are attracted to groups like Al Qa'ida, just as some of the many war-traumatised Tamil children in Sri Lanka might join the LTTE in order take revenge against "the Sinhalese"? In this more complex sense, perhaps, imperialist oppression legitimises terrorism and provides it with recruits.

For us, however, opposition to communal terrorism is a matter of survival, and this means we have to be equally opposed to the Bush camp. What, after all, do they stand for?

Imperialism—and this mean not merely economic exploitation but actual political and/or military subjugation, as even Lenin acknowledged—takes different forms. In South Asia it was relatively mild, certainly using sufficient brutality to subjugate the "natives", but not clearing them out with wholesale massacres. In the Americas and Australia, by contrast, the indigenous population was virtually wiped out by the European colonisers. Africa was devastated by the slave trade, in which tens of millions of Africans perished, apart from being colonised. Apartheid represents a half-way house between ethnic cleansing of the indigenous population and allowing them to remain where they are: they are herded into Bantustans from where their labour power can be used by the colonisers. Israel initially appeared to adopt the apartheid model, but more recently seems to be attempting to wipe out the Palestinians from Palestine altogether. The colonies of tsarist Russia briefly seemed to be destined for self-determination after the revolution, but Stalinism soon reverted to imperial domination over the Central Asian peoples, some of whom were ruthlessly massacred.

World War II ended with the dropping of nuclear bombs on Hiroshima and Nagasaki, proving (for those who needed proof) that it was not a war against fascism on the part of the Allies but an inter-imperialist war to re-divide the world between imperialist powers, where this crime against humanity could be justified as a demonstration of naked military might. Post-war, while one colony after another achieved independence, the Cold War provided the basis for a different type of imperialist strategy. In the name of the struggle against "communism", the US installed and propped up brutal fascist dictatorships throughout the world, from Latin America to Indonesia. Where these failed to hold up, as in Cuba and Vietnam, it intervened directly. Tens of millions were killed in these actions to stamp out democracy in the name of democracy. This is why, for most people in the world, the US and the "American way of life" are associated not with democracy and freedom but their very opposite: authoritarian dictatorships, rape, torture, death squads and massacres. The Soviet Union, for its part, mostly restricted its military interventions to the parts of the world that had been awarded to it as the spoils of war—its own empire in Central Asia, now extended by the "Eastern Bloc" in Eastern and Central Europe—while also attempting to extend its influence elsewhere. One of the few countries outside its own "sphere", which it invaded and occupied, was Afghanistan, in 1979.

Imperialism is premised on racism: the belief that humankind is divided into different "races", of whom the European or Caucasian or White or Aryan "race" is superior to all the rest. Only such a premise can legitimise the wholesale domination, enslavement or extermination of other peoples. Those who understand imperialism purely in terms of monopoly capitalism miss this dimension. No doubt capitalism is brutal and oppressive, and certainly contains an element of what might be called class racism in the way that the lives and health of workers, including child labourers, are treated. Yet the rationale of this is the production of profit and the accumulation of capital. The quest for control over sources of raw materials, markets and labour power is certainly an element in imperialism. Yet if this were its sole rationale, then one would expect populations in the colonies to be treated in the same way as those in the imperialist countries, and this has not been the case.

Thus although there was intensive bombing of Germany in the final stages of the war, the German people were not chosen as guinea-pigs to test the destructive potential of nuclear weapons. No European country was subjected to the intensive chemical warfare waged against Vietnam, where children were set on fire with napalm and others are still born with birth defects, and land is still unusable as a result of bombardment with Agent Orange. The bombing of Yugoslavia, representaive though it was, was not on anything like the same scale as the bombing of Iraq, nor was it followed by sanctions which took a similar toll on civilian life. I still remember how stunned I was to read a report of Madeleine Albright's response in 1996 to an interviewer who pointed out that half a million children had died as a result of sanctions against Iraq, and asked whether she thought it was worth it? She replied that although it was a hard choice, "We think the price is worth it." That's unbelievable, I thought; either this woman is a psychopath who could just as easily round up 500,000 European-American kids and kill them off at a rate of 1,000 per week, or she thinks of Iraqis—and probably coloured people in general—as some kind of sub-human species who can be slaughtered in the pursuit of political gain.

The same kind of racism is apparent in the treatment of Afghanistan, beginning with the Soviet occupation. It is estimated that at least a million Afghans died in the war against the Soviets, who also took the chance to litter the country with millions of anti-personnel landmines during their occupation, as a result of which civilians are still being blown up and crippled or killed every day. And now this new war. Who are being killed in this so-called war against terrorism, despite the blatant lies which White House and Pentagon officials are doubtless paid to put out? Even if we discount reports of hundreds of civilian casualities by the Taliban and Al-Jazeera TV (despite the fact that they are confirmed by lakhs of refugees fleeing the carnage, and foreign reporters who were invited in by the Taliban), doesn't it seem strange that one of the earliest strikes was against the UN mine-clearing facility in a civilian area, killing four workers and destroying the building along with the equipment? And this despite the fact that the UN had earlier notified the US of the location of its offices? Why was a Red Cross office with huge stores of food aid bombed, despite the fact that it could be identified by the huge red cross on its roof? There are only two ways these incidents can be explained: either the bombs are falling way off their supposed military targets and the Pentagon knows it, or civilian facilities and civilians are deliberately being targeted. Take your pick.

However, this is not the only death toll resulting from the bombing. Right from the beginning, aid agencies have been warning that unless massive amounts of food aid are transported to various locations, including remote villages, before the winter makes roads impassable by mid-November, up to seven-and-a-half million people could starve to death. Every day that bombing continues therefore means that lakhs more people will starve. The same agencies have pointed out that the surreal exercise of dropping food packets during bombing raids could at best keep some tens of thousands of people alive for one more day (after which they will die anyway); at worst it could result in people getting blown up by landmines as they run for the food. This may serve as a justification for people who can't count, or for pilots who would not like to think of themselves as murderers blowing up women with small children, the elderly, the crippled—i.e., those unable to run away from the bombing, but it is no use to the starving people of Afghanistan. Total civilian causalities as a result of the bombing are likely to be several millions. When you look at the NATO alliance backing the war, its racist nature becomes explicable. All the imperialist countries are there including, this time, Russia, represented by ex-KGB agent Putin. Why hasn't anyone suggested bombing the US to get rid of the right-wing militias which are apparently present in every state? What can explain these double standards, if not racism?

In other words, this type of terrorism and the kind represented by Al Qa'ida share some basic premises in common: all human beings are not born equal, and it is justifiable to kill innocent civilians in the pursuit of a political objective. This is what allows them to coexist and collaborate with each other so easily. It is what allowed the US to pour money, arms and training into the Pakistani ISI, and through them to the Taliban, the Northern warlords and Osama bin Laden from 1979 onwards, "aid" that has had a devastating fallout not only for the women of Afghanistan, but also for those of Pakistan and Kashmir, where for the first time women were recently subjected to acid attacks for not wearing a burqa. It is what allows the US to continue to have a close alliance with Saudi Arabia, where women are treated scarcely any better than they are by the Taliban—a cozy relationship best exemplified by the business association of Bush the father with bin Laden the father in the Carlyle Group, whose investments in armaments could mean that both fathers profit from the war declared by their sons! (see *Wall Street Journal*, 27/9/2001). It is what allowed the Israeli state to promote Hamas in its effort to undermine the secular elements in the Palestinin liberation struggle. Finally, it is also the reason why President Bush can still ally himself with the warlords of the Northern Alliance, none of whom accept voting rights for women and, as the Revolutionary Association of the Women of Afghanistan (RAWA) have repeatedly told us, raped, looted and massacred their way through the regions they captured after 1992.

At the same time, because these opposing forces are so similar to each other in their propensity to violate human and democratic rights, they also reinforce each other. There is credible evidence that the US was already planning an attack on the Taliban even before the September 11 events, but the terrorist strikes provided an excellent pretext for that attack. Many people who would have objected if the war appeared to be motivated by the desire to build an oil pipeline through Afghanistan, were disarmed by the claim that the purpose was a "war against terrorism". Those of us who still object have a much harder task to convince others that this war is a crime against humanity. Unlike the self-immolation of the Buddhist monks in Vietnam to draw the world's attention to the rape of their country, the September 11 gestures could easily be co-opted by the imperialist agenda. On the other side, Bush has reacted exactly as bin Laden would have wanted him to; if I were cartoonist, I would draw a picture of the former as a puppet with the latter pulling the strings. Millions of people around the world, some of whom can hardly have heard of Osama bin Laden before, now regard him as a hero; and if the CIA kills him without any convincing proof of his guilt, as they have now apparently been authorised to do, that will elevate him to the status of a martyr, silenced because he spoke up for the oppressed.

So the apparent choice—Bush or bin Laden—is really no choice at all. What alternative do we have?

A worldwide movement for human rights and democracy

Freedom from forced labour, freedom of expression and association, equal rights and opportunities, the right to elect one's representatives to government—these are usually referred to as "bourgeois democracy". The implication is that these are values upheld by the bourgeoisie, but I disagree. My contention is that these are values fought for spontaneously by working people throughout the world, especially working women, and supported only sporadically by the bourgeoisie, whose only values are the right to property and the freedom to exploit. One indication is provided by the struggle for universal adult suffrage. The original idea was that only males with property would have the right to vote; the dispossessed and women had to fight against these restrictions, and only working class women and those who supported them were steadfastly in favour of universal adult suffrage.

Another indication is the ease with which the bourgeoisie attacks so-called bourgeois democracy, and the fact that fascism too is a form of bourgeois rule, despite its negation of all the rights and freedoms listed earlier. The US, for all its tall claims to be a defender of democracy, has attacked it not only abroad but even at home. The McCarthy years saw a fascistic attack on democratic rights, and many observers have commented that similar forces are at work post-September 11—restrictions on the right to information, freedom of expression and association, the right to privacy, etc. A speaker at a meeting in Bombay who had recently returned from the US said that the ubiquitous Stars and Stripes reminded him of the Swastika displayed everywhere in Nazi Germany. Vicious attacks on dissenters, not only by the state but by other citizens, are evidence of fascism developing as a mass movement. And the fact that Congress, with the sole dissenting voice of Congresswoman Barbara Lee, voted to give unelected President George Bush, Jr. almost unlimited powers for military attacks on anyone, anywhere in the world, in violation of international law, the UN Charter and the US Constitution, suggests uncomfortable parallels with other regimes of absolute power. Let us be very clear: this may be the American way of life according to George Bush, but it is not democracy.

Both sides in the Cold War propagated the notion that socialism and communism were the opposite of democracy, yet when these ideals were first put forward, they constituted not a negation but a further development of democratic control over spheres from which it is normally excluded even under "bourgeois democracy", notably production relations and distribution of wealth, the repressive apparatus of the state, and international relations. However, the Soviet Union's use of these terms to describe policies which ruthlessly crushed democratic rights both at home and abroad, all but wiped out the memory of what these ideals had originally meant. If the destruction of Afghanistan is one of the tragic consequences of the Cold War, the destruction of the notions of democracy, socialism and communism are in a different way equally tragic, because they deprive us of a language in which to argue for the interests of the third social force, the working people of the world. Again, I reject the notion that these ideals are "alien" to us in the Third World. Perhaps they were articulated first by spokespeople like Kant, Marx and Sylvia Pankhurst because capitalism, and therefore the working class, had developed further in Europe than the rest of the world in the 18th, 19th and 20th centuries. But ordinary working people anywhere in the world can respond to them if they are explained in a comprehensible manner.

This, I think, is the task that faces us. We need to create a culture where these values are taken for granted, in opposition to the values of both communal and imperialist terrorism, and we need to do it on a global scale. That's a massive task, but let me suggest a few starting points here.

1. Given the present context, we need to take an absolutely clear stand on the politics of both types of terrorism, and explain why it is necessary to do so. We have to insist on secular states in our countries, neither Hindu, Islamic, Buddhist, Sinhala or Tamil, because a state that is tied to any particular religious or ethnic group cannot be democratic. In elections—for example, the forthcoming parliamentary elections in Sri Lanka and assembly elections in Uttar Pradesh in India, both of which will be crucially important—the record of every candidate and party in terms of human rights and secularism should be examined, and support extended or withheld accordingly. Sadly, there may be many cases where we have to make do with the lesser of two evils rather than a positive good, but there is always a choice. At the same time, we have to explain to those who

have illusions in the US (and that includes the majority of Americans!) why, as Gulf War resistor Jeff Paterson put it, "Now, more than ever, the people of the world are not safe from the US, and the people in the US are not safe from the US" ("A Message to Troops, Would-be Troops and Other Youth," 15/10/01)

2. Wherever there are ongoing conflicts, as in Sri Lanka, Kashmir and many other places in the subcontinent, we must insist that the first priority for any resolution must be to safeguard the human and democratic rights of all those concerned—national minorities as well as local minorities, women, etc—and this, again, cannot take place except within a genuinely secular state. Some 'peace' campaigners think it is possible to sidestep this issue, but any 'peace accord' which allows for continuing violation of fundamental rights will not last long.
3. Conflicts in other parts of the world affect us, as this latest crisis has shown, and we need to press for a just resolution of them too. In the current situation, the most urgent issues are: *(a) Afghanistan:* an immediate end to the bombing—since many legal experts have argued that it is illegal according to international law, and the death of civilians as a result of it constitute a crime against humanity—and resumption of food and other aid, protected by UN peace-keepers if necessary; prosecution of those responsible for the terrorist attack of September 11 as well as others who have committed crimes against humanity in the International Criminal Court. *(b) Iraq:* an immediate end to the bombing, and lifting of sanctions, so that adequate food, medicines and rebuilding of infrastructure takes place to end the appalling loss of life there. *(c) Palestine:* Implementation of numerous UN resolutions to bring about an Israeli evacuation (including settlers and the Israeli defence forces) from the Occupied Territories and the establishment of a secular, democratic Palestinian state with East Jerusalem as its capital, as well as ensuring the right of return of Palestinian refugees to their homeland. This would mean challenging the notion of Israel as a Jewish state. As Israel Shahak, a survivor of the Belsen concentration camp and citizen of Israel, writes,

"In my view, Israel as a Jewish state constitutes a danger not only to itself and its inhabitants, but to all Jews and to all other peoples and states in the Middle East and beyond," just as the self-definition of other states as "Arab" or "Muslim" also constitutes a danger. He points out that this communal definition resulted in close relations between zionists and anti-semites: "Perhaps the most shocking example of this type is the delight with which some Zionist leaders in Germany welcomed Hitler's rise to power, because they shared his belief in the primacy of "race" and his hostility to the assimilation of Jews among "Aryans" (*Jewish History, Jewish Religion*, Pluto Press, 1994, pp. 2, 71). So the transformation of Israel into a secular, democratic state would also be required. UN sanctions may be needed to press for these changes.

4. None of this could be achieved without an international movement for human rights and democracy, comprising supporters of these principles in all countries including the USA and Israel. There is also a need for international institutions capable of implementing them. Whether the UN can play this role remains to be seen. Although its role in this war has not been as shameful as in the Gulf War, where it merely rubber-stamped the slaughter of civilians, it has been side-lined completely so far. It seems obvious that as long as permanent members of the Security Council have veto powers, the UN cannot function in a democratic manner; so abolishing those veto powers is one reform which needs to be made in the long term. More immediately, however, the permanent International Criminal Court which was agreed upon in 1998 needs to be set up to deal with crimes against humanity including terrorism, war crimes and genocide. Other machinery is needed to deal with violations of fundamental rights (of women, workers, religious and ethnic minorities, indigenous people, dalits, etc.) where governments persistently fail to do so.
5. Finally, this crisis has shown the need for alternatives to the mainstream media as sources of information and communication. The internet can play such a role, but only if those who

have access to it also disseminate the information more widely, which involves translating it into local languages—a laborious task, but one without which a worldwide movement for human rights and democracy cannot grow.

Rohini Hensman is a writer and researcher active in the trade union, women's liberation and human rights movements, and the author of several articles and books, including To Do Something Beautiful, *a novel inspired by working women in Bombay.*

This essay first appeared in Pravada, *Vol. 7, Nos. 5 & 6, 2001. Published by the Social Scientists' Association, Colombo, Sri Lanka.*

Rubina Saigol

Ter-reign of terror: September 11 and its aftermath

Continuity or departure

It has become customary to talk as if history began on September 11, 2001. Everything that is happening in the world today began when those planes crashed dramatically into the symbols of global capitalism and military might. The tendency to view September 11 as a major discontinuity in world affairs obscures the fact that September 11 and the events that followed, in fact represent a continuity and, perhaps, even an intensification of global agendas that preceded that date by decades and even centuries. Colonialism, imperialism, globalization and militarization were not invented post-September 11; rather September 11 became a catalyst for global agendas that were festering long before then. It brought into the open and laid bare the fangs of military might, state terror and economic domination that were implicated in producing the events of September 11. I would go so far as to argue that in fact nothing has changed, at least not in any substantial way, and that what happened on September 11 and after only accelerated the pace of what was already underway prior to that fateful date.

Just examine the following facts: economic globalization, which in effect means the hegemony of rich and powerful states, was moving steadily forward despite Seattle, Genoa, Washington and Quebec where massive rallies opposed it. The US was already on its way to rejecting the Anti-Ballistic Missile treaty of 1972. The US has also steadily opposed the formation of the International Criminal Court for fear that its troops stationed in various countries will be held accountable for rape and other crimes. The US senate refused to ratify the Comprehensive Test Ban Treaty, thus weakening worldwide movements for banning nuclear testing. The US had already rejected the Kyoto Protocol on the environment despite the efforts of the EU, and in spite of being the world's biggest polluter. The decision to go ahead with the National Missile Defense Program was taken despite opposition by Russia, the EU and several other countries. The US had walked out of the international Conference on Racism in South Africa just prior to the events of September 11. All this was in the recent past, just prior to 9/11.

Let us examine events in the somewhat distant past. Israel occupied Palestinian land in the war of 1967, refused to return these territories and unleashed state terrorism upon the Palestinians. The US has the unique distinction of being the only country in the world that has used nuclear weapons on civilian populations in Hiroshima and Nagasaki. We all know about Iraqi children who have been killed in Iraq since 1991 due to the war, economic blockades and sanctions Let us recall that a pharmaceutical factory was destroyed in the bombing of Sudan in 1998, and hundreds of civilians were killed in Libya in the bombing of Tripoli in 1984. Approximately 20,000 people were killed in Lebanon in 1982, in which US weapons were used, thousands of civilians were killed in Vietnam in the 1960s and the 1970s, and in Afghanistan following the so-called "war against terror". The list is too long to cite every incident, but apart from this reign of terror there were other incidents such as attempted and successful murders of heads of state in covert operations by the CIA, support of illegal military rulers, dictators and monarchs such as Zia-ul Haq, Somoza, Pinochet, Musharraf, the Saudi dynasty and the Shah of Iran, against the wishes of their people, and a host of other acts with disastrous consequences, including the funding and assistance for the creation of the Mujahideen, and the Taliban and Osama bin Laden.

Ironically, nobody refers to Hiroshima or Vietnam as the defining moments of history. A much larger number of people died in Hiroshima than in NYC, and the damage to property was also on a much bigger scale. The attacks on Libya or Lebanon have not been referred to as earth-shaking events that changed the course of history, although in Lebanon at least, far greater numbers were killed. Why is the rhetoric of September 11 as the "biggest terrorist attack in history and a defining moment" being adopted by the entire world, even many intellectuals in poor countries? Why have Hiroshima and Nagasaki been forgotten as the biggest terrorist attacks in history? The answer does not lie simply in racism, or in the explanation advanced by many that when lives in the US are at stake, it is somehow more terrifying and morally unjustified than when the lives of Palestinians, Lebanese, the Japanese or Afghans are involved. There is certainly some truth in this but it does not explain the bloodthirsty American vengeance that resulted. Also, people of several nationalities were killed in the attack on WTC, not just white Americans.

An attack on symbols of power

The deep rage and desire for revenge that covered the pages and screens of the print and electronic media in red, came from something deeper than a crude form of racism. The twin towers of the World Trade Center and the Pentagon were symbolic of the twin powers of capital and the military. Not only was this an attack on American soil held sacred by the secular country, it was an attack on the sacred symbols of profit and might. It was an attack on the heart of what the Americans describe as "the American way", that is freedoms based on the so-called "free market" and a civilization rooted in raw muscle power deployed in the defence of profit. The fact that raw muscle power was unable to protect the icons of the American way of life outraged and frightened the sleeping giant into angrily stamping out everything in its way. What made it a "defining moment" and "the biggest terrorist attack in history" for CNN, Fox News and the rest of the US and global media, was not the loss of 3,000 or so innocent lives that it took but that it was an attack on the inviolate values of global economic domination, and global military domination.

September 11 left a great deal in its wake. What was lost that day was a lot more than the lives of various nationalities and the world's tallest buildings. Once the rubble is removed, new buildings and new structures announcing global economic and military might may be constructed; but those who construct knowledge and hold the power of making meaning, seized the moment to forever alter the way the world thinks about war, terror, rights, justice, legality and life itself.

The global media, those powerful makers of public meaning, managed to alter the very values and principles that used to guide the world. However flawed and toothless the UN might have been, it did have a moral agenda, at least in theory. There is the UN Charter, the Universal Declaration of Human Rights, the Convention on the Rights of the Child, the women's convention, the convention against racism, torture and inhuman punishment, convention on refugees, etc. Far from perfect or ideal, they nevertheless reflect certain moral norms that states have agreed to uphold. Prior to September 11, people living in occupied territories such as in Palestine, and those living under repressive regimes, e.g., Kashmiris in India, had recourse to an international body that could put pressure on the violating state to uphold its basic principles of self-determination.

One major effect of the events of September 11 and after, has been an increased faith in and reliance on the repressive apparatus of the state. State repression has varied inversely with the level of human rights acknowledged and practiced. In Pakistan the Anti-Terrorist Act was passed in 1997 and has been invoked with renewed vigour after September 11, to "hunt down and capture" Al Qa'ida and other "religious terrorists". This act has long been under fire by intellectuals and activists as being violative of basic human rights. In India the Prevention of Terrorism Ordinance (POTO) sparked off a major controversy, yet the Prevention of Terrorism Act was recently passed in a joint sitting of parliament. This act is widely believed to be an instrument of state power against the religious minorities in India. In Pakistan the state recently passed an ordinance which allows any premises to be searched by the police without a warrant from a magistrate. The police has been given sweeping powers under a recent police ordinance, ostensibly to enable the capture of "terrorists". In the US, there have been several newspaper reports about the constitution of military courts, the detention of foreigners without pressing charges, and other laws clearly reflecting a latent racism in official institutions. The media and government rhetoric of "hunting terrorists" has created an atmosphere where removing a confirmed passenger from airplanes becomes possible, and where beating up innocent people is allowed simply because they look Pakistani, or Arab, or Afghan or Muslim. The increased technology of surveillance and monitoring (at airports and public places), the most modern form of the application of power, erodes individual integrity by encroaching into a person's self. The steady erosion of civil rights and liberties' consciousness, both within state institutions and among the people, has led to lowered standards for human rights, globally. The actions of the Israeli government against the Palestinians and of the Indian government towards Kashmiris amply demonstrate the enhanced legitimacy of repression in the name of "fighting terrorism". The treatment of prisoners in Guantanamo Bay, deplored even by Mary Robinson and the UN Human Rights Commission, is a major attack on the rights of prisoners to be treated humanely.

In the post-Nazi era, at the end of World War II, the regime of rights and international norms and principles that were agreed upon by states, protected individuals against the state and ensured certain rights as inalienable, inviolate and universal. The globalization of the war on terrorism seems to have changed all that. Right and wrong, legal and illegal have come to be defined by each state, separately. This kind of cultural specificity and moral relativism is reflected in the insistence of the US government that those captured in Afghanistan are not prisoners of war but "illegal combatants". The latter category does not exist in international discourse, it was manufactured overnight by Rumsfeld and his band of men. The construction of such new categories to override internationally agreed upon terms and conditions diminishes the concept of the universality of human rights, the idea that all life is precious and all humans are to be given humane treatment compatible with human dignity, irrespective of caste, class, race, religion or nationality. The treatment meted out to prisoners in Guantanamo Bay contrasts sharply with the treatment of the eight aid workers held by the "uncivilized," "barbaric" and "violent" Taliban!

Like "civilization", other terms have also undergone a dangerous transformation. The most important of these is the word "terrorist", a highly racialized term which is now freely and irresponsibly used for anyone who disagrees with the US or looks Arab or Muslim. The media has turned the meaning of the word on its head—those who are living under illegal foreign occupation resulting from external aggression, have been branded "terrorists", and those raining bombs and rockets and missiles on those whom they subjugate, are now victims of terror. The UN human rights instruments used to recognize the right to self-determination and fighting for one's freedom as justifiable rights and activities. The current discourse makes it appear as though the Kashmiris and the Palestinians are terrorists, and Ariel Sharon and A.B. Vajpayee the hapless victims of terror! As Israel rains bombs and missiles on the Palestinians and Vajpayee maintains a force of 700, 000 in Kashmir to crush a freedom struggle, they invoke the US war against terrorism as a justification for state terror—while the latter category seems to have been erased from international discourse by the makers of knowledge and meaning in the world. Even as all this goes on, George Bush incessantly invokes the notion of the axis of evil and the like to characterize Iran, Iraq and North Korea—either communist or Muslim countries, thus trying to promote the facile "clash of civilizations" thesis.

Militarization and masculinity

This brings me to my next point. The so-called war against terror not only provided excuses to countries, such as India and Israel, to unleash terror upon dissenting populations in the name of "peace", it has suddenly provided seemingly justifiable reasons for enhanced militarization in many countries, including Pakistan, India, the US and almost all of Asia. The defence budgets of these countries have been hiked, and India and Pakistan are facing a military standoff on their borders. In order to support the budget of mobilization along the border, India has imposed a war surcharge on its already poor citizens, and Pakistani rulers have already started talking about increasing the defence budget in view of the border situation. Whenever defence expenditure is raised in poor countries, it is at the cost of expenditure on social sector development. The Public Sector Development Programme of Pakistan has been slashed several times in the name of "national interest", "national security" and defence.

The question is whose interests are "national interests", whose security is "national security" and who defines their agendas? Such questions are typically left unanswered by rulers who are usually engaged in saving only their own regimes. Vajpayee used the anti-Pakistan, Pakistan-as-terrorist rhetoric to win votes in crucial state and municipal elections, and Musharraf uses all kinds of internal and external threats as excuses to prolong his rule and remain in power. However, the BJP's massive losses in both the state and municipal elections reveal how sophisticated the public is, that it cannot be fooled by demagogues. Similarly, Musharraf's manipulated and engineered referendum may deliver a false victory, but it is widely known how the state and government machinery was deployed to ensure it. The public in both countries has declared that it wants social security, human security and rights—not more guns, more missiles, more tanks and more wars!

For Pakistan, one negative consequence of the country's forced participation in the so-called coalition against terror has been the legitimizing of an illegal, unconstitutional and highly repressive military regime. Countries such as the US and EU which, prior to September 11, had imposed economic and democratic sanctions on Pakistan, quickly moved to remove them. Even the Pressler Amendment, prohibiting arms sale to Pakistan, was lifted to enable western armament industries to reap profits. Within weeks, the Pressler, Symington and Glen Amendments were suspended and the way paved for yet another military regime to receive the approval and approbation of western powers. The IMF and the World Bank, too, began to look "favourably" on its economy. This intensified its structural adjustment agenda, and the Paris Club rescheduling of loans made it easier for the government to claim "economic stability". Within months the Poverty Reduction and Growth Facility of 1.3 billion dollars was made available to Pakistan, a step which made its people more indebted but was hailed as yet another glorious triumph of the military regime.

One was reminded of the 4.2 billion dollar aid that flowed into another Pakistani regime during the Reagan era (Afghan war), used to help create the jihadi groups and the Taliban in Afghanistan. As a mercenary state, Pakistan seems to create such groups when paid by the US to do so, then destroys them when paid by the US to do so. There is no sovereign policy, only the tendency to deliver upon payment! Repression, authori-tarianism and mercenary war have been internationally sanctioned within the new era of the globalization of the "war on terror". While the military government may have banned religious groups and sent them into hiding, one wonders how it plans to control the violence that is now likely to be unleashed within Pakistan by the banned groups operating surreptitiously on its territory. On the other hand, in a further attack on citizens' rights, the entire data collected by the National Database and Registration Authority, as well as other data (EPB, digital maps), have been handed over to the FBI, which operates in Pakistan as though it was the 51st state of the US! This encroachment into citizens' privacy through the advanced technology of surveillance represents a flagrant violation of human rights, as it allows Uncle Sam to examine the minutest details of people's lives.

One aspect of enhanced global militarization is that the US has been given bases in countries like Pakistan. The implications of this policy are far-reaching, especially for women who then become the source of R and R for the soldiers. Past experience shows that entire economies grow out of military bases—economies based on the flesh trade as in Thailand. At a more subtle level, women suffer in yet more ways. For example, societies that are either perpetually engaged in a low intensity war or full scale military engagement, tend to overemphasise the masculinist aspects of culture and undermine all that is defined as "feminine". Such societies, as is well known, eulogize physical valour, fighting capacity, martyrdom, heroism, masculinity—values normally associated with men, and undervalue peace, quiescence, pacifism and dialogue, often associated with women. While neither of these are the natural characteristics of men or women, societies engaged in war have a tendency to divide values along the masculine/feminine axis, and to attribute warlike virtues to males and weakness and fear to women. The intensified gendered division of war labour reinforces the idea that women are "naturally weaker" and less "valuable" to society because they cannot fight. This can happen despite the fact that increasing numbers of women are becoming direct combatants in war, as in Sri Lanka and even Palestine.

Terrible choice

The dichotomous choice that the global "war on terror" has left us with is highly problematic for feminists—either with us or with the terrorists! Only two choices, both in favour of terror, murder, genocide and war; neither one a choice for peace. If anyone felt that they were with neither side and condemned both the attacks on the WTC and the US bombing of Afghanistan, they were referred to as fence-sitters, or just plain confused. Even imagining a third possibility became at best, difficult, at worst, a crime. For long, feminists have condemned all forms of religion-based terror and especially the anti-women bias of such terror as epitomized by the Taliban. Feminists also have a long history of condemning rampant capitalism and unbridled militarism. Feminism has highlighted the hypermasculinist aspects of so-called "fundamentalism", capitalism and militarism! The need to oppose all forms of violence (which all three represent) means that feminists just cannot place themselves in the neat categories of Us and Them outlined by Mr. Bush. In fact, feminists have pointed out the similarities in the rhetoric of the Bushes and bin Ladens of this world—both claim to fight for justice, for freedom against evil, for the sake of good, and both are fighting a crusade/jihad.

Violence seems to inhere as much in the so-called advanced, modern, liberal, rational, technological, scientific, precise and secular rhetoric and actions of the US, as in the so-called "backward", ancient, pre-modern, religious, imprecise, irrational and conservative actions and discourse of the Taliban. Here, too, the two represent a continuity rather than a departure. The Taliban had less sophisticated weaponry only for lack of resources and access, not for lack of desire on their part. Technology, in its most destructive form, is worshipped no less by them than by the

Americans who prided themselves on the displays of death produced by their "Colourful" arsenal.

Feminist choices?

While challenging the choices offered between capitalist and religious terror, feminists also need to question the excessive moral relativism of the discourse on terror. An extreme celebration of "diversity" and the right of each state or society to act independently of the moral authority of other states, must be challenged. A number of states have engaged in terror based on the premise that "we have a right to defend ourselves". They have chosen to define who is a terrorist and what constitutes a "just war". Arguments from the point of view of cultural specificity are invariably arguments designed to deny rights and violate internationally accepted norms. Extreme moral and cultural relativism tend to turn into their opposite—moral absolutism. The latter leads Americans to say there is only one truth and it is on our side, and allows the Taliban to claim exactly the same! Some universally agreed upon standards, inclusive of women and everyone else, need to be devised so that no one claim immunity from their application. The UN already has instruments that embody a minimum universal moral code, but their implementation has been notoriously weak. The International Criminal Court seems to be one answer that promises to work.

Rubina Saigol has a doctorate in education from the University of Rochester, and has written widely on education and nationalism; and gender, feminism, nationalism and human rights. She is the author of Knowledge and Identity: Articulation of Curriculum, Pedagogy and Society, *and co-editor of* Engendering the Nation, *Volumes I and II and* Locating the Self: Women and Multiple Identity. *She has been engaged in curriculum development and teacher training on gender and human rights issues. She lives and works in Lahore, Pakistan.*

Rosalind P Petchesky

Phantom towers: feminist reflections on the battle between global capitalism and fundamentalist terrorism

These are trying times, hard times to know where we are from one day to the next. The attack on the World Trade Centre has left many kinds of damage in its wake, not the least of which is a gaping ethical and political confusion in the minds of many Americans who identify in some way as "progressive"—meaning anti-racist, feminist, democratic (small d), anti-war. While we have a responsibility to those who died in the disaster and their loved ones, and to ourselves, to mourn, it is urgent that we also begin the work of thinking through what kind of world we are now living in and what it demands of us. And we have to do this, even while we know our understanding at this time can only be very tentative and may well be invalidated in a year or even a month or a week from now by events we can't foresee or information now hidden from us.

I want to try to draw a picture or a kind of mapping of the global power dynamics as I see them at this moment, including their gendered and racialized dimensions. I want to ask whether there is some alternative, more humane and peaceable way out of these two unacceptable polarities now being presented to us: the permanent war machine (or permanent security state) and the regime of holy terror.

Let me make very clear that, when I pose the question whether we are presently facing a confrontation between global capitalism and an Islamist-fundamentalist brand of fascism, I do not mean to imply their equivalence. If, in fact, the attacks of September 11 were the work of bin Laden's Al Qa'ida network or something related and even larger—and for a moment I think we can assume this is a real possibility—then most of us in this room are *structurally positioned* in a way that gives us little choice about our identities. (For the Muslim Americans and Arab Americans among us, who are both opposed to terrorism and terrified to walk in our streets, the moral dilemma must be, I imagine, much more agonizing.) As an American, a woman, a feminist and a Jew, I have to recognize that the Bin Ladens of the world hate me and would like me dead: or, if they had power over me, would make my life a living hell. I have to wish them—these "perpetrators", "terrorists", whatever they are—apprehended, annulled, so I can breathe in some kind of peace. This is quite different from living at the very centre of global capitalism—which is more like living in a very dysfunctional family that fills you with shame and anger for its arrogance, greed and insensitivity but is, like it or not, your home and gives you both immense privileges and immense responsibilities.

Nor, however, do I succumb to the temptation of casting our current dilemma in the simplistic Manichean terms of cosmic Good vs. Evil. Currently this comes in two opposed but mirror-image versions: the narrative, advanced not only by the terrorists and their sympathizers but also by many on the left in the US and around the globe, that blames US cultural imperialism and economic hegemony for the "chickens coming home to roost"; versus the patriotic, right-wing version that casts US democracy and freedom as the innocent target of Islamist madness. Both these stories erase all the complexities that we must try to factor into a different, more inclusive ethical and political vision. The Manichean, apocalyptic rhetoric that echoed back and forth between Bush and bin Laden in the aftermath of the attacks—the pseudo-Islamic and the pseudo-Christian, the jihad and the crusade—both lie.

So, while I do not see terrorist networks and global capitalism as equivalents or the same, I do see some striking and disturbing parallels between them. I picture them as the phantom Twin Towers arising in the smoke clouds of the old—fraternal twins, not identical, locked in a battle over wealth, imperial aggrandizement and the meanings of masculinity. It is a battle that could well end in a stalemate, an interminable cycle of violence that neither can win because of their failure to see the Other clearly.

Feminist analysts and activists from many countries—whose voices have been inaudible thus far in the present crisis—have a lot of experience to draw from in making this double critique. Whether in the UN or national settings, we have been challenging the gender-biased and racialized dimensions of *both* neoliberal capitalism and various fundamentalisms for years, trying to steer a path between their double menace. The difference now is that they parade onto the world stage in their most extreme and violent forms. I see six areas where their posturing overlaps:

1. *Wealth:* Little needs to be said about the US as the world's wealthiest country nor the ways in which wealth-accumulation is the holy grail not only of our political system (think of the difficulty we have even in reforming campaign finance laws), but of our national ethos. We are the headquarters of the corporate and financial mega-empires that dominate global capitalism and influence the policies of international financial institutions (IMF, World Bank, WTO) that are its main governing bodies. This reality resonates around the globe in the symbolic pantheon of what the US stands for—from the McDonald's and Kentucky Fried Chicken ads sported by protesters in Genoa and Rawalpindi to the World Trade Center towers themselves. Acquisitiveness, whether individual or corporate, also lurks very closely behind the values that Bush and Rumsfeld mean when they say our "freedoms" and our "way of life" are being attacked and must be defended fiercely. (Why, as I'm writing this, do unsolicited messages about Wall Street investment opportunities or low fares to the Bahamas come spewing out of my fax machine?)

Wealth is also the driving force behind the Al Qa'ida network, whose principals are mainly the beneficiaries of upper-middle-class or elite financing and education. Bin Laden himself derives much of his power and influence from his family's vast fortune, and the cells of Arab-Afghan fighters in the 1980s war against the Soviets were bankrolled not only by the Pakistani secret police and the CIA—three billion dollars, writes Katha Pollitt in *The Nation,* "more money and expertise than for any other cause in CIA history"—but also by Saudi oil money. More important than this, though, are the values behind the terrorist organizations, which include—as bin Laden made clear in his famous 1998 interview—defending the "honor" and "property" of Muslims everywhere and "[fighting] the governments that are bent on attacking our religion and on stealing our wealth. . ." Political scientist Paul Amar, in a recent talk at Hunter College, rightly urges us not to confuse these wealthy networks—whose nepotism and ties to oil interests eerily resemble those of the Bush family—with impoverished and resistant social movements throughout the Middle East and Asia. There is no evidence that economic justice or equality figure anywhere in the terrorist programme.

2. *Imperial nationalism:* The Bush administration's initial reaction to the attacks exhibited the behaviour of a superpower that knows no limits, that issues ultimatums under the cover of "seeking cooperation." "Every nation in every region has a decision to make," pronounced Bush in his speech to the nation that was really a speech to the world; "Either you are with us or you are with the terrorists." "This is the world's fight, this is civilization's fight"—the US, then, becomes the leader and spokesman of "civilization," relegating not only the terrorists, but also those who refuse to join the fight, to the ranks of the uncivilized. To the Taliban and to every other regime that "harbors terrorists," he was the sheriff stonewalling the cattle rustlers: "Hand over all the terrorists or you will share in their fate." And a few days later we read "the American announcement that it would use Saudi Arabia as a headquarters for air operations against Afghanistan". As the war campaign progresses, its aims seem more openly imperialist: "Washington wants to offer [the small, also fundamentalist, drug-dealing mujahedeen mostly routed by the Taliban] a role in governing Afghanistan after the conflict," according to *The New York Times* of September 24, as if this were "Washington's" official role. Further, it and its allies are courting the octogenarian, long-forgotten Afghan king (now exiled in Italy) to join in a military operation to oust the Taliban and set up—what ? a kind of puppet government? Nothing here about internationally monitored elections, nothing about the UN, or any concept of the millions of Afghan people—within the country or in exile—as anything but voiceless, downtrodden victims or refugees.

Clearly, this offensive involves far more than rooting out and punishing terrorists. Though I don't want to reduce the situation to a crude Marxist scenario, one can't help wondering how it relates to the long-standing determination of the US to keep a dominant foothold in the Gulf region and to maintain control over oil supplies. At least one faction of the US "team," clamouring to go after Saddam Hussain as well, is clearly in this mindset. And let's not forget Pakistan and its concessions to the US demands for cooperation in return for lifting of US economic sanctions—and now, the assurance of a sizable IMF loan. In the tradition of a neo-imperial power, the US does not need to dominate countries politically or militarily to get the concessions it wants; its economic influence backed up by the capacity for military annihilation is sufficient. And, spurred by popular rage over the WTC attacks, all this is wrapped in the outpouring of nationalist patriotism and flag-waving that now envelops the American landscape.

Though lacking the actual imperial power of the US, the bin Laden forces mimic its imperial aspirations. If we ask, what are the terrorists seeking? we need to recognize their worldview as an extreme and vicious form of nationalism—a kind of fascism, I would argue, because of its reliance on terror to achieve its ends. In this respect, their goals, like those of the US, go beyond merely punishment. Amar says the whole history of Arab and Islamic nationalism has been one that transcended the colonially imposed boundaries of the nation-state, one that was always transnational and pan-Arabic, or pan-Muslim, in form. Although the terrorists have no social base or legitimacy in laying claim to this tradition, they clearly seek to usurp it. This seems evident in bin Laden's language invoking "the Arab nation," "the Arab peninsula," and a "brotherhood" reaching from Eastern Europe to Turkey and Albania, to the entire Middle East, South Asia and Kashmir. Their mission is to drive out "the infidels" and their Muslim supporters from something that looks like a third of the globe. Provoking the US to bomb Afghanistan and/or attempt ousting the Taliban would likely destabilize Pakistan and possibly catapult it into the hands of Taliban-like extremists, who would then control nuclear weapons—a big step toward their perverted and hijacked version of the pan-Muslim dream.

3. *Peudo-religion*: As many others have commented, the "clash of religions" or "clash of cultures" interpretation of the current scenario is utterly specious. What we have instead is an appropriation of religious symbolism and discourse for predominantly political purposes, and to justify permanent war and violence. So bin Laden declares a jihad, or holy war, against the US, its civilians as well as its soldiers; and Bush declares a crusade against the terrorists and all who harbor or support them. Bin Laden declares himself the "servant of Allah fighting for the sake of the religion of Allah" and to protect Islam's holy mosques, while Bush declares Washington the promoter of "infinite justice" and predicts certain victory, because "God is not neutral". (The Pentagon changed the "Operation Infinite Justice" label to "Operation Enduring Freedom" after Muslim Americans objected and three Christian clergymen warned that "infinite" presumed divinity, the "sin of pride.") But we have to question the authenticity of this religious discourse on both sides, however sincere its proponents. A "Statement from Scholars of the Islamic Religion," circulated after the attacks, firmly denounces terrorism—the wanton killing of innocent civilians—as contrary to Sh'aria law. And Bush's adoption of this apocalyptic discourse can only be seen as substituting a conservative, right-wing form of legitimization for the neoliberal internationalist discourse that conservatives reject. In either case, it is worth quoting the always wise Eduardo Galeano, writing in Mexico's *La Jornada*: "In the struggle of Good against Evil, it's always the people who get killed."

4. *Militarism:* Both the Bush administration and the bin Laden forces adopt the methods of war and violence to achieve their ends, but in very different ways. US militarism is of the ultra-high-tech variety that seeks to terrorize by the sheer might, volume and technical virtuosity of our armaments. Of course, as the history of Vietnam and the survival of Saddam Hussein attest, this is an illusion of the highest order. (Remember the "smart bombs" in the Gulf War that headed for soda machines?) But our military technology is also a vast and insatiable industry

for which profit, not strategy, is the driving rationale. As Jack Blum, a critic of US foreign policy, pointed out recently in the *Sacramento Bee*, “the national defense game is a systems and money operation” that has little, if any, relevance to terrorism. Missiles were designed to counter hostile states with their own fixed territories and weapons arsenals, not terrorists who sneak around the globe and whose “weapons of mass destruction” are human bodies and hijacked planes; nor the famously impervious terrain and piles of rubble that constitute Afghanistan. Even George W., in one of his most sensible comments to date, remarked that we’d know better than to aim “a $2 billion cruise missile at a $10 empty tent”. And yet four days after the attack the Democrats in Congress piled madness atop madness and withdrew their opposition to Bush’s costly and destructive “missile shield,” voting to restore $1.3 billion in spending authority for this misconceived and dangerous project. And the armament companies quickly started lining up to receive their big orders for the impending next war—the war, we are told, that will last a long time, maybe the rest of our lives. US militarism is not about rationality—not even about fighting terrorism—but about profits.

The war-mania and the rallying around the flag exhibited by the American people express desire, not for military profits, but for something else, something harder for feminist and anti-war dissidents to understand. Maybe it’s just the need to vent anger and feel avenged, or the more deep-rooted one to experience some sense of community and higher purpose in a society where we are so atomized and isolated from one another and the world. On September 25, Barbara Kingsolver wrote in the *San Franscisco Chronicle* that she and her husband reluctantly sent their five year old daughter to school dressed in red, white and blue like the other kids because they didn’t want to let jingoists and censors “steal the flag from us”. Their little girl probably echoed the longings of many less reflective grownups when she said that wearing the colors of the flag “means we’re a country; just people all together”.

The militarism of the terrorists is of a very different nature—based on the mythic figure of the Bedouin warrior, or the Ikhwan fighters of the early 20th century who enabled Ibn Saud to consolidate his dynastic rule. Their hallmark is individual courage and ferocity in battle; Malise Ruthven's *Islam in the World* quotes one Arab witness who described them, foreshadowing reports by Soviet veterans from the 1980s Afghan war, as: "utterly fearless of death, not caring how many fall, advancing rank upon rank with only one desire—the defeat and annihilation of the enemy". Of course, this image too, like every hyper-nationalist ideology, is rooted in a mythic golden past and has little to do with how real terrorists in the 21st century are recruited, trained and paid off. And, like high-tech militarism, terrorist low-tech militarism is also based on an illusion—that millions of believers will rise up, obey the fatwa and defeat the infidel. It's an illusion because it grossly underestimates the most powerful weapon in global capital's arsenal—not "infinite justice" or even nukes but infinite Nikes and CDs. And it also underestimates the local power of feminism, which the fundamentalists mistakenly confuse with the West. Iran today, in all its internal contradictions, shows the resilience and globalized/localized variety of both youth cultures and women's movements.

5. *Masculinism*: Militarism, nationalism and colonialism as terrains of power have always been in large part contests over the meanings of manhood. Feminist political scientist Cynthia Enloe remarks that "men's sense of their own masculinity, often tenuous, is as much a factor in international politics as is the flow of oil, cables, and military hardware". In the case of bin Laden's Taliban patrons, the form and excessiveness of the misogyny that goes hand in hand with state terrorism and extreme fundamentalism have been graphically documented. Just go to the website of the Revolutionary Association of the Women of Afghanistan, www.rawa.org, to view more photos of atrocities against women (and men) for sexual offenses, dress code offenses and other forms of deviance than you'll be able to stomach. According to John Burns, writing in the *NY Times Magazine* in 1990, the "rebel" leader in the Afghan war who received "the lion's share of American money and weapons"—and was not a Taliban—had been reputed to have "dispatched followers [during his student movement days] to throw vials of acid into the faces of women students who refused to wear veils".

In the case of transnational terrorists and bin Laden himself, their model of manliness is that of Islamic "brotherhood," the band of brothers bonded together in an agonistic commitment to fighting the enemy to the death. The CIA-Pakistani-Saudi-backed camps and training schools set up to support the "freedom fighters" (who later became "terrorists") in the anti-Soviet war were breeding grounds not only of a worldwide terrorist network but also of its masculinist, misogynist culture. Bin Laden clearly sees himself as a patriarchal tribal chief whose duty is to provide for and protect, not only his own retinue, wives and many children but also his whole network of lieutenants and recruits and their families. He is the legendary counterpart of the Godfather.

In contrast to this, can we say that the US as standard-bearer of global capitalism is "gender-neutral"? Don't we have a woman—indeed an African-American woman—at the helm of our National Security Council, the president's right hand in designing the permanent war machine? Despite reported "gender gaps" in polls about war, we know that women are not inherently more peace-loving than men. Remember all those suburban housewives with their yellow ribbons in midwestern airports and shopping malls during the Gulf War? Global capitalist masculinism is alive and well but concealed in its Eurocentric, racist guise of "rescuing" downtrodden Afghan women from the misogynist regime it helped bring to power. Feminists around the world, who have tried for so long to call attention to the plight of women and girls in Afghanistan, cannot feel consoled by the prospects of US warplanes and US-backed guerrilla chiefs coming to "save our Afghan sisters." Meanwhile, the US will send single mothers who signed up for the National Guard when welfare ended to fight and die in its holy war; US media remains silent about the activism and self-determination of groups like RAWA, Refugee Women in Development and NEGAR; and the US military establishment refuses accountability before an International Criminal Court for acts of rape and sexual assault committed by its soldiers stationed across the globe. Masculinism and misogyny take many forms, not always the most visible.

6. *Racism:* Of course, what I have named fascist fundamentalism, or transnational terrorism, is also saturated in racism,

but of a very specific, focused kind—which is anti-semitism. The WTC towers symbolized not only American capitalism, not only finance capitalism, but, for the terrorists, Jewish finance capitalism. We can see this in the misreporting of the September 11 attacks in Arabic-language newspapers in the Middle East as probably the work of the Israelis; their erroneous allegation that not a single person among the dead and missing was Jewish, so Jews must have had advance warning, etc. In his 1998 interview, bin Laden constantly refers to "Jews", not Israelis, in his accusations about plans to take over the whole Arab peninsula. He asserts that "the Americans and the Jews. . . represent the spearhead with which the members of our religion have been slaughtered. Any effort directed against America and the Jews yields positive and direct results." And finally, he rewrites history and collapses the diversity of Muslims in a warning to "western governments" to sever their ties to Jews: "the enmity between us and the Jews goes far back in time and is deep-rooted. There is no question that war between the two of us is inevitable. For this reason it is not in the interest of western governments to expose the interests of their people to all kinds of retaliation for almost nothing." (I cringe to realize I am part of the "nothing".)

US racism is much more diffuse but just as insidious; the pervasive racism and ethnocentrism that fester under the American skin always boil to the surface at times of national crisis. As Sumitha Reddy put it in a recent teach-in, the targeting of Sikhs and other Indians, Arabs and even tan Latinos and African-Americans in the wave of violent and abusive acts throughout the country since the disaster, signals an enlargement of the "zone of mistrust" in American racism beyond the usual black-white focus. Women who wear headscarves or saris are particularly vulnerable to harassment, but Arab and Indian men of all ages are the ones being murdered. The state pretends to abhor such incidents and threatens their full prosecution. But this is the same state that made the so-called Anti-Terrorism Act, passed in 1995 after the Oklahoma City bombing (an act committed by native white Christian terrorists), a pretext for rounding up and deporting immigrants of all kinds; and that is now once again waiving the civil liberties of immigrants in its zealous anti-terrorist manhunt.

Each day *The New York Times* publishes its rouges' gallery of police photos of the suspects, so reminiscent of those eugenic photographs of "criminal types" of an earlier era, and imprinting upon readers' minds a certain set of facial characteristics that they should now fear and blame. Racial profiling becomes a national pastime.

If we only look at terrorist tactics and the world's revulsion against them, then we might conclude rather optimistically that thuggery will never win out in the end. But we ignore the context in which terrorism operates at our peril, and that context includes not only racism and Eurocentrism but many other forms of social injustice. In thinking through a moral position on this crisis, we have to distinguish between *immediate causes* and *necessary conditions*. Neither the United States (as a state) nor the corporate and financial power structure that the World Trade Centers symbolized caused the horrors of September 11. Without question the outrageous, heinous murder, maiming and orphaning of so many innocent people—who were every race, ethnicity, colour, class, age, gender and some 60 odd nationalities—deserve some kind of just redress. On the other hand, the *conditions* in which transnational terrorism thrives, gains recruits and lays claim to moral legitimacy include many for which the US and its corporate/financial interests are directly responsible even if they don't for a minute excuse the attacks. It is often asked lately, why does the Third World hate us so much? Put another way, why do so many people, including my own friends in Asia, Africa, Latin America and the Middle East, express so much ambivalence about what happened, both lamenting an unforgivable criminal act and at the same time taking some satisfaction that Americans are finally suffering too? We make a fatal mistake if we attribute these mixed feelings only to envy or resentment of our wealth and freedoms and ignore a historical context of aggression, injustice and inequality. Consider these facts:

1. The United States is still the only country in the world to have *used* the most infamous weapons of mass destruction in the

nuclear bombing of innocent civilians—in Hiroshima and Nagasaki.

2. The US persists to this day in bombing Iraq, destroying the lives and food supplies of hundreds of thousands of civilian adults and children there. We bombed Belgrade—a dense capital city—for 80 straight days during the war in Kosovo, and supported bombing that killed untold civilians in El Salvador in the 1980s. In the name of fighting Communism, our CIA and military training apparatus sponsored paramilitary massacres, assassinations, tortures and disappearances in many Latin American and Central American countries in Operation Condor and the like in the 1970s, and had supported corrupt, authoritarian regimes in the Middle East, Southeast Asia and elsewhere—the Shah of Iran, Suharto in Indonesia, the Saudi dynasty, and let's not forget the Taliban regime itself. September 11 is also the date of the coup against the democratically elected Allende government in Chile and the beginning of the 25-year Pinochet dictatorship, again thanks to US support. Yes, a long history of state terrorism.
3. In the Middle East, which is the microcosm of the current conflagration, US military aid and the Bush administration's refusal to pressure the Sharon government are the sine qua non of continued Israeli government policies of attacks on villages, demolition of homes, destruction of olive orchards, restrictions on travel, assasination of political leaders, building of roads and enlarging of settlements—all of which exacerbate Palestinian despair and suicide bombings. The US therefore contributes to deepening the illegal occupation and "bantustanizing" the Palestinian terroritories and thus perpetuating hostilities.
4. Despite its pretense to uphold women's rights, the US is one of only around two dozen countries that have failed to ratify the UN Convention on the Elimination of All Forms of Discrimination Against Women, and the only country that hasn't ratified the UN Convention on the Rights of the Child. It is the most vocal opponent of the statute establishing an International Criminal Court as well as treaties banning landmines and germ

warfare; a principle subverter of a new multilateral treaty to combat illegal small arms trafficking; and the sole country in the world to threaten an unprecedented space-based defence system and imminent violation of the ABM treaty. So who is the "outlaw", the "rouge state"?

5. The US is the only major industrialized country to refuse to sign the Kyoto Protocol on Global Climate Change, despite compromises in the document designed to meet US objections. Meanwhile, a new global scientific study shows that the countries whose productivity will benefit most from the climate change are Canada, Russia and the US, while the biggest losers will be the countries that have contributed least to global climate change—i.e., most of Africa.
6. As even the World Bank and United Nations Development Programme attest, two decades of globalization have resulted in enlarging rather than shrinking the gaps between rich and poor, both within countries and among countries. The benefits of global market liberalization and integration have accrued disproportionately to wealthy Americans and Europeans (as well as small elites in the Third World). Despite the presumed democratizing effects of the Internet, a middle-class American "needs to save a month's salary to buy a computer; a Bangladeshi must save all his wages for eight years to do so". And despite its constant trumpeting of "free-trade" rhetoric, the US remains a persistent defender of protectionist policies for its farmers and steel and textile manufacturers. Meanwhile small producers throughout Asia, Africa and the Caribbean—a great many of whom are women—are squeezed out by US imports and relegated to the informal economy or sweatshop labor for multinationals.
7. The G-8 countries, of which the US is the senior partner, dominate decision-making in the IMF and the World Bank, whose structural adjustments and conditionalities for loans and debt relief help to keep many countries and their citizens locked in poverty.
8. In the aftermath of the September 11 attacks, the US Congress was able to come up with an immediate $40 billion for

> "anti-terrorism" activities, another $40 billion to bail out the airlines and a 20-year contract with Lockheed to produce military aircraft for $200 billion—enough to eliminate contagious diseases from the face of the earth. Yet our foreign assistance appropriations (except for military aid) have shrunk; we, the world's richest country, contribute only 1/7 of one per cent of our GNP to foreign aid—the least of any industrialized country. A recent WHO report tells us that the total cost of providing safe water and sanitation to all of sub-Saharan Africa would be only $11 billion, only no one can figure out where the money will come from; and the UN is still a long way off from raising a similar amount for its proclaimed World Global Fund to combat AIDS, malaria and TB. What kind of meanness is this? And what does it say about forms of racism, or "global apartheid" that value some lives—those in the US and Europe—far more than others in other parts of the globe?

And the list goes on, with McDonald's, Coca Cola, CNN and MTV and all the uninvited commercial detritus that proliferates everywhere on the face of the earth and offends the cultural and spiritual sensibilities of so many—including transnational feminist travelers like me, when we find pieces of our local shopping mall transplanted to central Manila, or Kuala Lumpur or Bangalore. But worse than the triviality and bad taste of these cultural and commercial barrages is the arrogant presumption that our "way of life" is the best on earth and ought to be welcome everywhere; or that our power and supposed advancement entitle us to dictate policies and strategies to the rest of the world. This is the face of imperialism in the 21st century.

None of this reckoning can comfort those who lost loved ones on September 11, or the thousands of attack victims who lost their jobs, homes and livelihoods; nor can it excuse the hideous crimes. As the Palestinian poet Mahmoud Darwish write, "nothing, nothing justifies terrorism". Still, in attempting to understand what has happened and think about how to prevent it happening again (which is probably a vain wish), we Americans have to take all these painful facts into account. The United States as the command center of global capitalism will remain ill-equipped to "stop terrorism" until it begins to recognize its own past and present responsibility for many of the conditions I've listed and to address them in a responsible way. But this would mean the United States becoming something different from itself, transforming itself, including abandoning the presumption that it should unilaterally police the world. This problem of transformation is at the heart of the vexing question of finding solutions different from all-out war. So let me turn to how we might think differently about power. Here is what I propose, tentatively, for now:

1. The slogan "War is not the Answer" is a practical as well as an ontological truth. Bombing or other military attacks on Afghanistan will not root out networks of terrorists who could be hiding deep in the mountains, or in Pakistan or Germany or Florida or New Jersey. It will only succeed in destroying an already decimated country, killing untold number of civilians as well as combatants and creating hundreds of thousands more refugees. And it is likely to arouse so much anger among Islamist sympathizers as to destabilize the entire region and perpetuate the cycle of retaliation and terrorist attacks. All the horror of the 20th century should surely teach us that war feeds on itself and that armed violence reflects, not an extension of politics by other means, but the failure of politics; not the defense of civilization, but the breakdown of civilization.
2. Tracking down and bringing the perpetrators of terrorism to justice, in some kind of international police action, is a reasonable aim but one fraught with dangers. Because the US is the world's only "superpower," its declaration of war against terrorism and its supporters everywhere says to other countries that we are once again taking over as global policemen, or, as Fidel Castro put it, a "world military dictatorship under the exclusive rule of force, irrespective of any international laws or institutions". Here at home a "national emergency" or "state of war"—*especially* when defined as different from any other war—means the curtailment of civil liberties, harassment of immigrants, racial profiling and withholding of information (censorship) or feeding of disinformation to the media, all without any time limits or accountability under the

dubious Office of Homeland Security and the "US Patriotic Act". We should oppose both US unilaterism and the permanent security state. We should urge our representatives in Congress to diligently defend the civil liberties of all.

3. I agree with the Afro-Asian Peoples Solidarity Organization (AAPSO) in Cairo that "this punishment should be inflicted according to the law and only upon those who were responsible for these events," and that it should be organized within the framework of the United Nations and international law, not unilaterally by the United States. This is not the same as the US getting unanimous approval from the Security Council to commandeer global security, which is a first step at best. Numerous treaties against terrorism and money-laundering already exist in international law. The pending International Criminal Court, whose establishment the US government has so stubbornly opposed, would be the logical body to try terrorist cases, with the cooperation of national police and surveillance systems. *We should demand that the US ratify the ICC statute.* In the meantime, a special tribunal under international auspices, like the ones for former Yugoslavia and Rwanda, could be set up, as well as an international agency to coordinate national police and intelligence efforts, with the US as one participating member. This is the power of international engagement and cooperation.
4. No amount of police action, however cooperative, can stop terrorism without addressing the conditions of misery and injustice that nourish and aggravate terrorism. The US has to undertake a serious examination of its values and its policies with regard not only to the Middle East but also to the larger world. It has to take responsibility for being in the world, including ways of sharing its wealth, resources and technology; democratizing decisions about global trade, finance and security; and assuring that access to "global public goods" like health care, housing, food, education, sanitation, water and freedom from racial and gender discrimination is given priority in international relations. What we even mean by "security" has to encompass all these aspects of well being, of "human security," and has to be universal in its reach.

Let me again quote from the poet Mahmoud Darwish's statement, which was published in the Palestinian daily *Al Ayyam* on September 17, and signed by many Palestinian writers and intellectuals.

> We know that the American wound is deep and we know that this tragic moment is a time for solidarity and the sharing of pain. But we also know that the horizons of the intellect can traverse landscapes of devastation. Terrorism has no location or boundaries, it does not reside in a geography of its own; its homeland is disillusionment and despair.
>
> The best weapon to eradicate terrorism from the soul lies in the solidarity of the international world, in respecting the rights of all people of this globe to live in harmony and by reducing the ever-increasing gap between the North and the South. And the most effective way to defend freedom is through fully realizing the meaning of justice.

What gives me hope is that this statement's sentiments are being voiced by growing numbers of groups here in the US, including the National Council of Churches, the Green Party, a coalition of 100 entertainers and civil rights leaders, huge coalitions of peace groups and students' organizations, New Yorkers Say No To War, black and white women celebrities featured in Oprah Winfrey's show, parents and spouses of attack victims, as well as some 500 petitioners from women's peace groups here and across the globe calling on the UN Security Council to "Stop the War, Rebuild a Just Society in Afghanistan, and Support Women's Human Rights." Maybe out of the ashes we will recover a new kind of solidarity; maybe the terrorists will force us not to mirror them, but to see the world and humanity as a whole.

Rosalind Petchesky is Distinguished Professor of Political Science at Hunter College and the Graduate Center, City University of New York.

This essay originated in a presentation given at Hunter College Political Science Department Teach-in, New York City, September 25, 2001.

Susan Hawthorne *September 21, 2001*

Terrorism, globalization, bio/diversity, survival: a feminist perspective

I have been thinking the last two weeks about the destruction of the twin towers of the World Trade Center in New York and the Pentagon in Washington. Even more, I have been thinking about the wanton destruction of life which is really the key loss in all of this. Buildings can be rebuilt, lives cannot be revived.

I have been researching globalisation for some years now, and writing my ideas about the connections between feminism, globalisation and biodiversity for a PhD I'm completing. The research has forced me to rethink a lot of things and it has reinforced some ideas. It has forced me to read economics and consider the different positions of peoples in different parts of the world, and in different social settings in Australia and the wider western world.

I am truly horrified by the devastation in New York and Washington, I know parts of these cities and know people living there whose shock, grief and loss affect me. But what horrifies me even more is the potential, not for one or two cities and their inhabitants to go up in flames, but the prospect that it could affect huge numbers of people across the world.

I deplore statements such as George W. Bush's "This is the first war of the 21st century." Where has he been? Does he see nothing outside his own tiny dominant culture (wealthy, white, male, American) experience? How insulting is his statement to the many thousands who have died in Palestine/Israel, Serbia/Kosovo, Macedonia/Albania, Sierra Leone, Fiji, West/East Timor, Aceh, Ambon, Afghanistan, just to name a few of the places most prominent in violent clashes around the world (although not all have had formal declarations of war).

Beyond that, there are then the many millions whose lives have been made worse, not better, under the new multilateral globalisation regimes which create more and more wealth for the US and US-based companies. There are victims—and they are dead, or living lives filled with horror and sadness—in every poor country, and among the poor of the wealthy countries too. They are slaves—many of them women and girls; they are the workers in the Export Processing Zones—many of them women and girls; they are those trafficked for the sexual pleasure of mobile men—the vast majority are women and girls; they are dependent on drugs, or handouts; they are starving, or homeless, or landless, or countryless; they have had their possessions, their land, their knowledge, their plants, their culture, even parts of their bodies stolen, appropriated, pirated, commodified. These people, too, are victims of another undeclared war in which the rich stand to gain, and the poor lose almost everything. And many of these people are women and girls, for whom the "war against women" as Marilyn French called it, has never really ceased, indeed it appears to have gained momentum.

War, formal declared war, will make the suffering of those already victimised by America's corporate self-seeking attitude even greater. Those who stand to gain are overwhelmingly men. They are rich men, mostly white, but male elites from other cultures are welcome to join the club. They represent a very narrow view of the world, one which has little contact with real life, with daily activities such as buying milk or bread, such as staying up with a sick child, such as talking with a friend about relationships or politics, such as comforting another who has suffered loss, such as planting trees or flowers or harvesting fruits or milking the goats. This narrow view is what I have come to call Dominant Culture Stupidities: the more dominant cultures one belongs to the more socially and politically insensitive and stupid one is. American corporate, military and mainstream political culture tends to think that the rest of world wants what they value.

The military might of the US is intimately connected with its corporate might. Their economies feed one another with goods and multimillion dollar contracts. General Electric did not get rich on refrigerators or kitchen appliances; its nuclear plants are much more profitable.

Where are the women in the structures of power? They are not there (even with the few tokens who are). They do not have decision-making power. They do not provide the financial backing. No, the women—even the captains of industry or law—are outside of this place of hyperpower. Under the Taliban, women are rendered invisible, covered up. In the highest offices of the US corporate and military decision-making boardrooms, it is much the same.

So what does biodiversity have to do with all of this? I suggest, that were the planet to shift its focus from profit-making (and war-mongering is a part of that, as economists such as Marilyn Waring have shown) to biodiversity, many of these things would be undoable, unthinkable. To focus on life—an inherent feature of sustaining biodiversity—is to change scale, to change direction, and to change all the basic aspects of life activities. If biodiversity were our inspiration, we would not be building 110-storey buildings for people to die in. We would not be dispossessing people on the other side of the globe just so that we can have that cheap T-shirt, that computer on which I'm writing this, that next trip with its seductive frequent flyer rewards, that strawberry grown out of season and trucked or flown to me thousands of miles away. The garments industry, the electronics industry, the tourism industry, the industrialised farming industry are interfaces of globalisation. They are the small, incremental cuts supported by the American way of life. They—along with the bombs and economic sanctions—are the makers of despair.

We do not yet know who is responsible for the huge acts of violence, but it does appear likely that they are male; that they are backed by wealth; that they are highly mobile. If, and I say this with caution, if they are connected to CIA-trained Osama bin Laden, they too will have been surrounded by a grossly masculinised culture, one in which aggression is valorised, and death for a higher good seen to be the highest honour. If they have come from the madrassas, then their education too is pure masculinity. The boys passing through the madrassas are mostly orphans, war orphans, they do not know the company of mothers or sisters or aunts or grandmothers, or possibly even the woman passing on the street. They are politicised for violence, for unemotionality, and for reward in the afterlife. If they could turn their heads towards biodiversity, to the earth's context now, towards growing things, towards caring, towards sustenance and a belief in life then the world would be a different place.

The next step would be to move towards a principle based on biodiversity, a philosophy based in the local, in contextual richness which includes the principle of diversity—social, political and cultural diversity—alongside biodiversity. They would have to move outside their narrow groove, whether they are George W. Bush or the boys from the madrassas; they would have to learn to appreciate the small things, the ecosystems, the community arts programme, the local shopping area or market, the garden.

There is a long way to go. Getting there won't be achieved by bombs, or reconstructing 110-storey buildings. It will be achieved by those in the diversity sector who see life with greater richness than those who inhabit the masculinised world of war, profit and globalisation.

Afterword: September 24, 2001

The connection between biodiversity and feminism as forces opposing global corporate greed appeared in an email on my computer this morning. The alliance between those who favour military retaliation and globalisation (with its attendant promotion of biotechnology and GMO rhetoric "to feed the hungry of the world") is shown by the nastiest kind of slippage such as that promulgated by Andrew Apel's (From: Andrew Apel agbionews@earthlink.net to AgBioView, Subject: The Face of Terrorism) accusation that anti-globalization activists and those of us who are against industrialised farming practices are terrorists, is the usual kind of reversal (in Mary Daly's sense) that we can expect from the hypermasculine ideology of corporate and military men. Feminists and ecological activists are not war-mongers, neither is there much profit to be gained; by contrast those who favour global corporate power—whether it be directed to war contracts or industrialised farm contracts—reap huge profits, and are the ones whose minds are focused on destroying or distorting life.

Susan Hawthorne has been a feminist activist for thirty years. She is the author of Wild Politics (2002), *based on her PhD, which looks at issues around feminism, globalisation and bio/diversity. She is also the author of a novel,* The Falling Woman *(1992);* Bird *(1999) a collection of poems; and co-editor of numerous anthologies including* Cyber-Feminism *(with Renate Klein).*

Vandana Shiva *October 19, 2001*

Bioterror and biosafety

The reports of anthrax cases in Florida and New York have put a renewed focus on bioterror—the risks and hazards posed by biological agents. From the US to India, governments are on high alert. Even the World Health Organisation has issued warnings. Americans and Europeans have been stockpiling gas masks and antibiotics, and images of policemen and investigators in biohazard suits have started to make front-page appearances in newspapers and magazines.

The panic and fear being spread about biohazards in the post-September 11 period is so different from the complacency earlier, even though the threat to public health and the environment from hazardous biological agents is not new. If we have to respond adequately and consistently to bioterror, we need to take two basic issues into account. Firstly, infective biological agents cause disease and kill, irrespective of who spreads them and how they spread. The current paranoia arises from the fear that they could get into terrorist hands.

However, terrorists can get them because they are around, and they pose hazards even if they are not in terrorist hands. As Vaçlav Havel, President of the Czech Republic, said in his opening remarks at Forum 2000 in Prague on October 14, "bin Laden did not invent bacterial agents". They were invented in defence or corporate labs. Anthrax has been part of the ascend of biological warfare in the very states which are today worried about bioterrorism. And genetic engineering of biological organisms, both for warfare and food and agriculture, is creating new biohazards, both intended and unintended.

Secondly, it is fully recognised that stronger public health systems is the only response to bioterrorism. However, precisely at a time when public health reports are needed most, they are being dismantled under privatisation and trade liberalisation pressures. Bioterrorism should help governments recognise that we desperately need strong biosafety regulation and public health systems.

The global citizens' movement and the movement of concerned scientists for biosafety have been alerting governments to the ecological and health risks of genetic engineering and therefore the imperative to test, assess and regulate the release of genetically modified organisms (GMOs) into the environment. This basic conflict over the need to assess GMOs for biohazards was at the heart of negotiations that stretched over a decade under the aegis of the United Nations Convention on Biological Diversity, and were finally concluded in February 2000, in Montreal, with the Protocol on Biosafety. There are two major concerns for potential risks of biohazards from GMOs.

Firstly, the vectors used for introducing genes from one organism to another to make a GMO are highly infectious and virulent biological agents. It is, in fact, their infectious nature which makes them useful as vectors to introduce alien genes into biological organisms. The risks of the use of virulent vectors for engineering novel life forms have not been assessed. And their use for bioterrorism becomes easier as they spread commercially around the world.

Secondly, since GMOs are novel organisms which have not existed in nature, their impact on the environment and on human health is not known. Ignorance of the impact is being treated as proof of safety, a totally unscientific approach. This has been called a "don't look, don't see" approach to biosafety.

Biowarfare or bioterrorism is the deliberate use of living organisms to kill people. When economic policies based on trade liberalisation and globalisation deliberately spread fatal and infectious diseases such as AIDS, TB and malaria, by dismantling health and medical systems, they too become instruments of bioterror. This is the way citizens' groups have organised worldwide against the TRIPS (Trade Related Intellectual Property Rights) Agreement and GATS (General Agreement on Trade in Services) of the WTO. TRIPS imposes patents and monopolies on drugs, taking essential medicines beyond the reach of the poor.

For example, the AIDS medicine which costs $200 without patents, costs $20,000 with patents. TRIPS and patents on medicines become recipes for spreading disease and death because they take cure beyond people's reach. Similarly, privatisation of health systems as imposed by the World Bank under SAPS (Structural Adjustment Programmes) and also proposed in GATS, spreads infectious diseases because low cost, decentralised public health systems are withdrawn and dismantled. These are also forms of bioterror. They are different from the acts of terrorists only because they are perpetrated by the powerful, not the marginalised and the excluded, and they are committed for the fanaticism of the free market ideology, not fundamentalist religious ideologies. But in impact they are the same. They kill innocent people and species by spreading disease.

Stopping the spread of bioterror at all these levels requires stopping the proliferation of technologies which create potentially hazardous biological organisms. It also requires stopping the proliferation of economic and trade policies which are crippling public health systems, spreading infectious diseases and leaving societies more vulnerable to bioterrorism.

Vandana Shiva is founder-director of the Research Foundation for Science, Technology and Ecology, New Delhi. An active campaigner for farmers' rights and the rights of the poor and marginalised, she has written several books on ecology, development and biodiversity. Among the most influential are Staying Alive: Women, Ecology and Survival in India; Monocultures of the Mind; The Violence of the Green Revolution; *and* Ecology and the Politics of Survival. *She was awarded the Right Livelihood Award—also known as the Alternative Nobel Prize—in 1993.*

Originally published in The Hindu.

Barbara Ehrenreich *November 4, 2001*

Veiled threat

Key West, Fla.—Feminists can take some dim comfort from the fact that the Taliban's egregious misogyny has finally been noticed. For years, the oppression of Afghan women was a topic for exotic list serves and the occasional forlorn Internet petition. As recently as May, for example, President Bush congratulated the ruling Taliban for banning opium production and handed them a cheque for $43 million—never mind that their regime accords women a status somewhat below that of livestock. In the weeks after September 11, you could find escaped Afghan women on Oprah and longtime anti-Taliban activist Mavis Leno doing the cable talk shows. CNN has shown the documentary "Behind the Veil," and even Bush has seen fit to mention the Taliban's hostility towards women—although the regime's hospitality to Osama bin Laden is still seen as a far greater crime. Women's rights may play no part in US foreign policy, but we should perhaps be grateful that they have at least been important enough to deploy in the media mobilization for war. On the analytical front, though, the neglect of Taliban misogyny—and beyond that, Islamic fundamentalist misogyny, in general—remains almost total. If the extreme segregation and oppression of women do not stem from the Koran, as non-fundamentalist Muslims insist, if it is in fact something new, then why did it emerge when it did at the end of the twentieth century? Liberal and left-wing commentators have done a thorough job of explaining why the fundamentalists hate America, but no one has bothered to figure out why they hate women.

And "hate" is the operative verb here. Fundamentalists may claim that the sequestration and covering of women serves to "protect" the weaker, more rape-prone sex. Or that they "protect" men from having unclean thoughts. But the protection argument hardly applies to the fundamentalist groups in Pakistan and Kashmir that specialize in throwing acid in the faces of unveiled women. There's a difference between protection and a protection racket.

The mystery of fundamentalist misogyny deepens when you consider that that the anti-imperialist and anti-colonialist movements of 40 or 50 years ago were, for the most part, at least officially committed to women's rights. Women participated in Mao's Long March; they fought in the Algerian revolution and in the guerrilla armies of Mozambique, Angola and El Salvador. The ideologies of these movements—nationalist or socialist –were inclusive of women and open, theoretically anyway, to the idea of equality. Bin Laden is, of course, hardly a suitable heir to the Third World liberation movements of the mid-20th century, but he does purport to speak for the downtrodden and against Western capitalism and militarism. Except that his movement has nothing to offer the most downtrodden sex but the veil, and a life lived largely indoors.

Of those commentators who do bother with the subject, most explain the misogyny as part of the fundamentalists' wholesale rejection of "modernity" or "the West." Hollywood culture is filled with images of strong or at least sexually assertive women, hence, the reasoning goes, the Islamic fundamentalist impulse of reducing women to chattel. The only trouble with this explanation is that the fundamentalists have been otherwise notably selective in their rejection of the "modern." The 19 terrorists of September 11 studied aviation and communicated with each other by email. Bin Laden and the Taliban favour Kalashnikovs and Stingers over scimitars. If you're going to accept western technology, why throw out something that has contributed to western economic success—the participation of women in public life?

I don't know but I am willing to start a dialogue by risking a speculation: Maybe part of the answer lies in the ways that globalization has posed a particular threat to men. Western industry has displaced traditional crafts—female as well as male—and large-scale, multinational-controlled agriculture has downgraded the independent farmer to the status of hired hand. From West Africa to Southeast Asia, these trends have resulted in massive male displacement and, frequently, unemployment. At the same time, globalization has offered new opportunities for Third World women—in export-oriented manufacturing, where women are favoured for their presumed "nimble fingers," and more recently, as migrant domestics working in wealthy countries.

These are not, of course, opportunities for brilliant careers, but for extremely low paid work under frequently abusive conditions. Still, the demand for female labour on the "global assembly line" and in the homes of the affluent has been enough to generate a kind of global gender revolution. While males have lost their traditional status as farmers and breadwinners, women have been entering the market economy and gaining the marginal independence conferred even by a paltry wage. In Sri Lanka, according to anthropologist Michele Ruth Gamburd, where many women find work in factories or as migrant domestics, the decline of the male breadwinning role has led to male demoralizing, marked by idleness, drinking and gambling.

Add to the economic dislocation engendered by globalization the onslaught of western cultural imagery, and you have the makings of what sociologist Arlie Hochschild has called a "global masculinity crisis". The man who can no longer make a living, who may depend on his wife's earnings, can watch Hollywood sexpots on pirated videos and begin to think the world has been turned upside down. This is *Stiffed*—Susan Faludi's 1999 book on the decline of traditional manhood in America—gone global.

Or maybe the global assembly line has played only a minor role in generating Islamic fundamentalist misogyny. After all the Taliban's home country, Afghanistan, has not been a popular site for multinational manufacturing plants. There, we might look for an explanation involving the exigencies—and mythologies—of war. Afghans have fought each other and the Soviets for much of the last 20 years and, as Klaus Theweleit wrote in his brilliant late-1980s book, *Male Fantasies*, long-time warriors have a tendency to see women as a corrupting and debilitating force. Hence, perhaps, the all-male madrassas in Pakistan where boys as young as six are trained for jihad, far from the potentially softening influence of mothers and sisters. Or recall terrorist Mohammad Atta's specification, in his will, that no woman handle his corpse or approach his grave.

Then again, it could be a mistake to take Islamic fundamentalism out of the context of other fundamentalisms—Christian and Orthodox Jewish. All three aspire to restore women to the status they occupied—or are believed to have occupied—in certain ancient nomadic Middle Eastern tribes. Religious fundamentalism in general has been explained as a backlash against the modern, capitalist world, and fundamentalism everywhere is no friend to the female sex. To comprehend the full nature of the threats we face since September 11, we need to figure out why. Assuming women matter, that is.

Barbara Ehrenreich is a political essayist and social critic who tackles a brave and diverse range of issues in books and magazine articles. She is the author or co-author of twelve books, including Fear of Falling: The Inner Life of the Middle Class *(1989), and,* Blood Rites: Origins and History of the Passions of War *(1997). She has written for dozens of magazines, including* Ms., Harper's, The Nation, The Progressive, The New Republic, The Atlantic Monthly *and the* New YorkTimes Magazine. *Her forthcoming book is called* Nickel and Dimed: Surviving in Low-Wage America.

This article first appeared in the San Francisco Chronicle.

Suchita Vemuri

The hidden cost of war

On the ground, war translates into heartbreaking costs—a price that goes beyond the price of lives lost. Interrupted development means prolonged suffering for someone "out there". Directing investment into wartime requirements means someone pays for the additional cost through higher taxes, or by cutting back on consumption. Disruption in the movement of people and goods, including money, means someone suffers scarce access to essential goods; maybe someone dies from the lack of an essential commodity.

There is more than one school of thought that believes that war is a necessity—while some economists hold that war is a cyclical economic inevitability, some psychologists and anthropologists believe that all civilisations need periodic bloodletting.

For many, war is a time of peak activity—within a month of the September 11 attacks on the Pentagon in Washington and the World Trade Centre in New York, pharmaceutical companies were gearing up for maximum capacity production, and humanitarian agencies were planning additional recruitment.

But for the ordinary citizen, war is simply a time of disruption, anger, anxiety and fear. After the attack in the US, among the millions of people affected are:

- an Afghan villager, who will have to wait longer for safe drinking water;
- a poor Somali, who has lost access to her expatriate breadwinner, the only source of her livlihood;
- a middle-class Indian hardware assembler, who will pay more for computer components imported from the US;
- a New York UNICEF consultant, who lost two weeks' income as the WTC crash destroyed the bank of Internet servers;

- a resident of Islamabad, who has had to disrupt her life and move to Dubai in fear;
- an executive of the Students Islamic Movement of India (SIMI), who was jailed.

The value of the cost of lives lost in the attacks is incalculable, except in legal and insurance terms. The cost to lives left behind is equally non-quantifiable—the loss of income may be calculated but the emotional loss, the loss of a sense of security, remains hidden.

And as the US makes the "war against terrorism" a global war, the loss of security, real and felt, engulfs the international community. From the Afghan frantically digging a futile hole beneath his mud hut to shelter his family against a rain of bombs, to the American queuing up to test for anthrax contamination. A few other examples:

Afghanistan A Japanese well-digging project run by Peshawar-kai (Japan Medical Service), a Fukuoka-based non-governmental organisation (NGO) in drought-hit Afghanistan has been disrupted, raising concerns that villagers will remain without safe drinking water and be prone to epidemics. The project team planned to build about 1,000 wells by next spring. It had already completed more than 600 wells, mostly in eastern Afghanistan, when it was forced to evacuate the country for safety reasons. The 626 wells dug by early September helped prevent more than an estimated 10,000 people from leaving their villages, said Keiji Ishida, an engineer with the project. War-torn Afghanistan is also suffering its worst drought in three decades.

Somalia Led by Europe and the US, a number of bank accounts of organisations and individuals, suspected to have links with terrorists, were frozen soon after September 11. Among these are Al-Rashid Trust, a Pakistan-based charity which denied any terrorist links and claimed it helps feed more than 300,000 Afghans, and al-Itihad al-Islamiya, a Somalia-based Muslim group with a global network of bank branches, mainly in Somalia and the US. The bank allows Somalis living abroad to transfer money in seconds to a relative living almost anywhere in Somalia—last year, these handled around $500 million. The cost to thousands of poor Somalis, anxiously awaiting remittances to buy themselves food and medicine, is yet to be calculated.

World War I the final figures

Central Powers	Killed	Wounded	Missing/POW
Austria-Hungary	1,200,000	3,620,000	2,200,000
Bulgaria	87,500	152,390	27,029
Germany	1,773,700	4,216,058	1,152,800
Turkey	325,000	400,000	250,000
Entente & Allied	**Killed**	**Wounded**	**Missing/POW**
Belgium	13,716	44,686	34,659
British Empire	908,371	2,090,212	191,652
France	1,375,800	4,266,000	537,000
Greece	5,000	21,000	1,000
Italy	650,000	947,000	600,000
Japan	300	907	3
Montenegro	3,000	10,000	7,000
Portugal	7,222	13,751	12,318
Romania	335,706	120,000	80,000
Russia	1,700,000	4,950,000	2,500,000
Serbia	45,000	133,148	152,958
USA	116,516	204,002	4,500

Source: *Encyclopaedia Britannica*

Russian Losses in Afghanistan 1979–89

Killed in action	9,511
Died of wounds	2,386
Accidental deaths, suicides etc.	1,739
Died of disease	817
Total	14,453
Wounded	53,753
Sick	415,932
Total	469,685

Source: *Soviet Casualties and Combat Losses* by G.F. Krivosheev

India The first estimates of property and casualty damages in the World Trade Centre crashes put the cost at anything between US$40 billion and US$60 billion. And almost simultaneously, financial and stock markets worldwide went into shock, insurance premia shot up as did transport (especially shipping) costs. Currencies such as the Indian rupee—and our national economy is crucially dependent on trade with the US—lost around 10 per cent in value against internationally accepted currencies such as the Euro and the US dollar. For the country, already in a crisis with a mere 2.2 per cent growth registered in the first eight months of 2001, import costs have gone up and export earnings cut in one blow.

At another, more sweeping level, the International Monetary Fund (IMF) stated on September 26: "Clearly, recent events will have an impact on activity in the short term, and add to the already significant downside risks both in the US and elsewhere." The IMF statement was made on the occasion of the release of the second of its bi-annual *World Economic Outlook* report for 2001.

The report, which characterised the global economy as being "already on the brink of recession" before the September 11 attacks on the US, had forecast economic growth of just 2.6 per cent for 2001, without factoring in the attacks, which were too recent to be fully analysed. The impact of "recent events" will undoubtedly affect the economic outlook in the near future, an indication of which is already in, in the massive layoffs by multinationals worldwide.

A twist to this is that the layoff costs are compounded by recent US policies, which have, in large part, dismantled unemployment benefits. The irony is that the government had stepped up its call to people to spend, a call it had issued earlier, in the face of a slowdown in the past several months.

The IMF projection was already sharply lower than an April 2001 estimate of 3.2 per cent and well below the 4.7 per cent global growth in 2000. Economists view worldwide growth of 2.5 per cent as a level indicative of global recession. Since September 11, most Wall Street economists are reported to have downgraded their global forecasts to growth of less than 2.5 per cent.

In a statement released on October 1, the World Bank said: "The September 11 terrorist attacks in the US will hurt economic growth in developing countries worldwide in 2001 and 2002, condemning as many as 10 million more people to live in poverty next year, and hampering the fight against diseases and malnutrition."

In a preliminary economic assessment, the World Bank said that "before September 11" it "expected developing country growth to fall from 5.5 per cent in 2000 to 2.9 per cent in 2001 as a result of slowdowns in the US, Japan and Europe, and then rebound to 4.3 per cent in 2002." But "because the attacks will delay the rich countries recovery into 2002," the Bank has now warned "that developing countries' growth could be lower by 0.5–0.75 percentage points in 2002."

The longer-term economic consequences will be more subtle—the US has already announced an allocation of US$40 billion for Operation Enduring Freedom and will step up its already vast allocation of resources for security and defence, as will other countries. Much of this will be taken away from investments in development.

As analyst Don Mathews has said in *Pravda* (October 5, 2001): "The economic cost of the shift in resources is enormous. Resources poured into security cannot be used to produce houses, food, or medicine."

Or as World Bank President James D. Wolfensohn said:

> We have seen the human toll the recent attacks wrought in the US. . . But there is another human toll that is largely unseen and one that will be felt in all parts of the developing world, especially Africa. We estimate that tens of thousands more children will die worldwide and some 10 million more people are likely to be living below the poverty line of $1 a day because of the terrorist attacks. This is simply from lack of income. Many, many more people will be thrown into poverty if development strategies are disrupted.

A disruption that is already evident in the evacuation of the Japanese NGO which was drilling wells in Afghanistan.

The Bank went on to state: "The slower growth and recessions will hit the most vulnerable people in developing countries the hardest. The Bank estimates that an additional 20,000–40,000 children under five years old could die from the economic consequences of the September 11 attack as poverty worsens." There will be disruption also in exports, tourism, foreign investment... all affecting economies.

In the long term also, the cynical truth is that slowing economies will revive, as past experience of wartime economies has shown. War has an immediate beneficiary effect on industries such as engineering, armaments and pharmaceuticals, and ultimately on the overall economy. More immediately, there is a crisis as markets adjust to new realities.

In the money industry, for example, as governments move ahead on what US Treasury Secretary Paul O'Neill has called an "economic war on terrorism", banks are thinking about the effects on the entire financial system.

Even before the September 11 attacks, banks in European Union member countries had frozen close to US$100 million worth of Afghan assets since July, on preliminary information that these were linked to Osama bin Laden. Since the attacks, the United Kingdom has frozen another US$68 million.

Experts say a global clampdown on funds held by terrorist groups is no easy task due to loopholes in the world's financial system and informal methods of moving money. But the recent declarations (of an economic war against terrorism) beg the question—why wasn't any attempt made earlier to dry up the funds pipeline to the terrorists?

For decades, governments have been promising action against the money conduits to terrorists and the drug trade. The sudden clampdown post September 11, decided upon in haste, has affected organisations such as al-Itihad al-Islamiya of Somalia, which has never before been suspected to have terrorist links or included on any watchlist anywhere in the world.

Explaining why the organisation has been included in the economic war against terrorism, diplomats said, "The fear is that bin Laden and his sympathisers could use the network" to move assets independent of any American control. So that brings us to fear. The most insidious cost of war is the loss of security, real and percieved—real loss of security and the sense of its loss—and related loss of civil liberties. There is no way to calculate the cost of fear and mistrust.

There are reports that pilots on some airlines have refused to carry Muslim passengers from Asia. There are also reports that the Chinese government has sent out a directive that its national airline will not carry passengers from a long list of Islamic countries. This is not merely fear—this is paranoia, affecting the rights of people worldwide.

Also consider this: The first thought that arose worldwide (as reported in the media) immediately after the recent Russian Siberian Airline TU-154 crash into the Black Sea was that it could be a terrorist or warlike attack. The first reports, in fact, evoked the following response from Unity, a Ukrainian political group: "We have reason to suppose that there has been a terrorist act, though other versions cannot be excluded, including ones connected with maneuvers of Ukrainian anti-aircraft forces."

In the days before September 11, the first assumptions would have been systems failure!

The September 11 attacks and the subsequent anthrax, bomb and other scares in the US have led to what Los Angeles-based Reuters columnist Arthur Spiegelman describes as "a national nervous breakdown". How long before it becomes a global nervous breakdown? Already, some of the more affluent Pakistanis and Iranians, with resources in other countries, are fleeing their lands in fear of the theatre of war expanding. In India, a 14-year-old makes a hoax hijack threat call and it becomes 'news' of a terrorist attack worldwide. There is fear in the air—fear for oneself in our separate localities and fear for the collective global future.

With fear comes a readiness to accept draconian laws in the hope that this will drive away the bogeyman. Perhaps the biggest cost of war is the denial of civil rights—after September 11, the police reportedly detained a man for having a tattoo of Osama bin Laden on his chest.

India has issued an ordinance against terrorism, an ordinance that is a virtual repeat of an earlier law (TADA) that was found by an independent inquiry commission to have been "more abused than used". Hong Kong is pushing through legislation that seeks to do away with confidentiality in banking, a radical departure from normal financial practice that may well affect its business.

An opinion poll run by CNN found a sudden increase in the number of US citizens supporting US aid to Israel. From hovering around 40 per cent for years, the numbers jumped to nearly 55 per cent.

An Israeli government official gloated to the press that it appeared America no longer cared if Israel shot Palestinians dead in the streets. In the US, Israel's domestic lobby almost celebrated the attacks—in fact, five Israeli nationals were arrested by the US Federal Bureau of Investigation in New York for celebrating the event in the streets.

Violence, particularly anti-Islamic violence, seems to have become acceptable worldwide. From anti-Semitism to anti-Islam is not too long a step. In the days after September 11, dozens of Palestinians and Israelis have been killed in clashes—while the news did not go unnoticed, it certainly did not make the kind of headlines it once would have. Till an Israeli minister was killed, and Israel struck back to avenge his death.

Such are the 'hidden' and not-so-hidden costs of war. Borne by some and directed by others. For poets such as William Blake innocence turned to despair; but in the more cynical twenty-first century, with despair already the norm, perhaps humanity will emerge in the long term.

Suchita Vemuri is a senior journalist, having worked with various dailies, news and feature agencies and magazines in Bombay, Visakhapatnam and Delhi, before moving to consultant work in developing communications strategies and products. She works as a consultant with public affairs and public relations firms, as well as other private and multilateral organizations. She has also worked as a trade union lawyer in Bombay and as a researcher at the Bombay and Andhra Universities.

3
Saying No

Sunera Thobani *October 12, 2001*

War frenzy

My recent speech at a women's conference on violence against women has generated much controversy. In the aftermath of the terrible attacks of September 11, I argued that the US response of launching "America's new war" would increase violence against women. I situated the current crisis within the continuity of North/South relations, rooted in colonialism and imperialism. I criticized American foreign policy, as well as President Bush's racialized construction of the American nation. Finally, I spoke of the need for solidarity with the Afghan women's organizations as well as the urgent necessity for the women's movement in Canada to oppose the war.

Decontextualized and distorted media reports of my address have led to accusations of me being an academic imposter, morally bankrupt and engaged in hate-mongering. It has been fascinating to observe how my comments regarding American foreign policy, a record well documented by numerous sources whose accuracy or credentials cannot be faulted, have been dubbed "hate-speech". To speak about the indisputable record of US-backed coups, death squads, bombings, and killings ironically makes me a "hate-monger". I was even made the subject of a "hate-crime" complaint to the Royal Canadian Mounted Police (RCMP), alleging that my speech was a "hate-crime". Despite the virulence of these responses, I welcome the public discussion my speech has generated as an opportunity to further the public debate about Canada's support of America's new war. When I made the speech, I believed it was imperative to have this debate before any attacks were launched on any country. Events have overtaken us with the bombing of Afghanistan underway and military rule again having been declared in Pakistan in the recent past. The need for this discussion has now assumed greater urgency as reports of casualties are making their way into the news. My speech at the women's conference was aimed at mobilizing the women's movement against this war. I am now glad for this opportunity to address wider constituencies and in different forums.

First, however, a few words about my location: I place my work within the tradition of radical, politically engaged scholarship. I have always rejected the politics of academic elitism which insists that academics should remain above the fray of activism and use only disembodied, objectified language and a "properly" dispassionate professional demeanor to establish our intellectual credentials. My work is grounded in the politics, practices, and languages of the various communities I come from, and the social justice movements to which I am committed.

On American foreign policy

In the aftermath of the terrible September 11 attacks on the World Trade Center and the Pentagon, the Bush administration launched "America's War on Terrorism." Eschewing any role for the United Nations and the need to abide by international law, the US administration initiated an international alliance to justify its unilateral military action against Afghanistan. One of its early coalition partners was the Canadian government which committed its unequivocal support for whatever forms of assistance the United States might request. In this circumstance, it is entirely reasonable that people in Canada examine carefully the record of American foreign policy.

As I observed in my speech, this record is alarming and does not inspire confidence. In Chile, the CIA-backed coup against the democratically elected Allende government led to the deaths of over 30,000 people. In El Salvador, the US-backed regime used death squads to kill about 75,000 people. In Nicaragua, the US-sponsored terrorist Contra war led to the deaths of over 30,000 people. The initial bombing of Iraq left over 200,000 dead, and the bombings have continued for the last ten years. Unicef estimates that over one million Iraqis have died, and that 5,000 more die every month as a result of the US-imposed sanctions, enforced in their harshest form by US power. The list does not stop here. 150,000 were killed and 50,000 disappeared in Guatemala after the 1954 CIA-sponsored coup; over two million were killed in Vietnam; and 200,000 before that in the Hiroshima and Nagasaki nuclear attacks. Numerous authoritarian regimes have been backed by the United States including Saudi Arabia, Egypt, the apartheid regime in South Africa, Suharto's dictatorship in Indonesia, Marcos in the Philippines, and Israel's various occupations of Lebanon, the Golan Heights, and the Palestinian territories. The US pattern of foreign intervention has been to overthrow leftist governments and activists and to impose right-wing regimes, which in turn support US interests, even if this means training and using death squads and assassinating leftist politicians and activists. To this end, it has a record of treating civilians as entirely expendable.

It is in this context that I made my comment that the United States is the largest and most dangerous global force, unleashing horrific levels of violence around the world, and that the path of US foreign policy is soaked in blood. The controversy generated by this comment has surprisingly not addressed the veracity of this assessment of the US record. Instead, it has focused on my tone and choice of words (inflammatory, excessive, inelegant, unacademic, angry, etc.).

Now I have to admit that my use of the words "horrific violence" and "soaked in blood" is very deliberate and carefully considered. I do not use theses words lightly. To successive United States administrations the deaths resulting from its policies have been just so many statistics, just so much "collateral damage". Rendering invisible the humanity of the peoples targeted for attack is a strategy well used to hide the impact of colonialist and imperialist interventions. Perhaps there is no more potent a strategy of dehumanization than to proudly proclaim the accuracy and efficiency of "smart" weapons systems, and of surgical and technological precision, while rendering invisible the suffering bodies of these peoples as disembodied statistics and mere "collateral damage". The use of embodied language, grounded in the recognition of the actual blood running though these bodies, is an attempt to humanize these peoples in profoundly graphic terms.

It compels us to recognize the sheer corporality of the terrain upon which bombs rain and mass terror is waged. This language calls on "us" to recognize that "they" bleed just like "we" do, that "they" hurt and suffer just like "us." We are complicit in this blood-letting when we support American wars. Witness the power of this embodiment in the shocked and horrified responses to my voice and my words, rather than to the actual horror of these events. I will be the first to admit that it is extremely unnerving to "see" blood in the place of abstract, general categories and statistics. Yet this is what we need to be able to see if we are to see the terrible human costs of empire-building. We have all felt the shock and pain of repeatedly watching the searing images of violence unleashed upon those who died in New York and Washington. The stories we have heard from their loved ones have made us feel their terrible human loss. Yet where do we witness the pain of the victims of US aggression? How do we begin to grasp the extent of their loss? Whose humanity do we choose to recognize and empathize with, and who becomes just so much "collateral damage" to us? Anti-colonial and anti-imperialist movements and theorists have long insisted on placing the bodies and experiences of marginalized Others at the center of our analysis of the social world. To fail to do this at this moment in history would be unconscionable. In the aftermath of the responses to my speech, I am more convinced than ever of the need to engage in the language and politics of embodied thinking and speaking. After all, it is the lives, and deaths, of millions of human beings we are discussing. This is neither a controversial nor a recent demand. Feminists (such as Mahasweta Devi, Toni Morrison, Gayatri Spivak, and Patricia Williams) have forcefully drawn our attention to what is actually done to women's bodies in the course of mapping out racist colonial relations. Frantz Fanon, one of the foremost theorists of decolonization, studied and wrote about the role of violence in colonial social organization and about the psychology of oppression; but he described just as readily the bloodied, violated black bodies and the "searing bullets" and "blood-stained knives" which were the order of the day in the colonial world. Eduardo Galeano entitled one of his books, *The Open Veins of Latin America,* and the post-colonial theorist Achille Mbembe talks of the "mortification of the flesh," of the "mutilation" and "decapitation" of oppressed bodies. Aime Cesaire's poetry pulses with the physicality of blood, pain, fury, and rage in his outcry against the domination of African bodies. Even Karl Marx, recognized as one of the founding fathers of the modern social sciences, wrote trenchant critiques of capital, exploitation, and classical political economy, and did not flinch from naming the economic system he was studying "vampire capitalism". In attempting to draw attention to the violent effects of abstract and impersonal policies, I claim a proud intellectual pedgree.

Invoking the American nation

In my speech I argued that in order to legitimize the imperialist aggression which the Bush administration is undertaking, the President is invoking an American nation and people as being vengeful and bloodthirsty. It is *de riguer* in the social sciences to acknowledge that the notion of a "nation" or a "people" is socially constructed. The American nation is no exception.

If we consider the language used by Bush and his administration to mobilize this nation for war, we encounter the following: launching a crusade; operation infinite justice; fighting the forces of evil and darkness; fighting the barbarians; hunting down the evil-doers; draining the swamps of the Middle East, etc., etc. This language is very familiar to peoples who have been colonized by Europe. Its use at this moment in time reveals the nature of the fundamentalist and racialized western ideology which is being mobilized to rally the troops and to build a national and international consensus in defense of "civilization". It suggests that anyone who hesitates to join in is also "evil" and "uncivilized". In this vein, I have repeatedly been accused of supporting extremist Islamist regimes merely for criticizing US foreign policy and western colonialism.

Another tactic to mobilize support for the war has been the manipulation of public opinion. Polls conducted in the immediate aftermath of the September 11 attacks were used repeatedly to inform us that the overwhelming majority of Americans allegedly supported a strong military retaliation. They did not know against whom, but they purportedly supported this strategy anyway. In both the use of language and these polls, we are witnessing what Noam Chomsky has called the "manufacture of consent". Richard Lowry, editor of the *National Review* opined, "If we flatten part of Damascus or Tehran or whatever it takes, this is part of the solution." President Bush stated, "We will bear no distinction between those who commit the terrorist attacks and those who harbour them." Even as the bombing began, he declared that the war is "broader" than against Afghanistan, that other nations have to decide if they side with his administration or if they are "murderers and outlaws themselves". We have been asked by most public commentators to accept these calls for military aggression against "evil-doers" as natural, understandable, and even reasonable, given the attacks on the United States. I reject this position. It would be just as understandable a response to re-examine American foreign policy, to address the root causes of the violent attacks on the United States, and to make a commitment to abide by international law. In my speech, I urged women to break through this discourse of "naturalizing" the military aggression, and recognize it for what it is: vengeful retribution and an opportunity for a crude display of American military might. We are entitled to ask: Who will make the decision regarding which "nations" are to be labeled "murderers" and "outlaws"? Which notions of "justice" are to be upheld? Will the Bush administration set the standard, even as it is overtly institutionalizing racial profiling across the United States?

I make very clear distinctions between people in America and their government's call for war. Many people in America are seeking to contest the "national" consensus being manufactured by speaking out and by organizing rallies and peace marches in major cities, about which there has been very little coverage in Canada. Irresponsible media reporting of my comments which referred to Bush's invocation of the American nation as a vengeful one deliberately took my words out of this context, repeating them in one television broadcast after another in a grossly distorted fashion.

My choice of language was, again, deliberate. I wanted to bring attention to Bush's right-wing, fundamentalist leanings and to the neo-colonialist/imperialist practices of his administration. The words "bloodthirsty" and "vengeful" are designations most people are quite comfortable with attributing to "savages" and to the "uncivilized", while the United States is represented as the beacon of democracy and civilization. The words "bloodthirsty" and "vengeful" make us confront the nature of the ideological justification for this war, as well as its historical roots, unsettling and discomfiting as that might be.

The politics of liberating women

I have been taken to task for stating that there will be no emancipation for women anywhere until western domination of the planet is ended. In my speech I pointed to the importance of Afghanistan for its strategic location near central Asia's vast resources of oil and natural gas. I think that there is very little argument that the West continues to dominate and consume a vast share of the earth's resources. This is not a controversial statement. Many prominent intellectuals, journalists and activists alike, have pointed out that this domination is rooted in the history of colonialism and rests on the ongoing maintenance of the North/South divide, and that it will continue to provoke violence and resistance across the planet. I argued that in the current climate of escalating militarism, there will be precious little emancipation for women, either in the countries of the North or the South.

In the specific case of Afghanistan, it was the American administration's economic and political interests which led to its initial support for, and arming of, Hekmatyar's Hezb i Islami and its support for Pakistan's collaboration in and organization of the Taliban regime in the mid-1990s. According to the Pakistani journalist Ahmed Rashid, the United States and Unocal conducted negotiations for years with the Taliban for an oil pipeline through Afghanistan in the mid-1990s. We have seen the horrendous consequences this has had for women in Afghanistan. When Afghan women's groups were calling attention to this US support as a major factor in the Taliban regime's coming to power, we did not heed them. We did not realize that Afghan women's groups were in the front line resisting the Taliban and its Islamist predecessors, including the present militias of the Northern Alliance. Instead, we chose to see them only as "victims" of "Islamic culture," to be pitied and "saved" by the West. Time and time again, Third World feminists have pointed out to us the pitfalls of rendering invisible the agency and resistance of the women of the South, and of reducing women's oppression to various Third World "cultures". Many continue to ignore these insights. Now, the US administration has thrown its support behind the Northern Alliance, even as Afghan women's groups oppose the US military attacks on Afghanistan, and raise serious concerns about the record of the Northern Alliance in perpetrating human rights abuses and violence against women in the country. If we listen to the voices of these women, we will very quickly be disabused of the notion that US intervention is going to lead to the emancipation of women in Afghanistan. Even before the bombings began, hundreds of thousands of Afghan women were compelled to flee their homes and communities, and to become refugees. The bombings of Kabul, Kandahar, Jalalabad and other cities in the country will result in further loss of life, including the lives of women and children. Over three million Afghan refugees are now on the move in the wake of US attacks. How on earth can we justify theses bombings in the name of furthering women's emancipation?

My second point was that imperialism and militarism do not further women's liberation in western countries either. Women have to be brought into line to support racist imperialist goals and practices, and they have to live with the men who have been brutalized in the waging of war when these men come back. Men who kill women and children abroad are hardly likely to come back cured of the effects of this brutalization. Again, this is not a very controversial point of view. Women are taught to support military aggression, which is then presented as being in their "national" interest. These are hardly the conditions in which women's freedoms can be furthered. As a very small illustration, just witness the very public vilification I have been subjected to for speaking out in opposition to this war.

I have been asked by my detractors that if I, as a woman, am so critical of western domination, why do I live here? It could just as readily be asked of them that if they are so contemptuous of the non-western world, why do they so fervently desire the oil, trade, cheap labour and other resources of that world? Challenges to our presence in the West have long been answered by people of color who say, We are here because you were (are?) there! Migrants find ourselves in multiple locations for a myriad of reasons, personal, historical and political. Wherever we resided, however, we claim the right to speak and participate in public life.

Closing words

My speech was made to rally the women's movement in Canada to oppose the war. Journalists and editors across the country have called me idiotic, foolish, stupid, and just plain nutty. While a few journalists have attempted balanced coverage of my speech, too many sectors of the media have resorted to vicious personal attacks. Like others, I must express a concern that this passes for intelligent commentary in the mainstream media.

The manner in which I have been vilified is difficult to understand unless one sees it as a visceral response to an "ungrateful immigrant" or an uppity woman of colour who dares to speak out. Vituperation and ridicule are two of the most common forms of silencing dissent. The subsequent harassment and intimidation which I have experienced, as have some of my colleagues, confirms that the suppression of debate is more important to many supporters of the current frenzied war rhetoric than is the open discussion of policy and its effects. Fortunately, I have also received strong messages of support. Day by day the opposition to this unconscionable war is growing in Canada and all over the world.

I would like to thank all of my family, friends, colleagues, and allies who have supported and encouraged me.

I have since learnt from my lawyer that the Ottawa police have dismissed the complaint against me. While I am glad that the police have decided not to proceed with the case, I believe we cannot discount the effect this incident has had on creating a chilly and fearful climate for anti-racist, feminist, and anti-war organising in the country. Nor can we discount the serious personal and financial consequences to activists who stand up against this form of harassment.

Sunera Thobani is cross-appointed to the Center for Research in Women's Studies and Gender Relations and the Women's Studies programme at the University of British Columbia. She is Past President of the National Action Committee on the Status of Women (1993–96), and the first woman of colour to hold this position.

Susan Sontag October 17, 2001

'The traitor' fires back

An interview with David Talbot, *Salon*

Writer Susan Sontag has produced many texts during her four-decade career, including historical novels and reflections on cancer, photography and the war in Bosnia. But it was a brief essay, less than 100 words long, in the September 24, 2001 issue of the New Yorker *that created the biggest uproar of her life.*

In the piece that she wrote shortly after the terror attacks of September 11, Sontag dissected the political and media blather that poured out of the television in the hours after the explosions of violence. After subjecting herself to what she calls "an overdose of CNN,*" Sontag reacted with a coldly furious burst of analysis, savaging political leaders and media mandarins for trying to convince the country that everything was okay, that our attackers were simply cowards, and that our childlike view of the world need not be disturbed.*

As if to prove her point, a furious chorus of sharp-tongued pundits immediately decended on Sontag, outraged that she had broken from the ranks of the soothingly platitudinouss. She was called an "America-hater," a "moral idiot," a "traitor" who deserved to be driven into "the wilderness," never more to be heard. The bellicose right predictably tried to lump her in with the usual left-wing peace crusaders, whose programmed pacifism has sidelined them during the current political debates.

But this tarbrush doesn't stick. As a thinker, Sontag is rigourously, sometimes abrasively, independent. She has offended the left as often as the right (political terms, she points out, that have become increasingly useless), alienating some idealogues when she attacked communism as "facism with a human face" during the uprising of the Polish shipyard workers in the 1980s, and again during the US bombing campaign against the Serbian dictatorship, which she strongly supported.

Sontag, 68, remains characteristically unrepentant in the face of the recent attacks. On Monday, she talked with us by phone from her home in Manhattan, reflecting on the controversy, the Bush war effort and the media's surrender to what she views as a national conformity campaign.

Did the storm of reaction to your brief essay in the New Yorker *take you by surprise?*

Absolutely. I mean, I am aware of what a radical point of view is; very occasionally I have espoused one. But I did not think for a moment my essay was radical or even particularly dissenting. It seemed very commonsense. I have been amazed by the ferocity of how I've been attacked, and it goes on and on. One article in the *New Republic*, a magazine for which I have written, began: "What do Osama bin Laden, Saddam Hussein and Susan Sontag have in common?" I have to say my jaw dropped. Apparently, we are all in favour of the dismantling of America. There's a kind of rhetorical overkill aimed at me that is astonishing. There has been a demonization which is ludicrous.

What has been constructed is this sort of grotesque trinity comprised of myself, Bill Maher and Noam Chomsky. In the Saturday *New York Times*, Frank Rich tried in his way to defend us by arguing for our complete lack of importance, by saying that any substitute weather forecaster on TV has more influence than any of us. Well, it's not true, of course. Excuse me, but Noam Chomsky is quite a bit more than a distinguished linguist. Our critics are up in arms against us because we do have a degree of influence. But our own "defenders" are reduced to saying, "Well, leave the poor things alone, they're quite obscure anyway."

Look, I have nothing in common with Bill Maher, whom I had never heard of before. And I don't agree with Noam Chomsky, whom I am very familiar with. My position is decidedly not the Chomsky position.

How do you differ from Chomsky?

First of all, I'll take the American "empire" any day over the empire of what my pal Chris Hitchens calls "Islamic fascism." I'm not against fighting this enemy—it is an enemy and I'm not pacifist. I think what happened on September 11 was an appalling crime and I am astonished that I even have to say that, to reassure people that that I feel that way. But I do feel that the Gulf War revisited is not the way to fight the enemy.

There was a very confident, orotund piece by Stanley Hoffman in the *New York Review of Books*—he's a very senior wise man in the George Kennan mold, certainly no radical. And I felt I could agree with every word he was saying. He was saying bombing Afghanistan is not the solution. We have to understand what is going on in the Middle East, we have to rethink what's going on, our foreign policy. In fact, since September 11, we are already seeing the most radical realignment of policies.

Bill Maher has abjectly apologized for his remarks—but you don't seem to be getting any more docile in the face of this storm of criticism. Why not?

Well, I'm not an institution, and I don't have a job to lose. I just get lots of very nasty letters and read lots of very nasty things in the press.

What do the letters say?

That I'm a traitor. The *New York Post*, or so I have been told, has called for me to be drawn and quartered. And then there was this Ted Koppel show—the producer invited me onto the show over a week ago. It's not my thing but I did it. And they got someone from the Heritage Foundation [Todd Gaziano], who practically foamed at the mouth and said at one point, "Susan Sontag should not be permitted to speak in honourable intellectual circles ever again." And then Koppel said, "Whoa, you really mean she shouldn't be allowed to speak?" and he said, well maybe not silenced, but disgraced and "properly discounted for her crazy views".

So there is a serious attempt to stifle debate. But, of course, God bless the Net. I keep getting more articles of various dissenting opinions e-mailed to me; naturally some of them are crazy and some I don't agree with at all. But you can't shut everyone up. The big media have been very intimidated, but not the Web.

I don't want to get defensive, but of course I am a little defensive because I am so stunned by the way my remarks were viewed. What I published in the *New Yorker* was written literally 48 hours after the September 11 attacks. I was in Berlin at the time and I was watching CNN for 48 hours straight. You might say that I had overdosed on CNN. And what I wrote was a howl of dismay at all the nonsense that I was hearing. That people were in a state of great pain and bewilderment and fear I certainly understood. But I thought, "Uh-oh, here comes a sort of revival of Cold War rhetoric and something very sanctimonious, that is going to make it very difficult for us to figure out how best to deal with this." And I have to say that my fears have been borne out.

What do you think of the Bush administration's efforts to control the media, in particular its requests that TV networks not show bin Laden and Al Qa'ida's video statements?

Excuse me, but does anyone over the age of six really think that the way Osama bin Laden has to communicate with his agents abroad is by posing in that Flintstone set of his, and pulling on his left earlobe instead of his right to send secret signals? Now, I don't believe that Condoleezza Rice and the rest of the administration really think that. At least I hope to hell that they don't. I assume they have another reason for trying to stop the TV networks from showing bin Laden's videotapes, which is they just don't want people to see his message, whatever it is. They think, why should we give him free publicity? Something very primitive like that. Which is ridiculous, because anyone online can see these tapes for themselves. Although I see the BBC, our British cousins, who are of course ever servile, are discussing whether to broadcast the tapes. We can always count on the Brits to fall in line.

Why has the media been so willing to go along with the White House's censorship efforts?

Well, when people like me are being lambasted and excoriated for saying very mild things, no wonder the media is cowed. Here's something that no one has commented on, that I continue to puzzle over: Who decided that no gruesome pictures of the World Trade Center site were to be published anywhere? Now I don't think there was a single directive coming from anywhere. But I think there was an extraordinary consenus, a kind of self-censorship by media executives who concluded that these images would be too demoralizing for the country. I think it's rather interesting that that could happen. There apparently has been only one exception: one day the *New York Daily News* showed a severed hand. But the photo appeared in only one edition and it was immediately pulled. I think that degree of unanimity within the media is pretty extraordinary.

What is your position on the war against terrorism? How should the US fight back?

My position is that I don't like throwing biscuits and peanut butter and jam and napkins, little snack packages produced in a small city in Texas, to Afghani citizens, so we can say, "Look, we're doing something humanitarian." These wretched packages of food that are grotesquely inadequate—there's apparently enough food for half a day's rations. And then the people run out to get them, into these minefields. Afghanistan has more landmines per capita than any country in the world. I don't like the way that humanitarianism is once again being used in this unholy way as a pretext for war.

As a woman, of course, I've always been appalled by the Taliban regime and would dearly like to see them toppled. I was a public critic of the regime long before the war started. But I've been told that the Northern Alliance is absolutely no better when it comes to the issue of women. The crimes against women in Afghanistan are just unthinkable; there's never been anything like it in the history of the world. So of course I would love to see that government overthrown and something less appalling put in its place.

Do I think bombing is the way to do it? Of course I don't. It's not for me to speculate on this, but there are all sorts of realpolitik outcomes that one can imagine. Afghanistan could in the end become a sort of dependency of Pakistan, which of course wouldn't please India and China. They'd probably like a little country to annex themselves. So how in the world you're going to dethrone the Taliban without causing further trouble in that part of the world, is a very complicated question. And I'm sure bright and hard-nosed people in Washington are genuinely puzzled about how to do it.

Do you really think it could be done without bombing?

Absolutely. But it's a complicated and long process—and the United States is not very experienced in these matters. The point is, as I said in my *New Yorker* piece, there's a great disconnect between reality and what people in government and the media are saying of the reality. I have no doubt that there are real debates among military and political leaders going on both there and elsewhere. But what is being peddled to the public is a fairy tale. And the atmosphere of intimidation is quite extraordinary.

And I think our protectors have been incredibly inept. In any other country the top officials of the FBI would have resigned or been fired by now. I mean, [key hijacking suspect] Mohammad Atta was on the FBI surveillance list, but this was never communicated to the airlines.

The authorities are now responding to the anthrax scare—to what I think are 99 per cent certain to be just domestic copycat crazies on their own warpath—by spreading more fear. We have Vice President Cheney saying, "Well, these people could be part of the same terrorist network that produced September 11." Well, excuse me, but we have no reason to think that.

As a result of these alarming statements from authorities, the public is terrified. I live in New York and the streets were empty after the FBI announced that another terrorist attack was imminent. You have these idiots in the FBI saying they have "credible evidence"—I love that phrase—that an attack this weekend is "possible". Which means absolutely nothing. I mean it's possible there's a pink elephant in my living room right now, as I'm talking to you from my kitchen. I haven't checked recently, but it's not very possible.

And meanwhile our ridiculous President is telling us to shop and go to the theatre and lead normal lives. Normal? I could go 50 blocks, from one end of Manhattan to another, in five minutes because there was no one in the streets, nobody in the restaurants, nobody in the cars. You can't scare people and tell them to behave normally.

We also seem to be getting contradictory messages about Muslims in the US. We're told that not all Islamic people are our enemy, but at the same time there is a fairly wide dragnet, which some civil liberties defenders have criticized as indiscriminate, aimed at rounding up Islamic suspects.

Well, people are very scared and Americans are not used to being scared. There's an American exceptionalism; we're supposed to be exempt from the calamities and terrors and anxieties that beset other countries. But now people here are scared, and it's interesting how fast they are moving in another direction. The feeling is, and I've heard this from people, about Islamic taxi drivers and shopkeepers and other people—we really ought to deport all the Muslims. Sure they're not all terrorists and some of it will be unfair, but after all we have to protect ourselves. Racial and ethnic profiling is now seen as common-sense itself. I mean, how could you not want that if you're going to take an airplane and you don't want a fellow in a turban and a beard to sit next to you?

What I live in fear of is there will be another terror attack—not a sick joke like the powder in the envelope, but something real that takes more lives, that has the stamp of something more professional and thought out. It could be another symbolically targeted building—maybe not in New York this time, but in Chicago or some other heartland city that scares the rest of the country. And then you could get something like martial law here. Many Americans, who as I say are so used to not being afraid, would willingly accede to great abridgements of freedom. Because they're afraid.

You call the president "robotic" in your New Yorker *essay. But the* New York Times, *among other media observers, has editorialized that Bush has shown a new "gravitas" since Sept. 11. Do you think the president has grown more commanding since the terror attacks?*

I saw that in the *Times*—I love that, gravitas. Has Bush grown into his role of president? No, I think he's acquired legitimacy since September 11, that's all—I don't call that "growing" at all. I think what we obviously have in Washington is some kind of regency, run presumably by Cheney and Rumsfeld and maybe Powell, although Powell is much more of an organization man than a real leader. It's all very veiled. And Cheney has not been much seen lately—is this because his is ill? It's all very mysterious. I hate to see everything become so opaque.

It seems important to the Times and other major media to shore up the president's image these days. . .

Yes, I just don't understand why debate equals dissent, and dissent equals lack of patrotism now. I mean, look, I cry every morning real tears, I mean down-the-cheek tears, when I read those small obituaries that the *New York Times* publishes of the people who died in the World Trade Center. I read them faithfully, every last one of them, and I cry. I live near a firehouse that lost a lot of men, and I've brought them things. And I'm genuinely and profoundly, exactly like everyone else, really moved, really wounded, and really in mourning. I didn't know anyone personally who died. But my son [journalist David Rieff] had a former classmate who worked for Cantor Fitzgerald who died. A number of people I know lost friends or loved ones.

I want to make one thing very clear, because I've been accused of this by some critics. I do not feel that the Sept. 11 attacks were the pursuit of legitimate grievances by illegitimate means. I think that's the position of some people, but not me. It may even be the position of Chomsky, although it's not for me to say. But it's certainly not my position.

Speaking of your son, he seems to favor a tougher military response to Islamic terrorism than you do.

Well, I don't want to go deeply into it, but clearly we don't see it exactly the same way. Whatever David thinks is tremendously important to me, but we do start from a different point of view. I feel that it's just a difference of emphasis, but without speaking for him, he feels it's deeper than that. But he's still the love of my life, so I won't criticize him.

This is one thing I do completely agree with David on: if tomorrow Israel announced a unilateral withdrawal of its forces from the West Bank and the Gaza Strip—which I am absolutely in favor of—followed by the proclamation of a Palestinian state, I don't believe it would make a dent in the forces that are supporting bin Laden's al-Qaida. I think Israel is a pretext for these people.

I do believe in the unilateral withdrawal of Israel from the Palestinian territories, which is of course the radical view held by a minority of Israeli citizens, but certainly not by the Sharon government. And it's a view I expressed when I received the Jerusalem Prize there in May, which created quite a storm. But just because I am a critic of Israeli policy—and in particular the Occupation, simply because it is untenable, it creates a border that cannot be defended—that does not mean I believe the US has brought this terrorism on itself because it supports Israel. I believe bin Laden and his supporters are using this as a pretext. If we were to change our support for Israel overnight, we would not stop these attacks.

I don't think this is what it's really about. I think it truly is a jihad, I think there is such a thing. There are many levels to Islamic rage. But what we're dealing with here is a view of the US as a secular, sinful society that must be humbled, and this has nothing to do with any particular aspect of American policy. So I don't think we have brought this upon ourselves, which is of course a view that has been attributed to me.

Let me ask you about another part of your essay that has riled your critics. You said the hijackers displayed more courage than those, presumably in the US military, who bomb their enemies from a safe distance.

No, I did not use the word "courage"—I did use my words carefully. I said they were not to be called cowards. I believe that courage is morally neutral. I can well imagine wicked people being brave and good people being timid or afraid. I don't consider it a moral virtue.

My feeling about this type of safe bombing goes back to the US air campaign against the Serbs in Kosovo, which I strongly supported, though I was criticized by many of my friends on the left for being too bellicose. I did support the bombing of the Serb forces because I had been in Sarajevo for three years during the siege, and I wanted the Serbs checked and rebuked. I wanted them out of Kosovo as I had wanted them out of Bosnia.

When the US campaign in Kosovo began, I happened to be staying with a close friend in a town on the tip of Italy, the boot, about 40 miles across from Albania, and the Apache helicopters wre literally passing over my head. They landed at the Tirana air base in Italy, but they never took off for Kosovo because it was calculated that they might be shot down and the crew killed. And the US was unwilling to accept these casualties.

But in order to bomb precisely, without hitting hospitals and other civilian targets, you have to fly low to the ground with aircraft like these. And you have to risk being brought down by anti-aircraft fire. So I was dismayed by the loss of civilian life in the US bombing campaign, which I had hoped would be very precise.

And so, thinking about this as I was writing my essay for the *New Yorker*, I became very angry. And I wrote, if you're going to use the word "cowardly", let's talk about the people who bomb from so high up that they're out of the range of any retaliation and therefore cause more civilian casualties than they otherwise would, in what is supposedly a limited military bombing.

What about those in the antiwar camp who see a moral equivalence between the destruction of the World Trade Center and the US bombing of Afghanistan?

Well, I don't share that view. I'm not a pacifist, but I am against bombing. And I do think that if you want to conduct a military operation, you have to be willing to take casualties. There are not, strictly speaking, very many military targets in Afghanistan. We're talking about one of the poorest countries in the world.

What they can do is bomb the soldiers, the camps where the Taliban soldiers are based. And you can imagine who they are, it's a lot of kids. We can drop a lot of napalm, and uranium-tipped bombs, and kill many thousands of people. We haven't been doing a lot of that yet. That's next. And then we'll get these other awful people to come in, this Northern Alliance, and it will be horrible.

Susan Sontag is one of America's finest political essayists, and author of the influential Against Interpretation, Illness as Metaphor, *and the novel*, The Volcano Lover. *She is a regular contributor to the* New York Review of Books.

David Talbot is founder and editor in chief of Salon, *where this interview originally appeared.*

Madeleine Bunting *November 19, 2001*

Intolerance of debate

Over the past few days, I've been ordered on to a strict diet of my words. A stream of emails arrived from American readers with plenty of advice (get laid, get pregnant, shut your fat legs, shut up) and prognostications for my future (you'll be fired). One told me that I made them feel sick: "untouched by our tragedy, yet [you] feel the right to criticise our country's actions". One asked if "you have a molecule of shame or humility within your entire being?" and promised to pray for me. Another asked: "How stupid do you feel now?. . . this is one of the best wars ever fought", and another asked: "As the US war on terror becomes increasingly successful, could the world say 'thank you'?"

Thank God for the volume of sea-water which puts these kind of nutters on another continent. It's not so much the fine line in misogynistic abuse from US patriots, but the intolerance of debate and diversity of opinion which is really frightening. But the truth is that this kind of emotional intensity has also seeped into the war on this side of the Atlantic—entrenched camps for and against are waging a bitter war of words over the heads of a majority who are worried and confused, but see no alternative to war.

Fear drives this kind of emotional intensity. It is a pitifully short time, only two months, since we learned of a ruthlessness born of fanaticism which we had not thought possible; our perception of human nature is having to painfully readjust to the revelation of a capacity for calmly premeditated brutality. I'm sure that fear has influenced my continuing conviction that waging war on Afghanistan is unlikely in the long term to defeat that kind of ruthless Islamist terrorism, and is very likely to have disastrous consequences for the poor benighted country itself. I very much hope I will be proved wrong.

It must have been so comforting to have been swept up in the emotional euphoria of VK day. It was the ultimate Disney ending after a month of nation-builders' storytelling. If only it were that simple. But even on VK day, the excited reporters and commentators surrounded by a telegenic rabble of curious boys at television cameras found no echo among anxious Afghan women, most of whom remained behind their burqas.

Nor did the VK story last long, quickly replaced by the tension of warlords struggling to position themselves; in Jalalabad, young men jostled around the cameras, their eyes, cartridge belts and guns all gleaming, poised for what they know best—waging war.

And yet, it's not even those Jalalabad warriors that have made the last week's events so troubling, but the growing appreciation of just how ruthless and ambitious the US is likely to become in its war against terrorism. What the events of the past few days have starkly revealed is that the US had only one interest in this war in Afghanistan, capturing bin Laden and destroying al-Qa'ida; that imperative outstripped all considerations of Afghanistan's future. So the timing of the attack was decided by US military preparedness rather than any coherent political strategy for the region, and the US war aim determined the crucial switch in tactics around November 4, when the US decided to throw its weight behind the unsavoury Northern Alliance by bombing the Taliban frontlines.

For the US, the whole country of Afghanistan is collateral damage. Or, to put it another way, a little hors d'oeuvre before they move on to the next course—Somalia, Yemen or, most worryingly of all, Iraq? The latter is already being openly touted in Washington as a possibility for the "second stage" and tension is growing in the Gulf region. Meanwhile, as far as the US is concerned, the UK with its nation-building agenda, the UN and everyone else is welcome to spend their soldiers' lives on the onerous task of clearing up the mess the US bombing has left behind, freeing it to concentrate on the next task.

All this strengthens the view that what we have to fear from September 11 is not just Islamist fanaticism, but the US response to it. Indeed, the latter could well prove a far greater threat to the stability of many countries, further stoking the Islamist fanaticism it seeks to extinguish. The template has been developed in Afghanistan: lavish bribery of neighbours, unchecked deployment of vicious military hardware, keep US soldiers out of it and use others to do the fighting. It is a foreign policy of brute force and it draws legitimacy within the US from a lethal combination of three factors: a profound sense of righteous anger, the reality of unchallenged economic and military power, and a pervasive ignorance of and indifference to the rest of the world.

To increase the danger, the US actions are unchecked by fear of another superpower and, at present, unchecked by its usually vibrant civil society where debate about the purposes or methods of the war against terrorism has been cowed into virtual silence in the mainstream. The result is that an ugly ruthlessness is creeping into US political culture. For example, "physical interrogation" or torture is proposed in the columns of *Newsweek,* while President Bush signs an order allowing military tribunals of suspected terrorists in private and without a jury, for the first time since the second world war.

In time we may come to see the disastrous timing of a rightwing presidency intent on asserting US unilateralism assuming power shortly before September 11: that tragic catastrophe has provided the moral mandate at home and the freedom for manoeuvre from allies for such a unilateralist policy. For all the US has needed western support for its war, we seem to have been singularly unsuccessful in extracting in return any compromises on US unilateralism. Putin's protestations on NMD are brushed off, and barely a murmur is raised in criticism of the US's failure to deliver its climate change plan while the world went ahead in Marrakesh last week.

From the start, this administration has been unabashed, denying any sense of responsibility to anyone other than its own citizens. Now, everyone has the almighty headache of how they are to tiptoe round and placate this raging colossus. Blair, white with exhaustion, has opted for the role of chief cheerleader, and while it may incense some that Britain, like every other country, is reduced to such impotence, the harsh reality is that it was AOS—all options stink. Bush will use and discard Blair, and the British prime minister is likely to be one among many casualties.

The Labour party has traditionally been deeply split over the conduct of US foreign policy. Vietnam, Central and Latin America and the Iran-contra affair all provoked intense controversy. That was bad enough, but we were not involved in playing the supporting role. At the risk of further incensing my American correspondents, the manipulation of the CIA in Central America could come to seem like child's play compared with what we are likely to glimpse over the next decade.

Madeleine Bunting is a columnist and lead writer for The Guardian, *London.*

Kalpana Sharma

World without colours

Last Sunday, thousands of people gathered in New York amidst the ruins of the World Trade Center and mourned for the dead. On the same day, a lone Afghan mother mourned alone for her dead children, the "collateral damage" of the increasingly senseless bombing of Afghanistan.

On both sides of the world, ordinary men and women continue to grieve even as politicians and men in uniform hunt for targets to bomb and boast of imminent victory in the "global war" against terrorism.

I have tried this last week to get away from "the war". But try as I might, I find that it creeps up on you from all sides. There is no escaping it. The world seems to have been bleached of all its colours; all of a sudden there is only black and white.

The world has changed after September 11. Words have lost their original meanings. Democracy does not denote freedom and individual rights any more.

In the name of democracy, our democratic countries are justifying laws that fly in the face of democratic and human rights. The United States, which counts itself amongst the "civilised" nations of the world, is justifying the most uncivilised behaviour in its hunt for accomplices of the terrorists who attacked it. Every day there are stories of people—Arabs, Indians, Pakistanis—being arrested, pulled out of trains and planes, being detained, questioned, harassed and traumatised.

In India, a Government that has failed to find political solutions to the problems in Kashmir and the North East is using the excuse of terrorism to introduce an unnecessary and draconian law that will seriously curb democratic freedom.

Even the media will now be told how it reports "terrorism". One can only hope that the "opposition" will unite for once and throw out this despicable piece of legislation.

And in Pakistan, a military general who claimed he was moving his country towards democracy has dropped all pretences and reintroduced military rule.

After many decades, we find ourselves once again in a polarised world. The lines of division do not follow national boundaries. They lie in the hearts of people, in how we view the world, and what we cherish as values that must be defended.

Shaded differences have been erased. We are divided into a civilised and uncivilised world; we are pro-terrorist or anti-terrorist, pro-Islamist or pro-western, pacifist or war-mongerer. You are told to choose which side you are on.

In fact, you are left with no choice. In a recent television programme, the discussion centred on conservative and moderate Muslims, a division that several participants pointed out was unnatural and dysfunctional.

The editor of a leading newspaper gave an interesting analogy. He said, that if as a Muslim he refuses an alcoholic drink, his non-Muslim media friends suggest that he must be a fundamentalist. He is not permitted the right to choose how much or how little of his religion he follows.

Yet, as he reminded us, Hindus who refuse to eat meat because it is against their religion are not considered fundamentalist.

We are also left with a permanently destabilised world. The war will spread, we are promised. Iraq might be the next target. Where next? Meanwhile, the war is not leaving countries outside the arena of battle alone. Indonesia and Pakistan are already witnessing the impact of the Afghan bombings.

And in India we now have the first inkling of what could follow with the riots in Malegaon in Maharashtra. There are many more communal tinderboxes that could explode in the next days.

But apart from these convulsions in our own societies that we have to be prepared to face, what happens to individuals who refuse these artificial divisions that are being forced upon us? Will this new, post-September 11 world order accommodate a dissenter, an individualist, a person who insists that there are many shades between black and white, and that there also many colours in the world?

In the US, the increasing intolerance towards people of Middle Eastern and Asian origin is also being extended to those who are critical of the US Government's "War on global terrorism".

And if you happen to be a person of South Asian origin, a woman, and a critic of the US Government, you are in deep trouble. A noted Canadian academic, Professor Sunera Thobani, for instance, has been called "idiotic, foolish, stupid and just plain nutty" and a "hate-mongerer" by the press for making statements critical of US foreign policy. Others had not said anything that she said before. But those others were part of the American majority, and she is from an immigrant minority. So she is now denied the right to raise uncomfortable questions in a country that swears by democracy.

What people like Prof. Thobani are experiencing today is not very different from what some Muslim intellectuals in this country have felt for decades. If they criticised the Government's policy in Kashmir, for instance, they were considered sympathetic to the militants, and to Pakistan. And today if they, or even non-Muslims, criticise the Government for banning a group like the Students' Islamic Movement in India (SIMI) on grounds that it is not being even-handed, they will be accused of being pro-SIMI. There is no middle ground.

For women, this obliteration of the middle ground, of the shades and nuances that are so much a part of our lives, must necessarily mean the beginning of much greater intolerance in all spheres.

Initially, this might express itself in matters political. But inevitably it will invade women's autonomy in all societies.

Kalpana Sharma is Deputy Editor of The Hindu. *As a journalist and columnist, she writes on developmental and environmental issues with a special focus on women. She is co-editor (with Ammu Joseph) of* Whose News? The Media and Women's Issues *(1994) and the author of* Rediscovering Dharavi: Stories From Asia's Largest Slum *(2000).*

Kamila Shamsie November 1, 2001

My home is not the place you see on TV

Last week, I returned to Pakistan for the first time since September 11. As I walked through the doors of Jinnah Airport's international terminal in Karachi, I was jolted by a shock of revulsion: a vast McDonald's had sprung up right across from the terminal, ensuring that the golden arches would henceforth dominate all visitors' first glimpse of the city. But all else seemed much as ever: no added security, no riots on the periphery of my vision, no stones being hurled my way because I was in trousers and a T-shirt. In short, McDonald's aside, Karachi seemed exactly as I had expected it to when I left London the day before. How nice, I thought, to finally be home where I won't have to spend every day telling people not to believe what they hear in the news about Pakistan being closer than ever to an Islamic revolution. (Pakistan may be closer than ever to an Islamic revolution; but since it's never been close to any such revolution, that relative term "closer" carries little urgency.)

Here, there is much anger about what everyone else in the world hears in the news about Pakistan. Almost everyone I have spoken to has mentioned the slanted coverage of the BBC and CNN, which get beamed via satellite to a great many households in Pakistan. It was partly to counter this partial reporting that a rally under the banner "Voices of the Silent Majority" was organised the day I returned. According to first-hand reports, about 200 people showed up, with placards saying "No to Extremism", "Pakistan First", "Yes to Jihad against Illiteracy". Speeches were made, doves were released (actually, they were pigeons, but let's not get bogged down by details). The whole event had acquired a slightly farcical sheen before it started, due to the fact that many of the people who were most fired up about the rally are better known for their fashion sense than their political sense. The march of the trendies, one of my friends dubbed it, while another predicted the placards would read: "The well-dressed women of Pakistan oppose terrorism". In the end, though, it was journalists and educators rather than models and beauty consultants who spoke. Neither the BBC nor CNN covered the event. And why should they? After all, it was just 200 people representing a tiny portion of society.

Well, when 200 protesters who represent a tiny portion of society start throwing stones at policemen and burning effigies of George Bush, the cameras can't stop rolling. Every day, the media teaches us lessons best left unlearned about the power of violence to capture people's attention. The truth of the matter is that in this country, which is often divided along so many lines—sectarian, ethnic, economic, political—there does seem to be something approaching a general consensus on two matters: the destruction of the World Trade Centre was sickeningly awful; the bombing of Afghanistan is sickeningly awful. Pakistanis were asked in a recent poll if they support the US or the Taliban in the war. More than 80% answered in favour of the Taliban. But—putting aside the question of how, exactly, the data was compiled—the question itself reflects an absurd "you're either with us or with them" reasoning which quite overlooks the complexity of Pak-Afghan-US relations. The poll didn't bother to ask if Pakistanis believe the Taliban are in any way responsible for what happened on September 11. It seems a fair guess that more than 80% would answer "no". Nor did it ask if the deaths of hundreds of Afghan civilians and the mass influx of refugees into Pakistan, a country already straining to cope with the million plus refugees that were here prior to September 11, was acceptable "collateral damage". Again, the answer would be an overwhelming "no". Looked at in this light, the opposition to US bombing in no way translates to a support for the terrorist attacks in the US. From here, this seems a self-evident truth.

There are frequent, non-violent rallies throughout Pakistan opposing the bombing. Most of these are rallies for peace, not for holy war. This is not to deny that the extremists who are calling for the overthrow of General Musharraf's government are a well-armed and dangerous minority—but the belief in most sections of Pakistan is still strong that the President has much cause to be concerned about an assassin's bullet and little reason to fear a popular revolution that will topple his government. This is not a nation of extremists. But it is not an unconflicted nation either—it says much for the difficult position Pakistan finds itself in that the people who show up at rallies to declare solidarity with the government which promised "unstinted support" to the US are often the same people at the rallies demanding an end to the bombing.

It seems I have been repeating all of this endlessly to friends in the UK and the US. All of them have listened with understanding, intelligence and compassion. In Karachi, I encounter somewhat surprised reactions when I say that of the many American friends I gathered in my years at university on the east coast, none of those who have written to me in the last two months hold views that are substantially different to mine when it comes to the bombing of Afghanistan. Just as Pakistan looks like an extremist monolith if you watch news reports in the US, so the US looks like an arrogant nation baying for blood and willing to bypass due process if you watch news reports here. The interesting point is this: the same news channels which broadcast images of Pakistan to the US also broadcast images of the US to Pakistan. That is, we watch CNN and we think it's showing us a complete picture of America. But having lived in the US, having spoken to friends who've written articles criticising US policy for the print media in the US and found those pieces "edited" or not published, I know that there is a voice of opposition within America which finds itself completely shut out by the mainstream media. Paradoxically, if the US media allowed those voices to come through to the rest of the world there might be less anger towards the US in places such as Pakistan.

I'm told that any criticism of US policy these days is seen by some as a justification for the terrorism of September 11. Let me make one thing perfectly clear: September 11 has long been a national holiday in Pakistan. It marks the death of Mohammed Ali Jinnah, the founder of Pakistan, a man who used his inaugural address to the nation to speak of the need for tolerance and freedom. September 11 is a day of mourning in Pakistan. It will continue to be a day of mourning in Pakistan.

Kamila Shamsie contributes regularly to The Guardian *newspapers and is the author of a number of books including* Salt and Saffron *and* Kartography.

4
Motherland/Fatherland

Martha Nussbaum

Can patriotism be compassionate?

In the aftermath of September 11, we have all experienced strong emotions for our country: fear, outrage, grief, astonishment. Our media portray the disaster as a tragedy that has happened to our nation, and that is how we very naturally see it. So too the ensuing war: it is called "America's New War," and most news reports focus on the meaning of events for us and our nation. We think these events are important because they concern us—not just human lives, but American lives. In one way, the crisis has expanded our imaginations. We find ourselves feeling sympathy for many people who did not even cross our minds before: New York firefighters, that gay rugby player who helped bring down the fourth plane, bereaved families of so many national and ethnic origins. We even sometimes notice with a new attention the lives of Arab-Americans among us, or feel sympathy for a Sikh taxi driver who complains about customers who tell him to go home to "his country," even though he came to the United States as a political refugee from Punjab. Sometimes our compassion even crosses that biggest line of all, the national boundary. Events have led many Americans to sympathize with the women and girls of Afghanistan, for example, in a way that many feminists had been trying to get people to do for a long time, without success.

All too often, however, our imaginations remain oriented to the local; indeed, this orientation is implicit in the unusual level of our alarm. The world has come to a stop in a way that it never has for Americans when disaster has befallen human beings in other places. Floods, earthquakes, cyclones—and the daily deaths of thousands from preventable malnutrition and disease—none of these typically make the American world come to a standstill, none elicit a tremendous outpouring of grief and compassion.

The plight of innocent civilians in the current war evokes a similarly uneven and flickering response.

And worse: our sense that the "us" is all that matters can easily flip over into a demonizing of an imagined "them," a group of outsiders who are imagined as enemies of the invulnerability and the pride of the all-important "us". Just as parents' compassion for their own children can all too easily slide into an attitude that promotes the defeat of other people's children, so too with patriotism: compassion for our fellow Americans can all too easily slide over into an attitude that wants America to come out on top, defeating or subordinating other peoples or nations. Anger at the terrorists themselves is perfectly appropriate; so is the attempt to bring them to justice. But "us versus them" thinking doesn't always stay focused on the original issue; it too easily becomes a general call for American supremacy, the humiliation of "the other."

One vivid example of this slide took place at a baseball game I went to at Chicago's Comiskey Park, the first game played there after September 11—and a game against the Yankees, so there was a heightened awareness of the situation of New York and its people. Things began well, with a moving ceremony commemorating the firefighters who had lost their lives and honouring local firefighters who had gone to New York afterward to help out. There was even a lot of cheering when the Yankees took the field, a highly unusual transcendence of local attachments. But as the game went on and the beer flowed, one heard, increasingly, "U-S-A, U-S-A," echoing the chant from the 1980 Olympic hockey match in which the United States defeated Russia. This chant seemed to express a wish for America to defeat, abase, humiliate its enemies. Indeed, it soon became a general way of expressing the desire to crush one's enemies, whoever they were. When the umpire made a bad call that went against the Sox, the same group in the stands turned to him, chanting "U-S-A." In other words, anyone who crosses us is evil, and should be crushed. It's not surprising that Stoic philosopher and Roman emperor Marcus Aurelius, trying to educate himself to have an equal respect for all human beings, reported that his first lesson was "not to be a fan of the Greens or Blues at the races, or the light-armed or heavy-armed gladiators at the Circus."

Compassion is an emotion rooted, probably, in our biological heritage. (Although biologists once portrayed animal behavior as egoistic, primatologists by now recognize the existence of altruistic emotion in apes, and it may exist in other species as well.) But this history does not mean that compassion is devoid of thought. In fact, as Aristotle argued long ago, human compassion standardly requires three thoughts: that a serious bad thing has happened to someone else; that this bad event was not (or not entirely) the person's own fault; and that we ourselves are vulnerable in similar ways. Thus compassion forms a psychological link between our own self-interest and the reality of another person's good or ill. For that reason it is a morally valuable emotion—when it gets things right. Often, however, the thoughts involved in the emotion, and therefore the emotion itself, go astray, failing to link people at a distance to one's own current possibilities and vulnerabilities. (Rousseau said that kings don't feel compassion for their subjects because they count on never being human, subject to the vicissitudes of life.) Sometimes, too, compassion goes wrong by getting the seriousness of the bad event wrong: sometimes, for example, we just don't take very seriously the hunger and illness of people who are distant from us. These errors are likely to be built into the nature of compassion as it develops in childhood and then adulthood: we form intense attachments to the local first, and only gradually learn to have compassion for people who are outside our own immediate circle. For many Americans, that expansion of moral concern stops at the national boundary.

Most of us are brought up to believe that all human beings have equal worth. At least the world's major religions and most secular philosophies tell us so. But our emotions don't believe it. We mourn for those we know, not for those we don't know. And most of us feel deep emotions about America, emotions we don't feel about India or Russia or Rwanda. In and of itself, this narrowness of our emotional lives is probably acceptable and maybe even good. We need to build outward from meanings we understand, or else our moral life would be empty of urgency. Aristotle long ago said, plausibly, that the citizens in Plato's ideal city, asked to care for all citizens equally, would actually care for none, since care is learned in small groups with their more intense attachments. Reading Marcus Aurelius bears this out: The project of weaning his imagination from its intense erotic attachments to the familial and the local gradually turns into the rather alarming project of weaning his heart from deep investment in the world. He finds that the only way to be utterly evenhanded is to cultivate a kind of death within life, seeing all people as distant and shadow-like, "vain images in a procession." If we want our life with others to contain strong passions—for justice in a world of injustice, for aid in a world where many go without what they need—we would do well to begin, at least, with our familiar strong emotions toward family, city and country. But concern should not stop with these local attachments.

Americans, unfortunately, are prone to such emotional narrowness. So are all people, but because of the power and geographical size of America, isolationism has particularly strong roots here. When at least some others were finding ways to rescue the Jews during the Holocaust, America's inactivity and general lack of concern were culpable, especially in proportion to American power. It took Pearl Harbor to get us even to come to the aid of our allies. When genocide was afoot in Rwanda, our own sense of self-sufficiency and invulnerability stopped us from imagining the Rwandans as people who might be us; we were therefore culpably inactive toward them. So too in the present situation. Sometimes we see a very laudable recognition of the interconnectedness of all peoples, and of the fact that we must join forces with people in all nations to defeat terrorists and bring them to justice. At other times, however, we see simplifying slogans ("America Fights Back") that portray the situation in terms of a good "us" crusading against an evil "them"—failing to acknowledge, for instance, that people in all nations have strong reasons to oppose terrorism, and that the fight has many active allies.

Such simplistic thinking is morally wrong, because it encourages us to ignore the impact of our actions on innocent civilians and to focus too little on the all-important project of humanitarian relief. It is also counterproductive. We now understand, or ought to, that if we had thought more about support for the educational and humanitarian infrastructure of Pakistan, for example, funding good local non-governmental organizations there the way several European nations have done in India, young people in Pakistan might possibly have been educated in a climate of respect for religious pluralism, the equality of women and other values that we rightly prize instead of having fundamentalist *madrassas* as their only educational option. Our policy in South Asia has exhibited for many years a gross failure of imagination and sympathy; we basically thought in terms of cold war values, ignoring the real lives of people to whose prospects our actions could make a great difference. Such crude thinking is morally obtuse; it is also badly calculated to advance any good cause we wish to embrace, in a world where all human lives are increasingly interdependent.

Compassion begins with the local. But if our moral natures and our emotional natures are to live in any sort of harmony, we must find devices through which to extend our strong emotions—and our ability to imagine the situation of others—to the world of human life as a whole. Since compassion contains thought, it can be educated. We can take this disaster as occasion for narrowing our focus, distrusting the rest of the world and feeling solidarity with Americans alone. Or we can take it as an occasion for expansion of our ethical horizons. Seeing how vulnerable our great country is, we can learn something about the vulnerability that all human beings share, about what it is like for distant others to lose those they love to a disaster not of their own making, whether it is hunger or flood or war.

Because human beings find the meaning of life in attachments that are local, we should not ask of people that they renounce patriotism, any more than we now ask them to renounce the love of their parents and children. But we typically do ask parents not to try to humiliate or thwart other people's children, and we work (at least sometimes) for schools that develop the abilities of all children, that try to make it possible for everyone to support themselves and find rewarding work. So too with the world: we may love our own nation most, but we should also strive for a world in which the capacities of human beings will not be blighted by hunger or misogyny or lack of education—or by being in the vicinity of a war one has not caused. We should therefore demand an education that does what it can to encourage the understanding of human predicaments—and also to teach children to recognize the many obstacles to that pursuit, the many pitfalls of the self-centered imagination as it tries to be just. There are hopeful signs in the present situation, particularly in attempts to educate the American public about Islam, about the histories of Afghanistan and Pakistan, and about the situation and attitudes of Arab-Americans in this country. But we need to make sure these educational efforts are consistent and systematic, not just fear-motivated responses to an immediate crisis.

Our media and our systems of education have long given us far too little information about lives outside our borders, stunting our moral imaginations. The situation of America's women and its racial, ethnic and sexual minorities has to some extent worked its way into curricula at various levels, and into our popular media. We have done less well with parts of the world that are unfamiliar. This is not surprising, because such teaching requires a lot of investment in new curricular initiative, and such television programming requires a certain temporary inattention to the competition for ratings. But we now know that we live in a complex, interconnected world, and we know our own ignorance. As Socrates said, this is at least the beginning of progress. At this time of national crisis we can renew our commitment to the equal worth of humanity, demanding media, and schools, that nourish and expand our imaginations by presenting non-American lives as deep, rich and compassion-worthy. "Thus from our weakness," said Rousseau of such an education, "our fragile happiness is born." Or, at least, it might be born.

Martha C Nussbaum is Ernst Freund Distinguished Professor of Law and Ethics at the University of Chicago. She is the author of Women and Human Development: The Capabilities Approach *(2000)*, Cultivating Humanity: A Classical Defense of Reform in Liberal Education; The Fragility of Goodness: Luck and Ethics in Greek Tragedy and Philosophy, *and* Sex and Social Justice.

Ellen Willis

Bringing the holy war home

It often happens that the lunatic right, in its feckless way, gets closer to the heart of the matter than the political mainstream, and so it was with Jerry Falwell's notorious response to September 11. In suggesting that the World Trade Center massacre was God's judgment on an America that tolerates abortion, homosexuality and feminism, Falwell—along with Pat Robertson, who concurred—exposed himself to the public's averted eye. For most Americans, from George W. Bush on down, resist the idea that the attack was an act of cultural war, and fewer still are willing to admit its intimate connection with the culture war at home.

Opponents of the "clash of civilizations" thesis are half right. There is such a clash, but it is not between East and West. The struggle of democratic secularism, religious tolerance, individual freedom and feminism against authoritarian patriarchal religion, culture and morality is going on all over the world—including the Islamic world, where dissidents are regularly jailed, killed, exiled or merely intimidated and silenced. In Iran the mullahs still have police power, but reformist President Khatami has overwhelming popular support and young people are in open revolt against the Islamic regime. In Pakistan the urban middle classes worry that their society may be Talibanized. Even in the belly of the fundamentalist beast, the clandestine Revolutionary Association of the Women of Afghanistan has opposed both the Taliban regime and the scarcely less thuggish Northern Alliance.

At the same time, religious and cultural reactionaries have mobilized to attack secular modernity in liberal democracies, from Israel to the post-Communist countries of Eastern Europe to the United States. Indeed, the culture war has been a centerpiece of American politics for thirty years or more, shaping our debates and our policies on everything from abortion, censorship and crime to race, education and social welfare. Nor, at this moment, does the government know whether foreign or domestic terrorists are responsible for the anthrax offensive. Yet we shrink from seeing the relationship between our own cultural conflicts and the logic of *jihad*. We are especially eager to absolve religion of any responsibility for the violence committed in its name: for that ubiquitous current cliché, "This has nothing to do with Islam," read "Anti-abortion terrorism has nothing to do with Christianity."

But why then do the great world religions all have brutal fundamentalist fringes that traduce their professed moral principles for the sake of power? The contradiction mirrors the conditions of the patriarchal culture with which these religions are intertwined—a culture that mandates the repression of desire and the control of women in the name of law and order, but which is nonetheless permeated with violence, from rape to war. Is this simply proof of innate evil, original sin, or is it rather that repression gives rise to hidden rage, which constantly seeks an outlet in sanctioned violence—the punishment of wayward children, women, enemies of the state? And of course there can be no violence more sanctioned than holy war.

This dynamic might explain why an undercurrent of sadism is always available to be tapped by demagogues seeking to exploit mass economic misery, the dislocation of war or other social crises. As with fascism, the rise of Islamic totalitarianism has partly to do with its populist appeal to the class resentments of an economically oppressed population and to anger at political subordination and humiliation. But, again like fascism, it is at bottom a violent defensive reaction against the liberal values of the Enlightenment. By its very intensity, moreover, that reaction suggests a defense against not only an external threat but an inner temptation. If exposure to forbidden freedoms aroused in Osama bin Laden and his confreres' unconscious rage at their own repression, what better way to ward off the devil than to redirect that rage against it? And if the World Trade Center represented global capitalism—the engine of American might and economic inequality, but also of modernity itself, of all that is solid melting into air—wasn't there yet another, more primal brand of symbolism embodied in those twin phalluses? With one spectacular act, the hijackers could annihilate both the symbol of temptation and its real source—themselves.

Only a small minority of extremists will ever go that far. But throughout the Islamic world many more will admire, sympathize, tolerate and obstruct opposition. For along with the economic suffering and political complaints that terrorists exploit, most of the population shares a cultural formation grounded in the patriarchal conservatism that pervades everyday life in Islamic countries—including those with secular governments like Iraq and Turkey—especially outside the cities and the educated classes. Post-Enlightenment, post-Reformation, post-feminist, post-sexual revolution, liberal democratic America offers a far smaller pool of people in which abortion-clinic bombers and their ilk can hope to swim. Yet the legacy of patriarchalism still weighs on us: our institutions resist change and our psyches remain more conservative than the actual conditions of our lives. As a result we are deeply anxious and ambivalent about cultural issues, and one way we deal with this is to deny their importance, even sometimes their existence.

For the most part Americans speak of culture and politics as if they were two separate realms. Conservatives accuse the left of politicizing culture and see their own cultural-political offensive against the social movements of the 1960s as an effort to restore to culture its rightful autonomy. Centrists deplore the culture war as an artifact of "extremists on both sides" and continually pronounce it dead. The economic-justice left regards cultural politics as a distraction from its efforts to win support for a populist economic program. Multiculturalists pursue the political goal of equality and respect for minority and non-western cultures, but are reluctant to make political judgments about cultural practices: feminist universalists like Martha Nussbaum have been regularly attacked for "imposing western values" by criticizing genital mutilation and other forms of female subjection in the Third World.

The artificial separation of politics and culture is nowhere more pronounced than in the discourse of foreign policy and international affairs. For the US government, economic, geopolitical and military considerations determine our allies and our enemies. Democracy (almost always defined narrowly as a freely elected government, rather than as a way of life) and human rights (only recently construed as including even the most elementary of women's rights) are invoked by policy-makers mainly to justify alliances or antagonisms that already exist. While the cold war inspired much genuine passion on behalf of freedom and the open society, there's no denying that its fundamental motive was the spectre of an alternative to capitalism spreading across the globe and encouraging egalitarian heresies at home. The one cultural issue that seems genuinely to affect our relationship with foreign states is our mania for restricting the international drug supply (except when we ourselves are arming drug cartels for some strategic purpose). The left, meanwhile, criticizes the aims of American foreign policy; yet despite intensified concern with human rights in recent years, many leftists still share the government's assumptions about what kinds of issues are important: the neoliberal economic agenda and struggles over resources like oil; the maintenance of friendly client states versus national self-determination; and so on. And like the United States, leftists have displayed their own double standard on human rights, tending to gloss over the abuses of populist or anti-imperialist regimes.

Given these tropisms, it's unsurprising that the absence of religious and personal freedom, brutal suppression of dissent and extreme oppression of women in Islamic theocracies have never been a serious subject of foreign policy debates. Long before the Taliban, many feminists were upset by the single-minded cold war agenda that led the United States to support, even foment, Islamic fundamentalism in Afghanistan; yet this never became a public issue. Nor did well-publicized Taliban atrocities stop us from giving aid to the regime in return for a crackdown on poppy production. Even now our enthusiasm for the Northern Alliance, which is to the Taliban what Trotsky was to Stalin, is restrained only—irony of ironies!—by the ethnic objections of our new ally, that champion of religious freedom, Pakistan. While the Bush Administration makes self-congratulatory noises about Afghan women's liberation, it is in no hurry to stop fundamentalist warlords from reclaiming power.

Back in the 1950s, in pursuit of our cold war aims in Iran, we overthrew an elected secular government and installed the tyrannical and deeply unpopular Shah, then dumped him in the face of Khomeini's 1979 revolution. Except for feminists, the American left, with few exceptions, enthusiastically supported the revolution and brushed off worries about the Ayatollah, though he had made no secret of his theocratic aims: the important thing was to get rid of the Shah—other issues could be dealt with afterward. Ten years later, on the occasion of the *fatwa* against Salman Rushdie, the Bush I Administration appeared far more interested in appeasing Islamic governments and demonstrators offended by Rushdie's heretical book than in condemning Khomeini's death sentence, while an unnerving number of liberals and leftists accused Rushdie and his defenders of cultural imperialism and insensitivity to Muslim sensibilities. Throughout, both defenders and detractors of our alliance with "moderate" Saudi Arabia have ignored Saudi women's slavelike situation, regarding it as "their culture" and none of our business, except when it raises questions about how Americans stationed in the Gulf are expected to behave. It's as if, in discussing South Africa, apartheid had never been mentioned.

There are many things to be learned from the shock of September 11; surely one of the more important is that culture is not only a political matter, but a matter of life and death. It follows that a serious, long-range strategy against Islamic fundamentalist terrorism must entail open and emphatic opposition to theocracy and to the subjugation of women, backed up by support for the efforts of secular and religious liberals, modernizers, democrats and feminists to press for reforms in Middle Eastern and South Asian societies. We might start by including RAWA and other secular elements as players in the discussion of Afghanistan's future; and by giving active aid and comfort to the Iranian reformers and their increasingly rebellious constituents. So far, no Afghans associated with the secular leftist government that pre-dated the 1978 Soviet-backed coup have been party to the political negotiations—indeed, they are the great unmentionable. (While the

United States has no problem supporting warlords with gory histories of rape and pillage, evidently any whiff of association with Communism is still beyond the pale.) As for Iran, recent anti-government, anti-clerical, pro-American mass demonstrations in the wake of the World Cup soccer matches have been virtually ignored by the Bush Administration and, remarkably, have gotten almost no attention in the American press. This must change.

Yet to recognize that the enemy is fundamentalism itself—not "evil" anti-American fundamentalists, as opposed to the allegedly friendly kind—is also to make a statement about American cultural politics. Obviously nothing of the sort can be expected from Bush and Ashcroft. But our problem is not just leaders who are in bed with the Christian right. There is also the tendency of the left and the center to appease the right and downplay the culture war rather than make an uncompromising defense of freedom, feminism and the separation of church and state. It remains to be seen whether fear of terrorism will trump the fear of facing our own cultural contradictions.

Ellen Willis directs the Cultural Reporting and Criticism programme in the Department of Journalism at New York University. Her articles on feminism and contemporary politics and culture have appeared in such publications as The Nation, Dissent, *the* Boston Review *and* Salon. *Her most recent book is* Don't Think, Smile! Notes on a Decade of Denial *(1999).*

And our flag was still there

My daughter came home from kindergarten and announced, "Tomorrow we all have to wear red, white and blue."

"Why?" I asked, trying not to sound wary.

"For all the people that died when the airplanes hit the buildings."

I fear the sound of sabre-rattling, dread that not just my taxes but even my children are being dragged to the cause of death in the wake of death. I asked quietly, "Why not wear black then? Why the colours of the flag, what does that mean?"

"It means we are a country. Just all people together."

So we sent her to school in red, white and blue, because it felt to her like something she could do to help people who were hurting. And because my wise husband put a hand on my arm and said, "You can't let hateful people steal the flag from us."

He didn't mean terrorists, he meant Americans. Like the man in a city near us who went on a rampage crying "I'm an American" as he shot at foreign-born neighbours, killing a gentle Sikh man in a turban and terrifying every brown-skinned person I know. Or the talk show hosts, who are viciously bullying a handful of members of Congress for airing sensible scepticism at a time when the White House was announcing preposterous things in apparent self-interest, such as the "revelation" that terrorists had aimed to hunt down Air Force One with a hijacked commercial plane. Rep. Barbara Lee cast the House's only vote handing over virtually unlimited war powers to one man that a whole lot of us didn't vote for. As a consequence, so many red-blooded Americans have now threatened to kill her, she has to have additional bodyguards.

Patriotism seems to be falling to whoever claims it loudest, and we are left struggling to find a definition in a clamour of reaction. This is what I'm hearing: patriotism opposes the lone representative of democracy who was brave enough to vote her conscience instead of following an angry mob. (Several others have confessed they wanted to vote the same way, but chickened out.) Patriotism threatens free speech with death. It is infuriated by thoughtful hesitation, constructive criticism of our leaders and pleas for peace. It despises people of foreign birth who've spent years learning our culture and contributing their talents to our economy. It has specifically blamed homosexuals, feminists and the American Civil Liberties Union. In other words, the American flag stands for intimidation, censorship, violence, bigotry, sexism, homophobia, and shoving the Constitution through a paper shredder? Who are we calling terrorists here? Outsiders can destroy airplanes and buildings, but it is only we, the people, who have the power to demolish our own ideals.

It's a fact of our culture that the loudest mouths get the most airplay, and the loudmouths are saying now that in times of crisis it is treasonous to question our leaders. Nonsense. That kind of thinking let fascism grow out of the international depression of the 1930s. In critical times, our leaders need most to be influenced by the moderating force of dissent. That is the basis of democracy, in sickness and in health, and especially when national choices are difficult, and bear grave consequences.

It occurs to me that my patriotic duty is to recapture my flag from the men now waving it in the name of jingoism and censorship. This isn't easy for me.

The last time I looked at a flag with unambiguous pride, I was 13. Right after that, Vietnam began teaching me lessons in ambiguity, and the lessons have kept coming. I've learnt of things my government has done to the world that made me direly ashamed. I've been further alienated from my flag by people who wave it at me declaring I should love it or leave it. I search my soul and find I cannot love killing for any reason. When I look at the flag, I see it illuminated by the rocket's red glare.

This is why warmongers so easily gain the upper hand in the patriot game: our nation was established with a fight for independence, so our iconography grew out of war. Our national anthem celebrates it; our language of patriotism is inseparable from a battle cry. Our every military campaign is still launched with phrases about men dying for the freedoms we hold dear, even when this is impossible to square with reality. In the Persian Gulf War we rushed to the aid of Kuwait, a monarchy in which women enjoyed approximately the same rights as a 19th century American slave. The values we fought for and won there are best understood, I think, by oil companies. Meanwhile, a country of civilians was devastated, and remains destroyed.

Stating these realities does not violate the principles of liberty, equality, and freedom of speech; it exercises them, and by exercise we grow stronger. I would like to stand up for my flag and wave it over a few things I believe in including, but not limited to, the protection of dissenting points of view. After 225 years, I vote to retire the rocket's red glare and bullet wounds as obsolete symbols of Old Glory. We desperately need a new iconography of patriotism. I propose we rip strips of cloth from the uniforms of public servants who rescued the injured and the panic-stricken, remaining at their post until it fell down on them. The red glare of candles held in vigils everywhere as peace-loving people pray for the bereaved and plead for compassion and restraint. The blood donated to the Red Cross. The stars of film and theatre and music who are using their influence to raise money for recovery. The small hands of school children collecting pennies, toothpaste, teddy bears, anything they think might help the kids who've lost their moms and dads.

My town, Tucson, Arizona, has become famous for a simple gesture in which some 8,000 people wearing red, white or blue T-shirts assembled themselves in the shape of a flag on a baseball field and had their photograph taken from above. That picture has begun to turn up everywhere, but we saw it first on our newspaper's front page. Our family stood in silence for a minute looking at that photo of a human flag, trying to know what to make of it. Then my teenage daughter, who has a quick mind for numbers and a sensitive heart, did an interesting thing. She laid her hand over a quarter of the picture, leaving visible more or less 6,000 people, and said, "That many are dead." We stared at what that looked like—all those innocent souls, multi-coloured and packed into a conjoined destiny—and shuddered at the one simple truth behind all the noise, which is that so many beloved people have suddenly gone from us. That is my flag, and that's what it means: we're all just people together.

Barbara Kingsolver has written extensively for a variety of publications, including The Nation, The New York Times, *and* Smithsonian. *In 1986 she won an Arizona Press Club award for outstanding feature writing, and in 1995, after the publication of High Tide in Tucson, she was awarded an Honorary Doctorate of Letters from her alma mater, De Pauw University. For Kingsolver, writing is a form of political activism. Her publications include poetry,* Another America: Otra America *(1992, 1998),* The Poisonwood Bible *(1998),* Prodigal Summer *(2000) and* Small Wonder *(2002).*

Originally published in the San Francisco Chronicle, *September 25, 2001.*

Barbara Ehrenreich &
Rosa Ehrenreich Brooks

A twisted sense of duty and love

The other day, a friend told us that what shook her up the most after September 11 was the knowledge that many of the terrorists had lived peaceably among Americans for several years before their attacks, sending their children to our public schools, shopping at the supermarket, ordering pizza, waving a friendly good morning to their neighbors. "What chills me," she said, "is the thought that they hate us so much that not even all those daily interactions with Americans could humanize us for them." That's become the prevailing explanation of the terrorist attacks on September 11: we are up against an almost incomprehensible form of "hate" or "evil".

But although "hate" and "evil" are powerfully evocative words, they don't really tell us much. Indeed, we often haul them out precisely as a way to avoid grappling with more nuanced and troubling explanations for the horrific. On September 11, nineteen men knowingly went to their deaths in order to kill Americans, stymieing experts in terrorist profiling. These men were not desperate or bereft of hope: they had families, foreign language skills, opportunities. They were not unsophisticated, ignorant, or backward, "brainwashed" by simplistic promises of sloe-eyed virgins in the paradise to come; they were highly educated, cosmopolitan people who lived easily among foreigners, both in the US and in Germany. Was cruelty all they knew? No: those who met them say they seemed like ordinary people, studying, laughing, picking their children up at school.

Did they hate us in some particularly relentless, unreasoning way? Perhaps, but what we need to acknowledge is that the September 11 terrorists may also have been motivated by their own understanding of duty, honor, and sacrifice—the very same values that have motivated our own soldiers in wars we consider just and necessary. Perhaps they were motivated even by their own terrible, fiery, brand of love, just as conventional warriors have, throughout history, been sustained by love of country and comrades—to the point of both dying and killing for them.

We shrink from the idea that the terrorists could have been motivated by the same impulses that drive soldiers in respectable wars. But imagine growing up, even in a middle-class household, surrounded by suffering, hopelessness, poverty and pain, in the ruins of Kabul, in the Gaza Strip, in Algeria's ransacked towns, or the bleak streets of Baghdad; imagine being brought up to believe that the suffering you see around you is caused by the hypocrisy, greed, obtuseness and injustice of the arrogant and licentious American superpower.

For millions of people in the Third World (and, increasingly, in Europe, as well), it may seem that nothing can stop America from taking far more than its fair share of the world's wealth, or from trampling those with less power. America, after all, uses the lion's share of the world's non-renewable energy resources; we produce disproportionate quantities of dangerous and non-biodegradable waste; we send air strikes against any nation that angers us without being willing to risk the loss of our own troops; we selectively decry human rights abuses in countries we dislike but show little willingness to criticize allies such as Israel, much less turn the mirror upon ourselves; our dominance in the UN and other international forums imposes what many see as unfair trade balances and unduly harsh sanctions on nations such as Iraq—sanctions that have a devastating effect on civilians. Striking out to teach America a lesson might then, for some in the Middle East and elsewhere, come to seem like a necessary action, arising out of duty, compassion and, ultimately, love.

If this seems paradoxical we should remember that, although laws and moral precepts prohibiting attacks on civilians are as old as humanity itself, history and legend have repeatedly glamorized and praised the slaughter of innocents. While few legal, religious, or philosophical traditions are willing to absolve slaughter that is motivated solely by sadism, many are willing to tolerate "necessary" slaughter, however brutal—and definitions of "necessary" are usually disturbingly vague.

In Book I of Samuel, for example, God orders Saul to punish the Amalekites for their past actions against Israel: " 'Go and smite [them], and utterly destroy all that they have; do not spare them, but kill both man and woman, infant and suckling, ox and sheep, camel and ass.' " (Indeed, when Saul slaughters all the people but spares the king and most of the livestock, God is so angered at Saul's failure to follow through on the letter of his command that he rejects him as king of Israel.) The Romans put whole populations to the sword when "necessary" to take revenge for "treachery" against Rome. The Crusaders raped and pillaged as they fought their most Christian of wars, leaving Jerusalem, at one point, knee-deep in blood. Shakespeare's Henry the Fifth warns his enemies that if they do not surrender, he will license his men to sack the city:

. . . in a moment look to see
The blind and bloody soldier with foul hand
Defile the locks of your shrill shrieking daughters,
Your fathers taken by the silver beards
And their most reverend heads dashed to the walls,
Your naked infants spitted upon pikes. . . .

During the Civil War, Sherman justified the burning of crops and the bombardment of Southern cities by saying, "We are not only fighting hostile armies but a hostile people" who must be made "to feel the hard hand of war." And the fire-bombing of Dresden and other German cities by Allied forces killed several hundred thousand civilians. In Hiroshima, nearly 100,000 people—most of them civilians—died in a single hour after the dropping of the atomic bomb. Three days later, in Nagasaki, at least another 40,000 died when the United States dropped the second atomic bomb (only 250 of the dead were in the Japanese military).

Most of the men who fought these battles were not sadists. They did what they saw as their duty, and they did it as much out of love of city or religion or nation as out of hatred of the enemy. Many of them willingly gave their lives in the process.

To say that the September terrorists may have been motivated by the kinds of feelings we respect in conventional warriors is not to equate terrorism and war. In war, the potential victims have been formally warned that they are at risk. A state of war is known to exist, the warring parties have identified themselves, and although the date and nature of any particular attack is not known in advance by the victims, all are at least on notice of the existence of the threat.

The September terrorists didn't bother with any of these niceties. What is uniquely chilling about the attacks is precisely the absence of authorship: the attacks had no stated purpose, no one has accepted responsibility, and it is impossible to know what might prevent further acts of violence. Even for terrorists, this degree of indifference to public opinion is rare: most of the time, even terrorists at least declare themselves, make specific threats, and issue concrete demands that, if met, would at least theoretically end the terror. Mohammed Atta and his confederates evidently didn't care what lessons we drew from their actions.

Still, the possibility that they acted not out of hatred but out of a twisted sense of duty and love should make us pause before trying to decide how the United States should respond. If the attacks were motivated by a lofty sense of duty, then Bush's retaliatory strikes that are killing civilians in Afghanistan or elsewhere may merely harden the resolve of other terrorist "patriots" to come. We may unwittingly foster a new generation of would-be martyrs who grimly slaughter innocents in the belief that doing so is an act of sacrifice and love.

Dismissing terrorism as a product of hate and evil is a luxury we cannot afford. After all, if war is what we are getting into, the first rule of war is never to underestimate the enemy.

Rosa Ehrenreich Brooks is an associate professor of law at the University of Virginia School of Law, a former Senior Adviser at the State Department's Human Rights Bureau, and a consultant for the Open Society Institute. Barbara Ehrenreich is a columnist for The Progressive *and the author of several highly acclaimed books.*

Dubravka Ugrešić

Because we're just boys

1.

If a foreigner turns up in Zagreb, the "metropolis" of the freshly baked European state of Croatia, and particularly if he turns up on a Saturday morning, he will be startled by a scene which he would probably more readily associate with some Far Eastern city rather than a European one. On Saturday mornings the main square in Zagreb is filled with men. Men stand, often with newspapers in their hands, smoking, talking, strutting importantly up and down, smiling cheerfully at one another, patting each other on the back, the younger ones giving each other friendly shoves or hugs, all pattering about like a flock of penguins. If the foreigner directs his gaze towards one corner of the square he will see steps leading up to a flat space. That is Dolac, Zagreb's main market. Up and down the steps go women with serious expressions, carrying plastic bags of groceries. These are the female inhabitants of the new European "metropolis", hurrying home to cook the Saturday lunch.

. . .

3.

Yugo-man, the male inhabitant of the former Yugoslavia, hardly exists in the singular. He is rarely an isolated instance, a person, an individual, he is most frequently a group of men. Yugo-man is brought up in a group, he grows in a group, he lives in a group, he dies in a group. The male group is his natural habitat, without it he flounders and expires like a fish on dry land. "Because we're boys by the bar, meeting over a jar" goes the chorus of a popular Zagreb song. It seems that Yugo-men stroll through life mentally holding hands. And that's why contemporary supporters of masculinism, in their search for a lost male identity, need not travel to New Guinea. Tried and tested male identity is here, right in front of them.

4.

In the Yugo-male mindset one of the most important places belongs, of course, to woman. The "image" of woman has not been tarnished by either the political changes brought by the Second World War (in which women, for the most part highly educated, participated on an equal footing with men in the partisan movement), or almost fifty years of socialism (which made men and women equal, at least in law), or the dominance of women in some fields (education, medicine), or their presence in public life (journalism, universities, the arts), or the phenomenon of feminism, or the so-called democratic changes, or even the new war. In this male mindset woman has the fixed, unchanging status of an inferior being.

. . .

11.

We could acquaint our foreigner with an anthology of selections from Yugoslav literature which are not infrequently textbook examples of misogyny and patriarchalism. We could introduce our foreigner to our mass-media culture, popular culture, cartoons, newspapers, women's magazines, and then to statistical data. We could take him through political institutions, through editorial boards, we could oblige him to watch television, to visit publishers. . . Everywhere, both before and now, on the left and right, west and east, south and north, our foreigner would see the same scene: warm, friendly male togetherness, with the shadow of a woman somewhere in the corner: a silent secretary, a silent cleaning woman, the silent companion of the loud Yugo-male. The one place he will meet only women is in the children's playgroups. Let's add a small boy with wet trousers wailing, "Mummmyyy. . . look what I've done!" to the picture. Not because this little addition is necessarily authentic, but because we need it for the sake of another truth.

12.

And why have we thrown a thoughtful, ideal foreigner into the story at all? Because it seems that both the male and female inhabitants of the Yugoslav lands have become so accustomed to their cultural surroundings, their everyday reality, their unwritten rules, that they are no longer capable of registering their abnormality.

"It's your duty to write about the rapes carried out by the Serbs against your 'sisters', Muslims and Croats," said a colleague of mine recently, stressing the word *duty*.

"But wasn't it your 'brothers' who did the raping?" I asked.

My colleague stared, open-mouthed. That simple thought would never have crossed his mind. I believe he is still convinced that it is my duty because, for God's sake, rape is after all. . . "women's business".

13.

Talking with Yugo-men before the war, our imagined foreigner would have been amazed at the readiness with which men talked about two things. In their conversations, men always enjoyed recounting events from their army days, even if they had happened ten years earlier. The other subject was sexual exploits in which Yugo-men enjoyed exaggerating their own sexual prowess and mocking the sexual impotence of others, "fairies". In this Yugo-mythology there was a myth that the Croats "couldn't do it" the way the Serbs and the Montenegrins "could". Serbian Yugo-men found support for their thesis (that Croats were "fairies"), in language that in colloquial Croatian is synonyms for the word "penis". The male pack (army, sport, pub, workplace, etc.) and sex—those were the two priority areas in the life of Yugo-men.

The war simply activated what had always existed in the male mindset. Jokes and anecdotes at the expense of the (former) army were replaced by war heroism, "manliness", tests of courage, and stories of invincibility in the field of the bed shifted to the battlefront. War and sex were richly intertwined. Weaklings came to be called "poofters" ("poofter" is the wartime synonym for a coward). *Hrvatski vjesnik* (*The Croatian Herald*), a provincial newspaper, is full of homosexual pornographic caricatures in which the "poofters" are, of course, Serbs. An identical wartime pornographic male slang is in use on all warring sides. The traditional war-pornographic rhetoric is confirmed by the names of weapons (often women's names), war photographs (a fighter with his rifle sticking out, a soldier embracing the barrel of a fieldpiece) and the subculture of war (cartoons, "literature", jokes, humour). Propaganda usually projects war as an attractive, exciting male adventure, less often as a holy, ascetic struggle for the homeland. "War is shooting and shagging, screwing and killing", a returnee from the front is puported to have announced.

14.

In the male concept of war there is, of course, also the homeland. The homeland is, as always, a feminine gender word. On an abstract level, she is the "mother" ("the mother country"), and on a practical level, she is a large bank for the laundering of all kinds of "dirty money". But that's how it is in every war.

The dusty, outmoded rhetoric of patriotism continues to demonstrate its effectiveness. No one has written so many outmoded patriotic poems as contemporary poets on all the warring sides. The homeland ("You are my love, my holy Croatia", goes one Croatian line) is still the tormented mother, the holy mother, the Virgin Mother, whom "the murderers" (foreign men!) have dishonoured, soaked in blood, and so on and so forth. The homeland, of course, forgives everyone everything. "Mummmyyy, look what I've done!" and the homeland smiles tenderly, takes her little boy on her lap and "There, there, it's alright. . ."

15.

The homeland-mother is abstract, the child (now father, now child) is concrete. The day after the Serbian "leader", Slobodan Milošević, announced in an interview that his wife was a bad cook, some 200 women offered to go and cook for him.

16.

If someone gave me the chance to select the most terrible scenes of the twentieth century, the short-list would certainly include the television broadcast of a sitting of the Serbian (rump Yugoslav) parliament. The parliament was filled with men: ageing, overweight, mostly with puffy faces, mostly pudgy, all somewhat seedy, sweaty, with loose ties and half-unbuttoned shirts. At one moment, the man standing on the rostrum made a blunder by throwing a scrap of rolled-up paper at another who was sitting in the body of the house. At that moment it was as though an invisible magnet drew the faces towards the camera. Dozens of male faces looked at the camera and. . . grinned. Those faces *must have known* that their soldiers had been destroying Sarajevo for months, that they were raping, killing, burning, they *must have known* that Croatia and Bosnia had been destroyed with their blessings. They were the faces of the democratically elected representatives of those who were killed, but also of those who were rummaging through rubbish bins to find something to eat, or at that moment burying the bodies of their sons. The "leader" was grinning and the representatives of the people were grinning and suddenly everything was terribly funny. "Mummmyyy, look what I've done!" the faces gloated gravely, because they had all "done it", and there was no reason for them to be individually ashamed, because only adults feel shame. It was a grin of relief: how easy it all is, everything is possible, and who says politics means responsibility, and who says you have to answer to anyone for anything?

For me that television shot of the meeting of the Serbian parliament was like a photograph of a football team kicking around not balls but innumerable people's heads. And the team, "the boys", were having their picture taken with a cheery grin on their faces.

17.

The people responsible for the war in former Yugoslavia, as indeed for every war, are men. Men invented and provoked the war, men participated in the war.

In the autumn of 1991 women in Sarajevo protested against the war. "We are women and not nationalities! Generals, murderers!" they shouted, and, in front of the television cameras, the women demonstarated a short introduction to their future deaths. One held up a metal tag with a number engraved on it, showing how they place the tag in the mouth of the dead soldiers in order to identify them. A few days later hundreds of women from Croatia and Bosnia set off for Belgrade, where they were to be met by women from Serbia. They were all supposed to go together to the headquarters of the (by then already former) Yugoslav People's Army. The women had only one weapon in their hands: little photographs of their sons. The generals, realising for the first time that women after all amounted to half the population, roughly prevented them from meeting. Soldiers blocked the roads leading to Belgrade and the women returned to their homes, humiliated.

The very next day Serbian television showed pictures of weeping Serbian mothers joyfully sending their sons to the army. "This is the happiest day of my life," said one of them, wiping away her tears. On the third day other men, Croats, convinced their wives that they had no choice but to send their sons "to defend the motherland", for "liberty". On the fourth day, a group of women from Croatia was shown in a television shot in Germany, in audience with a leading German politician. Instead of little photographs of their sons, this time the women were carrying a large photograph of their President. It was a humiliating scene, no less humiliating than the one that was shown some months later when the man from the big photograph, the President, was handing out medals to the widows and mothers of *brave Croatian knights* who had *laid down their lives on the altar of their homeland*. On that occasion, one of them gratefully kissed the President's hand.

18.

One of the best-known theatre and film actresses in former Yugoslavia, a woman from Zagreb married to a man from Belgrade, was accused by the Croatian media of treason against the nation. The actress had written a moving anti-war article for the newspaper. Violent attacks followed; she left the country. For months afterwards the Croatian newspapers carried offensive articles, full of lies, with nude photographs of her, deeply offensive details from her private life, tasteless political accusations. The fury of the media attack could not be quenched. Everyone fanned the flames and brought their own twigs to add to the fire. To be fair, some people came with little pails of water, including the occasional male journalist. At the same time some of the actresses' friends and colleagues of a short time before (four of them) recorded a Croatian version of "Lily Marlene" for a record company. For the boys dying at the front, of course.

19.

About ten years ago, three over-excited young men on the streets of Pristina set fire to the skirt of a gypsy woman who was carrying a child in her arms. The case was reported only in the Slovene press. When asked by a journalist whether she intended to prosecute the men, the Gypsy was surprised: "It was only a joke," she said.

20.

In the war, women have lost homes, children, husbands. Women have been raped. First by one lot of men, then often by their own husbands ("No one drinks from a broken glass"), then by the foreign media, and then by the local media. . . At the moment these raped and deserted women and their children are being cared for. . . by other women. Not by men. Men have more important business. I imagine that they sometimes wonder how the money reaching the women from humanitarian organisations all over the world could be diverted, in a legal, legitimate way, to be "temporarily loaned" for more urgent purposes. For the purchase of "defensive" weapons, for instance.

21.

The war in Yugoslavia is a masculine war. In the war, women are post-boxes used to send messages to those other men, *the enemy*. And *enemies* who were their *brothers* until a short time before, at that.

"Rape in war is quite a normal thing, it's part of the male psychology, it's irrational. I hope you won't get me wrong, but it's a kind of a negative compliment to a woman, an ugly sexual blunder. But what is really monstrous is the deliberate Serbian impregnation of Croatian and Muslim women! Not merely rape, in other words, but forced impregnation. That's a Nazi concept. And only the Serbs could do such a thing!" said my colleague, a writer, with feeling.

Dubravka Ugrešić is the author of many books, including four that have been translated into English: In the Jaws of Life and Other Stories *(1993)*, Fording the Stream of Consciousness *(1993)*,

Have a Nice Day *(1994), and The Museum of Unconditional Surrender (1998). She was awarded the prestigious Charles Veillon Prize in 1996 for the* The Culture of Lies: Antipolitical Essays. *Since 1993 she has lived in Amsterdam in self-imposed exile from the former Yugoslavia.*

Excerpted from Dubravka Ugrešić, The Culture of Lies. © Dubravka Ugrešić, 1998.

5
The War on Women

Humera Khan

November 21, 2001

Freedom, fashion and an assault on the burqa

The war campaign in Afghanistan is progressing from the sublime to the ridiculous. First there were the not-so-smart bombs that destroyed hospitals, UN storage facilities and mosques. Then came the cluster bombs that killed many innocent civilians and left large swaths of the country unsafe for children to play in.

If the leaflets dropped by American planes as part of the propaganda war aimed at "winning hearts and minds" were offensive and in bad taste, the food packages—including peanut butter—certainly reflected the arrogance and insensitivity of the US-led coalition.

But of all the nasty things to drop from the skies upon the Afghan people in recent weeks, nothing is more insidious and more frightening than the anti-burqa propaganda message. This is due in no small measure to the fact that this latest weapon is being launched from the very heights of the White House and Downing Street.

The assault against the burqa by the US first lady and the UK's Cherie Blair lends credibility to the argument that the war campaign in Afghanistan is against Muslims and Islam, rather than terrorism. But what is it that has provoked these two capable and intelligent women to pick up this crusade?

Laura Bush does not have a history as a campaigner on the plight of her fellow sisters. "Had she been," according to one columnist, "she would, presumably, have laboured tirelessly for the millions of American women, most of them black or Hispanic, who live below the poverty line and whose chances of enjoying the life of a liberated modern woman are little better than those of women anywhere worldwide."

Cherie Blair, QC, on the other hand, can claim to be some kind of human rights champion. So the next campaign for the bright Mrs Blair could be to highlight the treatment of women in China. Beijing, as we all know, does not allow women to have more than one child, thereby implicitly encouraging them to kill their female babies. However, nobody expects bombs or statements directed from Downing Street to rain on the People's Republic of China merely because they murder female children.

Nobody is arguing against alleviating the plight of Afghan women. But any meaningful effort must be sensitive and respectful to their experiences, context and faith. Otherwise the result could be disastrous. The issue of the burqa in Afghanistan, or anywhere else in the Muslim world, is not about the garment itself. Women wore such clothing even before Islam and will continue to do so as a matter of choice.

Those western women like Mrs Bush and Mrs Blair, ostensibly offended by the sight of such attire, must learn to accept that the sight of scantily-clad women has the same effect on many in the world. In both extreme cases one must understand the notion of choice.

While the Taliban were imposing their beliefs and reducing freedom on one side, the same can be said of the male-dominated and often misogynistic fashion industry on the other. The question of which is the more ruthless form of persuasion, the lashes of the Taliban or the multimillion-pound advertising flashes of the fashion industry, remains a moot point.

Mrs Blair's concerns would have had more legitimacy if she had also been prepared to ask some serious questions about the situation in Afghanistan. Was the war, for instance, by the world's richest nations against the poorest, necessary? Is western support of the equally murderous and sexist forces of the Northern Alliance the only option available?

But perhaps before embarking on her burqa-bashing mission thousands of miles away, Cherie Blair should have asked a few questions at home.

"Dear Tony," she could have whispered, "does the government have any initiative aimed at improving the lot of British Muslim women?" Or perhaps, over an Indian meal, she could ask: "And, darling, where are the women when you meet spokesmen who claim to be representatives of the Muslim community?"

But then again, Tony might just be too busy reading a translation of the Koran he received from one of his male Muslim advisers.

Humera Khan is a member of the An-Nisa Women's Society and a columnist for the British Muslim magazine QNEWS.

Originally published in Guardian Unlimited.

Gayle Forman

Women in war

United Nations resolutions don't usually warrant birthday commemorations, but on October 30, women from three war-torn regions—Afghanistan, Kosovo and East Timor—honored the first anniversary of Resolution 1325, which seeks to address the particular problems faced by women in conflict zones, by testifying before the Security Council. Their stories, which were imbued with new urgency by the current crisis in Afghanistan, described a variety of abuses they and their countrywomen suffer on a daily basis. Sexual exploitation, in the form of rape, trafficking, forced prostitution and early marriage, has become as commonplace in modern conflicts as mines and sniper fire, as Haxhere Veseili, a 21-year-old from Kosovo, attested. "Thousands of children have been born of rape. I have friends who were raped," she said. "I know other girls who have relations with peacekeepers just so they can have some safety. Other young women exchange sex for money."

Women and children constitute 75 percent of war refugees. "And yet widows and single mothers in East Timor have received little or no aid," says Natia Godinho-Adams of East Timor.

Unfortunately, even after fighting ceases, all too often such dilemmas are disregarded or swept under the rug once the ink has dried on a peace accord, prolonging instability and misery for millions. Which is why perhaps the most important component of Resolution 1325 is the call for governments and international agencies to include women in peace negotiations and nation-building.

The progress in East Timor shows just how much difference some feminist consciousness can make. This past August, two years after East Timor ended its twenty-five-year civil war by passing a referendum to establish an independent state, the country held national elections. Women captured 27 per cent of elected seats and were subsequently appointed to two of ten Cabinet positions. Moreover, the progressive East Timorese constitution contains women-friendly provisions dealing with slavery and trafficking, forced prostitution and paid maternity leave. "Not even the United States goes this far," noted Godinho-Adams.

East Timorese women not only had a role in the UN-brokered referendum, but were also very active in the transitional administration. In the two years between the referendum and national elections, local grassroots

NGOs and UN agencies lobbied the political parties to run female candidates. These groups also identified women community leaders who would make strong potential candidates and provided leadership training and assistance. Now East Timor has twice the level of nationally elected female representatives as the United States, who in turn are more likely to address women's issues.

In Kosovo the situation for women is not as hopeful. In the two years since the war ended, the area has become a hotbed for sexual trafficking—a problem that seems to be growing worse. Last year the country held municipal elections, and in spite of quotas set up to ensure women's presence in government, some of the women who were elected resigned their posts to men, in part due to a lack of the kind of support or leadership training that went on in East Timor. It remains to be seen how things will change after the November 17 national elections, in which 358 of the 1,281 candidates are women.

If ever there were a time and place to invite women into the negotiating fray, it is in Afghanistan today. Now that Kabul has fallen, plans for a post-Taliban provisional government have assumed a new urgency. Lakhdar Brahimi, the UN's special representative for Afghanistan, is working to assemble a broad-based coalition that will apparently include the various tribal factions—the Pashtun, Tajiks, Hazaras and Uzbeks—as well as the spectrum of political persuasions. In spite of their repeated requests, women, who constitute 54 per cent of Afghanistan's population, have yet to be invited to the table.

Considering how women's subjugation in Afghanistan has become the political totem of the Taliban's repression, women's absence from these negotiations makes for bad symbolism—and even worse policy. Before the Taliban hid a nation full of females under house arrest and cover of the burqa, Afghan women were lawyers, judges, doctors, professors and government ministers. While the mujahedeen were off fighting the Soviet invasion in the 1980s and the civil war of the early 1990s, women were keeping the shops, the hospitals and the courts going. "Do they think that because women wear veils we do not have a voice?" Jamila, an Afghan human rights worker, asked. They may be invisible now, but those women have the experience and brainpower that will be necessary to rebuild what is now a thoroughly decimated country. Women's participation in the peace process is not just a matter of symbolic equality; it is a matter of ensuring peace and stability for all of Afghanistan.

Gayle Forman is a freelance journalist who writes about social justice issues pertaining to young people. She recently returned from Quetta, Pakistan, where she reported on Afghan refugees, and is currently at work on a book about subcultures and community.

Elizabeth Schulte

Is the US fighting for women's liberation?

> The scenes of joy in the streets of Kabul evoke nothing less than the images of Paris liberated from the Nazis. Women taking to the streets to bask in the Afghan sun, free at last to show their faces. Children gathering to fly kites, a once-forbidden pastime. Old people dancing to music, banned for many years. The liberation of Afghanistan from the tyranny of the Taliban is a watershed event that could reverberate for years. The warm embrace by ordinary people of the freedom to do ordinary things is a major victory for western humanist values. This victory of values, in the long run, may count for far more than the hunt for Osama bin Laden.

This is how *Business Week* magazine—its front cover featuring an unveiled Afghan woman beneath the word "Liberation"—described the fall of the Taliban government last month.

They must not have asked Abdul Abdullah for his opinion. Abdul's cousin Aziz Khan and his wife Fatma fled their home near Herat when fighting erupted between Taliban and Northern Alliance forces. On their way toward the Iranian border, Khan and his wife were stopped with 20 other families at a checkpoint set up by anti-Taliban warlords. The men were herded into the hills and shot. The women were taken away. Abdul doesn't know Fatma's fate. But given the appalling record of rape among Northern Alliance soldiers, he can guess. "I know they let most of the women go, but they kept the young and pretty ones," he told a reporter.

Stories like these expose the lie that Afghans have been "liberated" by the US government's brutal new allies. Western news reports regularly feature pictures of women appearing in public without a veil. "What the photos do not show is the women putting [the veils] back on again moments later," one reporter for Britain's *Guardian* wrote. "For the fact remains that the Alliance feels the same way about women as the Taliban did—they are chattel, to be tolerated but kept out of real life."

In fact, the *Observer* newspaper reported that the Taliban's retreat from Kabul had unleashed a wave of so-called "honor crimes"—in which relatives kill or maim young men and women for violating the strict Islamic code governing relationships. This should be no surprise. The warlords of the Northern Alliance have a miserable record of human rights abuses, especially against women.

One has only to ask Afghan women who remember when the warlords reigned before the Taliban came to power in 1996. "They're just as bad as the Taliban, and in some ways worse," explained Tahmeena Fayral, of the Revolutionary Association of the Women of Afghanistan, during a recent US speaking tour. "They looted museums and hospitals and schools, and sold what they found. They raped women and even children. They committed the worst crimes in Afghan history." The US government didn't let these well-established facts get in the way of backing the Northern Alliance—just as it ignored the Taliban's vicious repression of women when it was courting the regime in the mid-1990s.

And any talk about the U.S. going to war for women's liberation will come as a surprise to women in Saudi Arabia, which imposes Taliban-style restrictions as well.

The US media's interest in what life is like for Afghan women is sudden. Under the hard-line version of Islam followed by both the Taliban and the Northern Alliance warlords, women must dress in the head-to-toe shroud of the burqa, for fear of public beating or death. They aren't allowed to leave home unaccompanied by their husbands or other male family members and are banned from school and work. And underlying this is the grinding poverty that cripples the entire population of Afghanistan.

The many widows in a country brutalized by 23 years of war often resort to begging or prostitution to survive. Some 1,700 out of 100,000 Afghan women die during childbirth—the highest rate in the world. Life expectancy for women is about 45 years. Human rights groups like Amnesty International have tried for years to get the word out about the plight of Afghan women, but the mainstream media showed no interest. Now, because of Bush's war, the issue is splashed across the cover of *Time* magazine.

Even Laura Bush got into the act. "Because of our recent military gains in much of Afghanistan, women are no longer imprisoned in their homes," she said in her own radio address last week. "They can listen to music and teach their daughters without fear of punishment—the fight against terrorism is also a fight for the rights and dignity of women."

No one should forget who spoke these fine-sounding words. They should be seen for what they are—a cynical rationalization for a US war that has already murdered thousands of civilians, many of them women. That's why it's infuriating to see many liberals, and even radicals, backing Bush's campaign—in the name of liberating women. For example, the liberal group Feminist Majority has asked members to circulate a petition thanking Bush and his administration for its commitment to restoring the rights of Afghan women. "We have real momentum now in the drive to restore the rights of women," Feminist Majority President Eleanor Smeal told Congress last week. Are they talking about the same administration that, immediately on taking power last January, imposed a gag order on international family planning organizations from mentioning the word "abortion"—in one stroke of the pen relegating millions of women to poverty? And a few radicals are having second thoughts. Susan George, vice president of the French-based global justice group ATTAC, said recently that though she opposed the US bombing campaign, the media pictures of women celebrating in Kabul made her question her stand.

She should remember what she knows full well about the US government's long record of promoting injustice around the globe. The US military's own wartime abuses of women are well documented. During the Vietnam War, American soldiers earned the title of "double veterans" when they raped civilian women before murdering them. Accounts of the 1968 My Lai massacre describe an orgy of gang rape—followed by soldiers mowing down at least 400 people, most of them women and children.

The US military's culture of brutality against women is alive and well today, with several recent cases of US soldiers stationed in Okinawa, Japan, raping local teenagers. And this isn't to mention the rapes of women in the US military by fellow soldiers.

Conditions for Afghan women are far worse than for women in the US. But to hold up the US government—especially under the Bush administration—as a champion of women's rights is offensive. Bush has the nerve to denounce Islamic "fanatics" even after he appointed anti-abortion fanatics John Ashcroft as Attorney General and Tommy Thompson as head of Health and Human Services. And when Bush needed advice about life-saving stem cell research, he turned to anti-woman evangelist Billy Graham for guidance.

No one who wants Afghan women to achieve real freedom should support the US government's war. The decades-long intervention by the US and other western powers is to blame for the grinding poverty of Afghanistan and the vicious rule of tyrants and warlords—the perfect breeding ground for the cruel oppression of women.

They haven't suddenly become interested in liberation now. We have to expose the real aims of this US war for "liberation"—before they "liberate" other countries.

Elizabeth Schulte is a member of the International Socialist Organization in the US and a journalist for Socialist Worker *newspaper.*

Originally published in Socialist Worker, *December 7, 2001.*

Ayesha Khan

Song of war

The international community has rediscovered Afghanistan after ignoring the civil war that has raged there since 1992. The reason for this is yet another war, this time waged by the United States against the ruling Taliban and their guest Osama bin Laden. War fought in the name of peace is an unconvincing slogan to many, particularly those who reap the results of conflict, generation after generation. Women and children in Afghanistan know better than anyone else what war has brought them, and their stories are cautionary tales to those who believe in the healing powers of more violence and forced displacement.

When Hafeeza spoke to us about her experience of war and the Taliban from a refugee camp in Peshawar, it was in the year 2000, when the world's interest in Afghanistan had slipped to its lowest point ever. The UN international appeal for humanitarian aid brought in so little money that it embarrassed them to announce the figures. Pakistan had officially declared that it too was tired of supporting millions of destitute refugees when two decades had gone by with no hope of improvement. It had sealed the border with Afghanistan, turning back the new waves of drought-cum-war refugees at the border and rounding up illegal entrants to send them home. Half a million new refugees came into Pakistan that year. The Pakistan government refused them refugee status and asked the United Nations High Commissioner for Refugees (UNHCR) to set up the new refugee camps inside Afghanistan instead.

At that point the tale of Hafeeza proved that the condition of new refugees from Afghanistan was urgent and serious, meriting immediate international action and a more sympathetic consideration from the Pakistan government. While the latest Afghan war has certainly focused international attention on the plight of war victims, nonetheless humanitarian assistance is still falling short of targets and the Pakistan government is still refusing to open its borders to accept the displaced. But Hafeeza's story reminds us that in consequence of every political agenda and act of war there are people with unique and individual stories of suffering.

She tells us about her fate at the hands of the Taliban, a regime since demonised by the western world—but allowed by them to function at the time when she experienced their wrath. Her words also remind us that all those who have waged war in Afghanistan have committed atrocities against its people, suggesting that there is no guarantee the current war will be any different. And finally, Hafeeza's eloquence and passion in describing the trauma of displacement and the yearning to go home speak not for only the Afghans, but for all refugees fleeing modern warfare around the world.

The war trauma—Hafeeza's story

I was born in Parwan province, Bagram district. We used to have a good life until the war began. After the war and cruelties started, I have seen people from the Pashtoons to the Hazaras, Tajiks, Uzbeks, everyone began atrocities against each other. I lost my husband, my cousin, my aunt's son, and daughter-in-law. Now it is my four children and me alone. We all need to eat, wear clothes, and have a place to live and means to survive.

[My husband and son] were martyred seven years ago. He had a small shop close to the airport [in Kabul]. He and my elder son were in the shop when a rocket hit the front of the shop. They say it had come from Koh-i-Safi from Gulbudin [Hekmatyar] Sahib. Both were torn to pieces. It was lunchtime when some people brought them both on a wheelbarrow. It was the worst moment of my life. I wanted to jump off the roof. What would life be like without my husband and young son? I was tearing my hair, slapping myself on the face, cutting myself with my own nails and fingers. People around me were trying to calm me down. My late mother was saying, "It is God's will—now look after your other children."

I have seen lots of miseries in Afghanistan. A few days before that, my aunt's daughter and one of my aunt's grandchildren were killed in a similar way. They were walking in the street. I have seen so many deaths, sudden deaths and pieces of the human body lying around that now I have become cold-hearted against seeing corpses or wounded bodies.

With my [remaining] children, we found something to wear and sometimes we didn't. If I found a shirt there were no trousers. If I found a *chador* (shawl) for them then there were no shoes. Food-wise, if we found two meals a day we were lucky. If I found tea, then there was no sugar. If we found pepper then there was no salt. Nevertheless, we held ourselves together and sustained whatever hardships life brought upon us without my husband and elder son. We miss them a lot.

I had two sisters-in-law who got married. And [after my husband died] I was left alone in that house with my four children. I took my children under my own wing and led a widow's life, till the troubles and unrest began in Bagram. Each party in their own turn did their own brand of cruelties and atrocities on us. From Gulbudin to Burhanuddin, the Hazaras, the Dostumis, they did nothing but worsen people's lives. The worst among all of them were the Taliban. The mullahs turned to monsters.

God has given us a throat through which we must speak and eat something. God has given us life and is supplying something to live with. Gradually, I sold whatever we had. My two sons worked on daily labour. If they collected wheat for others in the evening they brought wheat, if they collected grapes then we had grapes. At times I bought or made things for them to sell in the street, like eggs, potatoes and with that and whatever I did we have made it so far.

Facing the Taliban

No, I didn't remarry. I know no one will accept the troubles and responsibilities of my four growing children. Father was too old, mother too was sick and old to accept four orphan children. I was young and strong enough to sustain them. I also had to keep my good name and reputation as a widow. My daughters were growing up and we needed to stick together and protect each other. I had to wear veil or *chador* and watch out for myself. When the Taliban came I couldn't work outside and in others' houses. They told everyone to stay at home and not be seen.

What could I have done even if I was afraid? I had no choice left. Yes, I was afraid every day, every hour. When, for example, shootings began, we all were trembling. We would hold the Holy Koran to our chests and pray to God to rescue us. We didn't know what to do, where to go, whom to go to. We always hid under the stairs as walls from all four sides protected them. We all held together shaking and praying till the blind rocketing or shooting ended. Several gun-shells, rockets landed close to the house and broke the windows, but God saved us.

Things became unbearable for my children and me when the Taliban came. They are worse than infidels. They practically kicked us out of our house. I was cooking in the kitchen. They walked in, armed, saying, "Out, out, get out." My children began crying and I begged them [saying] that they don't have anyone but me. Where should we go and why, what had we done wrong? It was of no use. Barefoot we just walked out and ended up in Pakistan.

All those who have come across to me all the way and in the camps, had similar stories of Taliban atrocities and mercilessness. At times people had to jump into rivers to escape the tortures inflicted by the Taliban. Thousands of elders, women and children, in hot or cold weather, had to leave their homes. Some had nowhere to go and no choice but to jump into a river and put an end to all their troubles and worries. One family told us that the Talibs went to a house in their village and held a child from his arm and asked where is the father. They even gave money to find out whose son the boy was. When they found out that he was the son of a commander, they tore the boy into two pieces.

Even the infidel Russians didn't do this. They used to enter houses and ask "doshman" (enemy) or "dost" (friend). If you said, "dost," then they left. I don't think Talibs are Muslims because they don't have the heart and mercy of a Mussalman.

Children have developed a song:

God has brought us the evil (*Khuda award bala ra*)
God has brought the Talib group (*Goroh-e-Taliba ra*)
They beat the women (*Kebal mezad zana ra*)
Where have you put the weapon (*Kuja mandi sala ra*)
Where have you put the gold (*Kuja mandi tela ra*)

Ask God, he knows who they are, what kind of people and from where. People say they are Kandaharis, some others say they are Jaji and Mangal. During the time we were there all we saw was cruelty and torture. I don't know what happened after we left. However, those people who come from home, they say the Talibs are unknown people, you don't know about their fathers and forefathers. You couldn't understand their language either.

Personally, I didn't see [them assault women] in Kabul. I cannot lie, but then I have also been away for a year.

Refugee living

One of my daughters [had] got married in Pakistan. My son-in-law invited us and sent some money to come to Pakistan. I left all my belongings with my neighbours and came to Pakistan. We saw lots of troubles on the way. We had to walk to most places especially in Nijrab up to Tagab. We did not have enough money to get donkeys. It was late in the evening when we reached Tagab, hungry and thirsty. We sat in front of a balcony of a shop. Someone passed by and spoke in Pushto: Mother, what are you doing here? I told him that we have to spend the night here and next day we would be going to Pakistan. Tomorrow we go to Peshawar. He did not understand and then brought a Farsi speaking man to talk with me. He asked where is your man and what are you doing? I said I have no man, I am a widow going to Pakistan with my children. Soon they came back and said there was a room where we could spend the night. We had some cold bread with us but the children didn't eat it as they were too tired and just lay down. Then I asked for some boiled water. They said 5,000 Afghanis. We had our own tea and teapot and made some sweet tea and bread before falling asleep.

In the morning we headed for Peshawar and reached Torkham by late afternoon, where again I rented a room to sleep with my children. In the morning, hungry and thirsty, we headed for Peshawar and finally reached my daughter's house. [We] have spent three years here. Things went from bad to worse. [I returned to Bagram because] I heard my mother was dead and one of my brothers had been martyred. I was very upset by all these tragedies happening to my family and relatives. But soon when I saw the atrocities of the Taliban I forgot about the past and returned.

We couldn't afford the rent and living expenses in Peshawar city. Then they guided us to go to Akora Khattak camp. We were told that they would give us a tent in the camp. We spent one year here in this camp. Two months ago they built a room for us. It is better than the tent for the time being but it is too wet and damp. We have no choice or option. God has brought this upon us and we have to endure it. There is no job and no ration except hope from God.

Everyone had his or her own troubles and burdens to carry. Those who had means and rich relatives went abroad in various directions. My relatives were poor and had nothing to share with me. Friendship and caring totally decreased. Now we are in this camp. If some war or trouble starts here we must go somewhere else. If things become unbearable here, we would certainly seek haven somewhere else. In the same manner our network of friends and relatives disintegrated. There remained nobody to help us.

God knows whose fault [the war] was and who is to blame. Everyone says it was the other one's fault. But they built their lives on the ashes of Afghanistan. They cut Afghanistan into small pieces. There are piles of ruins and graves in each village. All dwellings have been destroyed, now it doesn't matter whose fault it was. My homeland is in ruins. All I know is that the Taliban were the worst of them all and had no mercy on people, especially on women.

There is no place like home. Everyone loves his or her own fatherland. Animals love their nests. Once upon a time, there was a bird singing in a cage in the king's palace. The king wondered what it was singing about. So he released the bird and asked persons to follow it. Someone noticed that the bird went to the bank of a river and sat on a branch of a tree and started singing:

"Ai watan," Oh my homeland
"Bulbul watan," nightingale of my country
"Shakh-e-sunbul watan," the branch of a flower is my homeland.

After singing this song the bird fell down and died, because of happiness. Now, if animals love their homes this much, then human beings love them even more. We get burned in the hot weather and frozen in the cold weather of Pakistan. No other place exists or could be as sweet as our own homeland.

It is fine [in the camp]. In the summer it is like hell. Last year we were in a kaprak tent. It couldn't hold against the winds and rain and turned into an oven in the summer. This year it is better because we have a room. It is safer in the rain, wind and may be better in the summer too. My children sell water and tea. Lately they both work in one shop in Peshawar. They sleep in that shop. On weekends they return with some food and Rs 100-200 that we live on.

Everyone else from my family was martyred, but we have chosen to survive. I cannot let my children die. Enough is enough. I cannot allow my remaining children to be martyred.

Ayesha Khan is a freelance journalist and researcher based in Islamabad, Pakistan. This verbatim rendering of Hafeeza's story has been made possible by a group of people who remain unnamed.

Originally published in The News, May 17, 2001.

Fahima Akhtar

Jehadi and Taliban are both responsible for the human rights disaster*

First of all, on behalf of the Revolutionary Association of the Women of Afghanistan, I congratulate you on the 8th of March, International Women's Day. The 8th of March this year holds great significance because it is the first eighth of March of a new century. When we speak about the new century, we immediately think of such things as freedom, secularism, democracy, development, science and technology. We think of the people of the world, particularly women, who are advancing with new hopes and aspirations for the achievement of their rights. But now a flame is burning in my heart, because I belong to a country where the savage rulers don't consider women to be human beings. We will never forget that in many countries of the world the condition of women is deplorable. Now, before our eyes, the Kashmiri women are experiencing the most brutal oppression and treatment. But we still believe that the Kashmiri women are lucky, because they are fighting for independence. During the resistance war against the Russians, women of Afghanistan faced innumerable difficulties and types of oppression but remained unshaken in their resistance. Today, however, women are being deprieved of even their most basic rights. Women are not allowed to go to the doctor, or go shopping. It is unlawful and forbidden even for a woman's footsteps o be heard. Women are stoned to death and flogged in public to teach them the way of living in an Islamic Emirate!

The sufferings and sorrows of Afghan women can only be understood if you think of yourself in the place of an Afghan woman, and imagine that you are being flogged in front of your

**Abridged text of the speech of a member of RAWA. Translated from the Urdu.*

brother, husband or close relative, on the pretext that your trousers' opening is too wide, or that you are wearing high heel shoes, or that your burqa is too short—or too long.

Despite all these things, the tragedy of Afghanistan does not end here. The economic struture of the country has collapsed, and unemployment and inflation have peaked. The old, women, men and children, roam the streets from dawn to dusk just to find a breadcrumb. There are many families who are selling their sons and daughters because they cannot feed them. Many women have been forced into prostitution because they have only two options: either death from hunger or selling their bodies to survive. Our suffreings are doubled when we see the world remaining silent about our country's tragedy.

As you know there are now two groups in Afghanistan: Massoud and the Taliban. Both groups are blaming the current disastrous situation on external powers, but we continue to assert that these groups are only attempting to cover their own crimes and horrible records. In fact, they are so shameless that they are looking for military and economic support from almost any other country. If they had their own military and economic power, they would never give another country permission to interfere in the internal affairs of Afghanistan.

As I said before, our sadness and sorrow increases as we see the world witness the tragedy of the Afghan people and do nothing.

The UN, which is under the influence of the world powers, knows well that its policies have failed in Afghanistan. The UN, then and now, out of the utmost frustration has acknowledged its failure. Mr Mehmood Mestiri once called the Afghan fundamentalists "a gang of bandits" and UN envoy Lakhdar Brahimi has confessed that his efforts are useless and futile.

In addition to the above points, I want to make clear that the UN option is not ideal for the Afghan people and Afghan issue. Unfortunately, however, in the given situation and despite its failures and negative policies, the UN is our only alternative.

A point or a criticism which we hear again and again, and which it is our wish to convey to other people, is that in the Pakistan general election, the Jama'at Islami received just one chair in the parliament and was thrown out of the political circles of Pakistan. This in itself is a pleasant point. But on the other hand, we see this same Pakistan trying hard to install its puppets in Afghanistan—puppets who are anti-women, ignorant, anti-secularism, and against freedom and justice, even more than the Jama'at Islami and other Islamic parties of Pakistan. In such a situation, the Pakistani people cannot win the hearts of the Afghans. The friendship between Pakistan and Afghanistan will only strengthen on a democratic basis when a democracy-loving regime is established in Afghanistan. Pakistan can only prove itself the real friend of the Afghan people if it throws out the Taliban as it threw out Gulbuddin. It is most unfortunate for us that the Chief Executive of Pakistan wants to go to Kabul and find a solution to the Afghan issue. We believe that such action will not prove fruitful, and instead a handful of ignorant, anti–women, anti-democracy and anti-freedom creatures will end up with importance and prestige.

On the Osama question, the opposition of the Taliban towards their masters is an old trick by which they want to prove themselves "independent." But we all know that the life and death of the Taliban is dependent upon their masters. If they wish, they could bring the Taliban to collapse as they did to Gulbuddin.

The other critism which we have been hearing for a long time regards our use of the word "fundamentalism."

The first point is that fundamentalism is an expression which has found a specific meaning. If somebody suggests that we should avoid the use of this word, we ask him or her to please come forward and find or invent a word that we can use instead. In our view, based on our experiences, fundamentalism has become equivalent to: reaction + ignorance + hostility towards women + dependence upon foreign powers and terrorism. The words "fanatics," "medieval-minded" or "Islamist" do not describe the real nature of the Afghan fundamentalists.

RAWA and other democratic forces of Afghanistan have to face countless hardships in their struggle against fundamentalism. Our fundamentalists, while having a Koran in one hand and a kalashnikov in the other, want to bury Afghanistan in a trench of backwardness, obscurantism and suffering in order to run their Islamic Emirate.

It is most fortunate that here today among us are many Pakistani intellectuals, well-known personalities, and politicians. We hope they will continue their struggle and maintain their reolute stance against fundamentalism. We know that fundamentalism is spreading like a cancer. And if we compromise with it, it will continue to spread and strengthen.

Let us in the name of freedom, democracy and humanity stand together and fight against fundamentalism and uproot this cancer from our region forever.

Long live the struggle of the Afghan and other women of the world against fundamentalism.

Fatima Akhtar is a member of the Revolutionary Association of the Women of Afghanistan. Reproduced from their Special Bulletin on International Women's Day, March 2000.

Anuradha M. Chenoy

The politics of gender in the politics of hate

The politics of gender were integral to the making of the Hindutva militia that carried out the violent attacks on the minority Muslim community across the Indian state of Gujarat in the first quarter of 2002. The use, abuse and control of women were a critical aspect of the pogroms which involved the simultaneous resurgence of a politics of masculinity and militarism, asserted along with identity politics, at the level of both civil society and the state. Women's experiences during the violence were documented by both the media and human rights activists, thanks perhaps to increased public awareness of women's issues. Women were both targets of and participants in the carnage, widely viewed as a form of ethnic cleansing, if not genocide. Can there be an explanation for the cruelty inflicted on women and for the participation by women in the violence? Can the rapes and other crimes against women that took place during that period be linked to the metaphoric uses of gender representation? And what meaning does this have for social experience and action? This essay attempts to analyze some aspects of the gendered pogroms witnessed in Gujarat in February-March 2002.

Women as signifiers of the conflict

One way to examine the structural roots of the gender system is to move beyond women's experiences and analyze the metaphoric uses of gender representation. Studies of nationalism and nation states have often shown how nations express their goals in sexual terms. The use of the mother image as a metaphor for the nation has been part of nationalist discourse in India, as elsewhere. This sexual representation of a nation/community has an impact on social and personal experience.

A number of episodes in the Gujarat carnage reflect this use of the gendered metaphor. For instance, independent reports have established the fact that the tragic killing of railway passengers at Godhra on February 27 was preceded by provocative comments by the "kar sevaks" (Hindutva activists) who had been travelling to and from Ayodhya in connection with their agitation for the construction of a temple dedicated to Ram on the site where an ancient mosque (the Babri masjid) once stood. Their provocative behaviour was directed specifically towards those who bore ethnic/religious markings, especially women. Men with beards and women with veils, who appeared to be Muslims, were singled out for abuse and humiliation. The initial fracas at Godhra station that morning reportedly involved the teasing of a young Muslim girl. The mob of Muslim miscreants that allegedly set two coaches of the train on fire is believed to have been incensed by the rumour that "kar sevaks" had abducted and molested a Muslim woman, thereby "dishonouring" the Muslim community.

The reprehensible Godhra incident, resulting in the gruesome death of 58 travellers, most of them women and children, provoked widespread shock, anger and grief. Adding fuel to the simmering fire were rumours floated by newspapers like the Gujarati dailies, *Sandesh* and *Gujarat Samachar*, which on February 28 reported that religious fanatics had kidnapped some Hindu women. On March 1 *Sandesh* claimed that two Hindu women had been abducted from the train, gang-raped, mutilated and killed by Muslims, before their bodies—with breasts cut off—were dumped near Kalol, not far from Godhra. The police investigated the story and found it to be baseless, but the damage had been done. From February 28 onwards, as Hindu mobs began attacking Muslims and destroying their property in different parts of the state, many Muslim women were raped and some were subsequently burnt. A slogan used throughout the carnage spoke of avenging the rape of "our women".

Critical aspects of the methodology of the pogroms that were to follow became clear. By evoking symbols of women sexually abused by the enemy it was possible to arouse mass sentiment and pave the way to mass violence. The rape of women was seen as synonymous with dishonouring the community; it had to be avenged in kind. By constructing a myth involving the rape of Hindu women by Muslim men and by linking the latter to an external enemy (Pakistan), the Sangh Parivar and the communal press sharpened the religious divide, fostered notions of revenge, made the citizen into a warrior and turned the mob into a militia.

A statement by Pravin Togadia, international general secretary of the Vishwa Hindu Parishad (VHP, a militant organisation belonging to the Sangh Parivar), was telling: "Hindu society will avenge the Godhra killings. Muslims should accept the fact that Hindus are not wearing bangles. We will respond vigorously to all such incidents." The statement reflected the basic tenets of the Sangh's philosophy: cultural nationalism, militarism and masculinity. Women then became easy victims of the conflict. In fact, as women activists reported, the most extreme forms of sexual and gendered violence were perpetrated on women and even young girls during the carnage. The use of the myth and reality of rape is an old wartime tactic, the oldest means of dehumanizing the object. The "enemy other" is best hurt if "their women" are dishonoured through bodily abuse. As Susan Brownmiller noted about the Bosnian rapes: "In one act of aggressiveness, the collective spirit of women and the nation (in this case the community) is broken, leaving a reminder long after the troops depart." All these were steps towards the fulfilment of a militarized Hindutva agenda.

Hindu women who were found guilty of saving, or attempting to protect, Muslims were equally punished. The most famous case was that of Geetaben, married to a Muslim. Hindutva forces stripped her before stabbing her, because she had committed the crime of marrying and shielding a Muslim. This practice of stripping and shaming "erring" women has been followed quite often by fundamentalists as a lesson to women who have violated the set norms of the community. The humiliation of one woman warns and intimidates other women; it serves the purpose of maintaining gender hierarchy by limiting the autonomy of women. Also punished during the recent violence in Gujarat were those women who protested against the violence. Newspapers reported that a man killed his wife because she tried to stop him from joining a mob that was on a burning and rampaging mission.

In the case of Geetaben, she became a victim but also a martyr. Those who opposed the genocide celebrated her as a heroine, a symbol of communal amity and resistance: "In these troubled times when heroes are scarce and villains abound, Geetaben deserves to be worshipped. She is Gujarat's Jhansi-ki-Rani, its La Passionaria. I salute you Geetaben, from the bottom of my heart for your one brief moment of defiance," wrote one journalist.

The tendency to extol women as objects of veneration and elevate them as symbols of community honour places burdens on them as carriers of culture while simultaneously imposing controls on them. Restraining the autonomy of women lies at the heart of the Hindu fundamentalist agenda (as in other fundamentalist ideologies). The clear message to women is that they should conform to the strict confines of womanhood as defined by their religious/cultural codes. This is presented as a condition for the construction of an idealised vision of a society based on the Hindutva ideology.

Militarization is also an integral part of this agenda. Communal violence is used to maintain and strengthen differences between communities. In Gujarat the politics of revenge, victory, honour and humiliation was signified on and with women, just as it often is in wars. As women caught in the conflict told activists, "Yahan to yudh ho gaya" (There has been a war here). People spoke of "borders" demarcated in neighbourhoods, with makeshift fences physically separating the two communities. In some areas the "other" side was called Pakistan. Godhra itself was referred to as "mini-Pakistan." Thus imagery and language became militarized and values like force as power, violence as arbitrator, masculine hierarchy, and gender difference permeated society.

The binary "other" of this feminine signifier—i.e. of masculinity as power and lust—is an underlying theme of Sangh Parivar leaders and was sharpened during the conflict in Gujarat. Prof. Keshavram Kashiram Shastri, Chairman of the Gujarat unit of the Vishwa Hindu Parishad, who justified the violence as necessary, said in an interview, "Lust and anger are blind." He also drew a natural connection between masculinity, power and lust when he stated that the violent acts could not be condemned because they were, after all, done by "our" Hindu boys, who "were charged up because in Godhra women and children were burnt alive". Thus notions like "boys will be boys" and images of them as warriors formed part of the justification of the carnage.

Women's agency

Women's role in the Gujarat carnage as supporters of violence and looters of goods has been well-documented. Sangh leaders cited this phenomenon to prove the spontaneity and "mass character" of the movement. Women leaders of the Bharatiya Janata Party (BJP), the political party heading the state government as well as the coalition of parties ruling the country, feigned ignorance of the atrocities, including those against Muslim women. A women's fact-finding team reported, for instance, that Maya Kodnani, a BJP member of the state legislative assembly who has been named in the First Information Report as an accused, inciting and participating in violence in one of the worst hit areas (her own constituency), justified the incidents as "natural" anger against Muslims.

Several questions arise in the context of women's role in the violence. Did Kodnani, along with the rest of the Sangh Parivar, comprehend mass rape in terms of the everyday violence that is considered legitimate? Was women's participation in the violence seen as a sign of their empowerment? Or was it more than that? It appears that the Sangh Parivar saw the Gujarat events as a war, fought by a militia made up of their cadres, unhampered by rules regulating the treatment of the enemy. Since, in their scheme of things, Muslims are not even considered full citizens, they are obviously not worthy of human rights. Women of the Hindu Right were partners in this war, assuming perhaps that participation would "empower" them, give them agency in domestic affairs and raise the status of "womanhood" in the eyes of the Hindu militia. Through participation in violence, conflict and war, women of the Hindu Right demonstrated their aspiration for power and equality with men. They assumed they would benefit by proving their "sameness" and establishing their worth as partners in violence. In reality they were only reinforcing patriarchal patterns based on hierarchical power structures that have been used to keep women and others down through history.

The militarization of society is a gendered process. De-sensitization to violence and dehumanization of the potential opponent are core processes in this project. For male recruits, it includes a process of overt masculinization where the feminine is rejected as unworthy or the Other. Militarization for men also involves providing proof of manhood which can be shown in various ways, ranging from aggression and unmitigated violence, to initiation through rape. Women's place in a militarized institution is defined within the confines of gender, with women usually assigned to service and support roles.

The making of a militia?

The gendered carnage in Gujarat was in step with long years of the planning and propagation of the Sangh ideology. Sangh outfits have long used Gujarat as a test case for the agenda of Hindutva, concentrating their efforts in the region. Before and during the 2002 conflict the VHP openly distributed venomous leaflets that called for the economic and social boycott of Muslims. Gender tension was an underlying theme in almost all such hate literature, whether it addressed commerce, the construction of the Ram temple or national security. The pamphlets constantly referred to "thousands" of rapes of Hindu women by Muslim youth and to the deception of Hindu women by Muslim men. They called upon Hindu men to unite and pay back the Muslims for the apparent wrongs done to Hindus down the ages. Hindu men were told "to keep a watch on your girls" and to "save them" with the help of Hindu organizations. The most consistent theme underlying most of the pamphlets was the sanctity of Hindu women and the threat posed to them by Muslim men.

These lessons on commerce and sex do more than encourage a false sense of fear based on an imagined threat perception leading to prejudice and discrimination. The enemy in civil society can only be fought through war within civil society. The next logical step is to militarize civil society and create a male militia in every home. The VHP and the Bajrang Dal (another militant outfit belonging to the Sangh Parivar) have worked at this for years. They have distributed trishuls (tridents, symbolic of a holy war) in the thousands, with the clear message that these were to be used for the protection of the Hindu religion. They have organized camps for training in the martial arts, including special camps for women and children led by women of the Hindu Right, which have been openly advertised in newspapers. In fact, after one such camp, women trained in these skills are reported to have stated that they "felt empowered" in the process. The meaning of empowerment was thus transformed from the securing of equal rights to being armed and militarized.

Cynthia Enloe has examined the case of Bosnian Serb men in the militia and how they were simultaneously masculinized, militarized and ethnically politicized. In this case, Serb men learnt from their elders of how Muslims (their neighbours) had oppressed their ancestors. The militia were also taught that Muslims—from the Ottoman past to the present—were to blame for their current problems and failures. It was men like them who decided to form armed militia rather than trust civilian parties or the weak state. The warrior element was also central to the construction of the Serbian ideal of masculinity. Femininity was constructed to bolster masculinity. The Serbs had collectively managed to convince individual men that their manhood would be validated only if they performed as soldiers, either in the state army or in autonomous forces. This process undoubtedly assisted in militarizing ethnic nationalism and creating the Serb militia that carried out the infamous ethnic cleansing, genocide and mass rape that took place in that part of the world.

Striking similarities between the VHP/Bajrang Dal groups can be found not just with the militias in former Yugoslavia but also with militia organizations of the 1930s in fascist Italy, like the Italian Balilla and Avanguardisti. These groups organized youth on para-military lines and were based on an ideology of cultural superiority that excluded other religious and ethnic minorities from the concept of the nation. They used symbols of past greatness and blamed minorities for historical wrongs, seeking revenge for the past in the present. They placed women lower in their hierarchic organizations, with specific roles as supporters of the cause and reproducers for the nation. The forces of the RSS, VHP and Bajrang Dal are parallels of such militarized politics. These organizations have large cadres in Gujarat and follow a similar trajectory, with specific variations. The construction of the male as warrior is a constant theme with them, from the highest to the local levels.

Conclusion

The media, citizens' groups, women's groups and political parties opposed to the politics of the BJP and Sangh Parivar, have all expressed horror and anguish at the events in Gujarat in early 2002. NGOs, including women's organisations, worked in the 103 makeshift camps which housed over 150,000 displaced persons, primarily Muslim. Citizens' groups conducted fact-finding missions and set up a citizens' tribunal to listen to and record the experiences of victims. All this was necessitated by the inadequate response of the central government, and because the state administration attempted to not only cover up the genocide but even protect the guilty. Fact-finding teams of women found that the crimes against women during the carnage had been grossly under-reported, and that sexual violence had been made largely invisible even by the media which had covered other forms of violence in considerable detail. In addition, the police and others in positions of authority failed to take notice of these crimes or initiate any action against the perpetrators.

The Gujarat carnage has shown how the forces of Hindutva distort cultural definitions of gender by using gender representations during times of conflict. As such cultural notions of gender differences get heightened, and women as a category get dehumanized. The attempts and struggles of women's movements that are engaged in making real changes for women suffer a setback as this retrogressive ideology, which prevents real change in the name of "honouring" women as nation/goddess, gains ascendancy. Before the Gujarat carnage, and during it, there has been a continuous subtext that points to the control of women's sexuality and the simultaneous assertion of masculinity. The metaphor of mother/woman as nation/religious/ethnic symbol is closely linked to this distinction. The need to arouse masculinity to protect and control this identity is the basis of the making of the militia.

Civil society in Gujarat, as indeed civil society in all of India, has become sharply polarized. On the one side is a pseudo-Hinduism under the guise of a Hindutva ideology that threatens to devour not only everything the Indian nation and Constitution stand for, but also civil society and, eventually, Hinduism itself. On the other side are the secular, multi-ethnic urges and forces of Indian society. Progressive women's movements in India are a critical part of the latter; they have to take the lead in this contestation for the sake of the country's women, whose future existence and well-being are threatened by multiple fundamentalisms, chief among them the ideology of Hindutva.

Anuradha M. Chenoy is Professor in International Studies, Jawaharlal Nehru University, New Delhi. She is an activist on gender and social issues and has written many articles and books, including Militarisation and Women in South Asia *(2001)*, The Making of New Russia *(2001) and* India Under Siege: Challenges Within and Without *(co-authored, 1994).*

6
Displaced/Dispossessed

Sonia Jabbar

Spirit of place

1. The path

It is autumn and I'm hovering somewhere between the 9th and 14th centuries, recovering some of Kashmir's rich past in my explorations of ancient sites and still more ancient people—amateur historians, mythologists, anchorites, all. It is truly fascinating and far more engaging than the dreadful accounting of killings and tortures that has occupied me all year. The weather is gorgeous. Brilliant sunshine and a cold that nips pleasurably. The gigantic chinars and poplars are turning to rust and gold. Great flocks of sheep and long-haired goat swarm down from the high pastures, flooding the plains, drowning the highways so that even now, on this road to Ganderbal, the Maruti and the bus in front are transformed into little islands in this vast woolly sea lapping and eddying around us. It is a while before the shepherds, the Gujjars, with their great curving noses and hennaed beards whistle their flock into remarkable discipline.

The wait, though, isn't without some trepidation. Kumarji and I sitting in front, could pass off as anybody—we have nothing that distinguishes our religion. But the ladies crammed into the back seat, the old ladies who have gossiped and giggled and sung bhajans off-key this past hour? Sari clad, tikas, and worse still, the unmistakable mark of the Kashmiri Pandit woman, the *dejehor*, heavy triangular earrings suspended by a complex system of gold chains. In Srinagar this would have been passable, but we are in Ganderbal and Lar is only a stone's throw away. The same Lar which, according to some, could be Kandahar, so infested is it with Afghan Mujahideen, their fingers welded to hair-triggers. But the ladies are sanguine. "Bhagvati kare theek," they shrug, and we are, after all, going to visit Bhagvati, Devi,

Ragni, Khir Bhavani, the great benign mother in her shrine at Tula Mula. It is this spirit of optimism and resilience that has kept the handful of Kashmiri Pandits—17,860 to be precise—in the Valley. I am tending to spend more and more time with them these days, watching them negotiate and nourish the old relationships with the Muslims, worn thin by the decade of war, dirty politics and mistrust. Watching also, their anger and disbelief at being scorned and targeted by the Pandits who fled the Valley in the early '90s to become refugees in camps in Jammu and Delhi.

It was at a refugee settlement in Jammu that I first realised the importance of Khir Bhavani for the Kashmiri Pandits. My host was Shekhar, a soft-spoken, bespectacled, middle-aged man. I'd thought of spending an hour or so with him but ended up five hours later, unable to tear myself away from the unending stream of stories, anecdotes, myths, histories. How different he seemed now from his earlier avatar that I had encountered in various fora on Kashmir: the strident Dr. Agnishekhar, convener of Panun Kashmir, demagogue, agitator for a separate Pandit homeland. We had kept our respective politics intact and yet laughed quietly together this afternoon. Now we were parting as friends. "Wait. Don't go yet. I want to show you something," he slipped into his slippers and walked out of the front door into the warm evening, "I know you'll enjoy this." We walked up the narrow street, negotiating piles of building material. The colony was desolate, a treeless wasteland. On either side were the newly built, single-storeyed, pill-box like homes of the refugees, abject substitutes for the ancient, soaring four-tiered houses of Anantnag, or Safa Kadal, Bijbehara or Sattu Barbarshah: delicately brickworked, latticed-windowed, wooden-tile-roofed structures gravitating lovingly towards each other.

"What's this?" I said as we stood under a small rise on top of which I could see the marble trikoned canopy of a temple. We trotted up the steps, Shekhar greeting the evening temple-goers. At last we stood at the gate and with a great theatrical swoop of the arm, he said, "Welcome to Khir Bhavani, Jammu." I entered speechless and stood silently watching a few men and women at prayer, the gaudy fairy lights illuminating their faces, deeply absorbed in devotion. In front of me stood an exact replica of Khir Bhavani— smaller than the original, but faithful in detail. The holy spring out of which the original temple grew was replaced here by a marble tank filled with tap water. All form and no content. A wave of sadness washed over me. It was suddenly perfectly clear. This wasn't any old temple. They missed Kashmir so badly that they tried to replicate it here, like children with their doll's houses, entering a world at once real and make-believe. It was like the old Pandit woman in a camp in Delhi who confessed that she could only make it through the hideous summers by sitting in front of the cooler, closing her eyes tightly and imagining that it was cool Kashmiri rain and not the wet machine-propelled air caressing her face. The rage follows quickly after disappointment when the eyes fly open and it is not Kashmir at all but a stinking cooler in a stinking room in a stinking refugee camp far, far away from Kashmir. At some point each one must have realised that it is not a question of a few weeks or months but perhaps forever that the gates of Kashmir have been slammed shut behind them. Now that I have lived in Kashmir I understand their irreparable sense of loss and longing, of betrayal and heartbreak. I understand now the anger of the refugees, their bitterness towards all who were fortunate enough to remain in the Valley, be they Muslims or Hindus.

I don't know what is worse: to lose a beloved, to lose a father or son, or to lose one's entire universe.

2. The circumambulation

Ravan had the audacity to try and bribe the Goddess to work the forces of the universe on his side as Ram battered down the gates of Lanka with his army of monkeys. The Goddess, appalled by Ravan's evil deeds, was in no mood to be propitiated and flew into a rage. Ravan tried his best to appease her but She would have none of it, or of him or of Lanka, and ordered Hanuman to fly her out of the wretched isle as far away as possible. They flew far north into the Himalayas—Hanuman, the Goddess and her 360 serpents and alighted, it seems, in the most felicitous of places, Tula Mula, where the Goddess has remained since.

But it wasn't until a pious brahman, Krishna Pandit—in some unspecified period of antiquity—had a visitation by the Devas, that the site became known to humans.

"How shall I find the spring?" he asked the Gods, trembling with excitement.

"Engage a boat as far as Shadipor, and from there a serpent will guide you. Thus shall you know."

He did as he was told, engaged a boat and came as far as Shadipor, and behold! a snake was seen to be swimming in the waters of the swamp. The boat followed the snake. The snake halted at particular places where Krishna Pandit fixed long sticks into the swamp to demarcate the area. Thus was the divine spring discovered. Then the intrepid Krishna Pandit set about reclaiming the land by dumping dry earth into the marsh. When the ground was prepared, he brought wide-eyed devotees from Srinagar to worship the Goddess. As soon as the puja ended Krishna Pandit opened his eyes and found a piece of birch bark floating on the waters of the spring. On retrieving it he found a sloka written on it, describing the divine form of the goddess Ragni.

I make obeisance to that one Goddess who,
having taken the position of the Supreme God
is the Queen in reality, whose form is made of light and is
adorned by (the lustre of) twelve suns,
who cannot be observed through senses,
who is seated on a throne and is wrapped with serpents.

It is said that the spring was once surrounded by 360 springs. Now it is surrounded by the bunkers of the Border Security Force. Gaily painted signs welcome us as we approach a sandbagged booth to sign ourselves in. Name, State, M/F, Time In, Time Out, Sign. It feels like the register at the heavily guarded gates of the secretariat in Srinagar. But nothing can spoil our mood, and I follow the excited chattering old ladies into an enclosed area at the edge of the temple wall that says "For Women Only". In no time they have stripped down to their underwear, great breasts flapping against wobbling stomachs as they plunge into the icy waters of the canal to purify themselves. I realise with some alarm that I am expected to follow suit. It is far too cold and I decide to put up with their withering glances instead. I bring the women fistsful of earth that serves as soap, and also help one of the toothless ladies out of the contraptions that hold her broken old body together: neck collar, spine brace, left knee brace, right knee brace, elastic crepe bandage around the left ankle. She chuckles loudly at my obvious discomfiture before pinching the tip of her nose, taking a voluminous gulp of air and disappearing under the dark waters of the Gangkhai.

. . .

I first heard about Hamid the Fish after he had been shot dead by the security forces. They claimed that it was he who had masterminded the killing of 23 Pandits in Wandhama in January of '98. It was spring and I think the event was sandwiched between reports of Fidayeen attacks and the dreadful massacre of Chittisinghpora. It would have escaped my notice except that the local newspapers had made much of the fact of him ducking the security dragnet for eleven years. There were just a handful of the old guard left among the militants. Most had been killed by the army and paramilitary or by rival Mujahideen groups just a few years into the insurgency. The cleverer ones surrendered, joined the pro-state Ikhwan, only to be picked off one by one by determined assassins over the years. The cleverest were like Hamid the Fish, or Yusuf Chopan of Bandipora, Robin Hood like characters, determined, incorruptible, striking terror into the hearts of their enemies but never, it is said, harassing innocents, silently cheered on by the villagers of the area they controlled. A forest of legends grew up swiftly around them, so that it was impossible to hear a story about one or the other without the appellation of *ferishta*, or angel, added to their names. This is rare in Kashmir: one usually hears the army and the militants being cursed in the same breath.

"Even in death Yusuf Chopan was compassionate and heroic," Haleema had said softly, "the army had cordoned the house. He knew that they would have used mortars and blown us all up if he'd remained holed up inside. So he made a dash of it with the other guy. They leapt out of this window. The snow was deep and the dawn light made them easy targets, dark silhouettes against the whiteness. . ."

She pointed to the field behind the house, "This is where they fell. There was fresh snow, white, pure white. But they pumped so many bullets into him to make sure he was dead, that the field turned red."

"So, when did they take your husband away?"

"Right after. They accused us of being accomplices but what could we do? Yusuf came at 3 in the morning and demanded food. They have guns too. I woke up and fed him and allowed him to rest for a bit, that's all. What could we do?"

This is Buthu, Bandipora District in North Kashmir, a couple of hours hard climb through the forest from the shrine of Aham Sharif. Because there is no road the village remains isolated and at the mercy of both the militants and security forces who swoop down with tiresome frequency.

Shaafi and I sat eating hot rotis and a delicious local *saag*. We were famished after the walk. It was a warm summer night and I was propped drowsily against the window half-listening to the delightfully secular young Maulvi's monologue and drifting into a delicious feeling of well-being. A fat buttery moon painted the pine-covered hillsides in dramatic shades of silver and shadow. Suddenly, I thought I heard something which made me sit bolt upright, straining to hear above the conversation, the clinks from the kitchen and the insistent chirping of crickets. A half minute went by before I heard it again. A ghostly wail which echoed in the hills and made my hair stand on end.

"What's that?" I said

The men looked up quizzically, unwilling to break the talk.

"Listen," I said with a growing sense of unease.

Nothing. After a few minutes of politely humouring me they return to the gossiping. I begin to feel a bit foolish when I hear it again. And again.

"Listen! what was that?!!"

"Probably jackals. . ."

The man at the hookah giggles nervously.

"Ha didi, it's probably *chudails* or ghosts!" Shaafi teases.

But then they hear it. The Maulvi jumps up and walks swiftly outside, stands on the step frowning, but perfectly still. The wail echoes again and the Maulvi explodes into life, rushing inside and shuttering the windows. Like a well-rehearsed drill all the actors, without a word spoken to each other, leap up and dash about.

"What. . . what's going on. . . Shaafi, what is it dammit? Someone say something."

Everyone is tightlipped and I hear the banging of doors and windows, creaking of bolts sliding shut, thumping of seven or eight pairs of little feet on wooden stairs as the children run to hide in the attic. Then, silence and stillness, but for the women weeping and whimpering in each others' arms in the corners. The lamps are turned out. We sit quietly in the darkness, neck-deep in fear. I can feel my heart slow down, my breath shallow, my senses expanded.

"It sounds like something's happening in the mohalla above us," the Maulvi whispers.

"What?"

"I don't know. Maybe an RR raid."

"At this hour?"

"Always at this hour."

We wait. The minutes drag on. We hear the shrieking again, clearer this time, inhuman cries. I can't bear it any longer and get up.

"Where d'you think you're going?" the Maulvi hisses.

"I have to find out. I must see. . ."

"Sit down," he pulls me roughly by the wrist, "don't be foolish. We'll find out in the morning."

A couple of hours later a group of wailing women and men come down the path in front of the house. It seems it is safe now to step out. The Maulvi is soon surrounded by them and speaks in low comforting tones. They hold mashaals, burning torches, in their hands, the flickering light throwing ghostly shadows on their tear-stained faces. The story unfolds jerkily, but in the end I gather that the paramilitary Rashtriya Rifles did a cordon and search operation. A couple of rough Ikhwanis went in first looking for Manzoor Ahmed Reshi while the RR stood guard outside. He was asleep. They woke him up, told him to dress at gunpoint, while the women wailed and pleaded with them not to take him away.

"Don't worry. The sahab just wants to ask him a few questions outside. He'll be back after 5 or 10 minutes," one of the men said soothingly. Then the whole lot disappeared swiftly into the night. That's when the wails and screams started. The village had had some experience of this. The Maulvi's brother had been taken one night a couple of years ago in exactly the same manner. They found him the next morning, face down, barely a hundred yards from the village with a bullet through his head.

Poor Manzoor Ahmed Reshi, the carpenter who can no longer ply his trade. The man whose arm hangs limply at his side because it was shot up in the cross-fire five years ago by god alone knows whose bullets. The same man who was picked up a year ago and shown a photograph.

"Know this face?"

"Yes."

"Is he with you?"

"No."

"Does he come often?"

"Yes."

"Go now and when Chopan comes into the village next I want you to inform us."

When Chopan was killed retribution followed swiftly. They picked up Reshi one night and beat him mercilessly. He pleaded with the militants to let him go, that he was innocent and had nothing to do with Chopan's betrayal. Perhaps they believed him because he returned bleeding and battered, but alive.

Sitting in the dusty courtyard the morning following the nightmare I had witnessed, I promised Reshi's young wife that I'd follow up on the case, and that she shouldn't lose heart, that I was sure he'd return just fine, words I have repeated so often these last five years. Earnestly. Then I went to see Haleema up the hill.

The house was double-storeyed, as Kashmiri peasant houses tend to be, with a large courtyard full of clucking chickens. The woman looked worn out and frail as she recounted the tale of Chopan's last stand and the subsequent arrest of her husband.

The room was neat and gaily painted. On one wall, in red paint, in English, neatly printed, with laurels in green on either side, was written: *You only live once, but if you live right once is enough.*

"Who wrote this?" I asked, struck by the terrible irony.

"I did," Haleema's sixteen year old son, Hilal, said shyly.

"Your English is very good, as is your writing, but your wisdom is even better."

He smiled, "Actually, my father used to say that."

I turned to Haleema just before I left, "By the way, what charge did they take your husband on?"

She excused herself for a few minutes and rummaging in an old trunk pulled out a copy of the FIR. It had been lodged by the Naib Subedar, S.S. Rawat of the 14 Rashtriya Rifles camped at Chittarnar, under the Indian Arms Act 7/25 and Act 307—212 RPC. It recommended 9 months for Wali under the Public Safety Act. Naib Subedar Rawat accused Wali Mohammed Reshi of sedition: "Mohd. Wali Reshi incites militants against India."

3. The gates

This is marvellous. My neck starts to hurt because I've been looking up in wonder for the last five minutes. The chinars were planted with some design in mind because now, several hundred years later, together they form a grand marquee. The sky shows only in tiny irregular fragments of blue. The light filtering in is a cool green. The flagstones are so cold that they hurt my naked feet. Behind me is the Gangkhai arcing around the periphery of the temple, forming a natural moat. I turn to look at the ducks quacking and fussing among the reeds when a voice says, "The canal protects the temple. Whenever it has been attacked the bullets and shells have landed harmlessly in these waters."

I turn to see the man who has been selling Kumarji flowers and incense, grinning at me. "Really, it's true," he says emphatically, "this place is very special."

I grin back and buy a plateful of flowers from him. The old ladies are making a huge racket ringing the temple bells vigorously. I follow behind them, touching the temple bell above me to announce my presence to the Goddess gingerly. I don't really believe but I've always been a sucker for ritual.

The temple is actually no temple. A wide courtyard with flagstones and the chinars surrounds the spring which is no more than twenty-five feet long and fifteen wide. The spring is an irregular septagon with its apex at the east curiously called, *Pad*, or feet. On its opposite end is the *Sher* or head. The northern and southern sides are longer. On an island in the centre is a tiny shrine to the Goddess. Once a mulberry tree grew here ("Tul=Mulberry, and Mul= Roots," Kumarji told me.) Yellow and orange marigold overflow from it, tumbling into the spring. The Goddess peeks out from among them: a small delicate figurine in bronze, said to have been recovered from the waters. Facing the shrine at the edge of the spring is a narrow pavilion in which we stand now, hands folded, heads bowed. The purohit is chanting raucously in Sanskrit. Kumarji and I exchange glances, "The Mahant is on leave today so we'll have to make do with the BSF purohit," he whispers. I steal a glance at the old ladies. They are blissed out: eyes closed, beatific smiles, swaying to the grating voice of the purohit. From time to time he instructs us to light the diyas, drop flowers or pour *lota*s of milk which we've brought along into the spring. We have to step around a large man to do that. He sits praying in front of a stack of handwritten notes lit by a single diya. Something about him makes me believe he's been at this for a long time. But I know we are disturbing him by the frown that creases his forehead. At one point the purohit steps around him and attempts to light a diya from the one illuminating the notebook. The man explodes wordlessly, hissing and waving him off like he would an irritating blue-bottle. The purohit slinks off into his own corner without a peep and rummages in his pockets for matches. Just desserts, I think with some amusement. At the gates I had seen him bullying a small wretched-looking man in a prayer cap and pheran. The same man who would later prove useful to me.

The puja ends with a dreadful rendition of Om Jai Jagdish Hare. I groan inwardly. I had been expecting a traditional Kashmiri Pandit hymn. I have *never* heard this bhajan being sung tunefully and the group here was being faithful to the tradition.

"Om jay-aa jag-a-deesh a-hare-swaami-jayaa-jag-a deesh-hare," they squawked, dragging the tortured syllables painfully behind them. I grab the opportunity to slip away, and it is then that I realise that the pile of rags among the tins of ghee in one corner had a pair of round glasses, a flowing grey beard and a wide toothless smile.

"Come, sit," he says patting a sack into a seat, "let's take a look at your hand."

I hesitate only for a moment before making myself comfortable and offering him my palms to read.

"Hmm," he growls disapprovingly, "Shani. Saturn rules. You married?"

"No."

"Good thing. But you should have according to your hand, at twenty-eight."

He holds my palm close to his face. "What do you do?"

"I write. . ."

"Ah! Journalist. Silly profession. No integrity," he says the last in English. "According to your hand you should spend your life in spiritual activity."

"Join your profession?"

He throws back his head and laughs. "My profession, my *profession*," he repeats, delighted with the joke. "I tell you, you're right, *diksha* and *bheek,* begging for alms is no longer what it was supposed to be but has become big business. When I first became a sadhu and hung out at the Kumbh I made a friend, an older sadhu. Every day we used to step off the ghat into the river and then spend the rest of the time hanging out with the other sadhus, smoking ganja at the akharas. One day my friend pointed at the sea of sadhus and spat in disgust, 'Look Rajen,' he said, 'mark them carefully. They are like the oil the halwai uses over and over again to fry pakoras, black and sour and without potency.'

"Then I thought, here I am, a sadhu and I eat for free, but nothing is for free. I owe the universe."

Kumarji joins us and they greet each other effusively. "You've met Rajen Maharaj, I see," he says squatting besides me. The purohit comes around with a platter, spots my forehead with a vermilion tilak, pours dates and misri into Rajen Maharaj's lap and leaves the temple. His work is over for the day.

"Babaji is from Bengal and has been here for the last forty years," Kumarji tells me. I am intrigued. I thought I'd detected a Bengali accent and now try out my meagre store of Bengali on him. It is his turn to be delighted, and the Bengali seems to nudge a torrent of stories out of him. "I was at the Calcutta University, very involved in student politics. CPI in those days, the undivided Communist Party of India. Before everything started to be divided... Bengal, the Party, the country for God's sake! For years, even as a sadhu I was known as the Communist Sadhu. Tea... tea was wonderful then. We used to get Flowery Orange Pekoe at 6 rupees a pound. Very good stuff, and we'd drink it like gentlemen, not like the sherbet they serve you in Kashmir. Pah! Came here in '58 after Amarnath but settled finally in '60. As I was telling you nothing is for free, so I started working. Cut grass every morning and went around from house to house feeding the cows..." he pauses. "Earlier it was the Hindu cows but after the Pandits left, it was the Muslim cows." He collapses into laughter at his own joke.

"So, how come you came here, to Kashmir, to Khir Bhavani?"

He gives me a look, ignores my question and continues. "You see politics is supposed to serve the country, the people. But I soon realised that it was the politics of frustration. So I became a monk. Left the party and became a monk to serve people. Was in Belur Mutt for many years. Did you know Bose wanted to become a monk at Belur Mutt? No? Well, he did. And he was denied permission so he went on to form the INA. You think the British would've left without the INA? Hah! Gandhi and Nehru were all very well, but if it wasn't for Bose and the Indian National Army... Here, eat," he offers the dates.

"Why did I come here? Well, because of Swamiji. Swamiji inspired me. His life inspired me. And finally he chucked up everything because of the Devi right here" he says triumphantly.

"Er... which Swamiji?" I venture

"Swami Vivekanand, of course. Look I don't believe in a personal god. Never have. Maybe because I was Communist or maybe because I became a Vedantist. All I know is that to concentrate the mind you need a personal god. I'm 88. I should know."

"And Swamiji. . ."

"Hmm. Swamiji had all sorts of plans and ventures, all kinds of ambitions before he came to Kashmir and stood before HER. One day standing right here—*right here*—in worship he thought, 'The Goddess has been manifesting in this wonderful place for centuries and when the Mohammedans came they destroyed her temple. Yet the people here did nothing to protect it.' The Swamiji was thinking these thoughts, thinking if he was here he surely would have protected the temple. Just then, just as he was thinking these thoughts, a voice thundered in his head, 'Ho! Phellow?' Babaji was jumping about his seat now, enacting the ancient drama vigorously, speaking in English 'Ho! The temple was destroyed because *I willed it so*,' it was the Divine Mother speaking, he whispered, eyes swimming large in his spectacles, 'If I wished I could live in a golden temple seven stories high but I prefer it this way. You, phellow! *You will take care of me or I you?*'"

This, according to the Babaji, prompted the Swami to take early retirement from proselytising.

"So it doesn't matter?" I asked quietly, thinking of all the ultimately useless acts of vengeance from the Babri Masjid to the ravaged temples of Kashmir.

"It doesn't. These are simply cycles. . ." he smiled, drawing a circle through the air with an arthritic finger.

The old ladies were fidgeting now and sighing meaningfully. It was time to go and I stood up reluctantly. "Babaji, what d'you think about Kashmir? I mean the situation, you've been here forty years. . ."

"You know how to make curd?"

"Well. . ."

"If you did then you'd know that you can't make sweet curd out of curd that is sour. . . Goodbye and Bless You!"

I followed the old ladies out and waved goodbye to Babaji. The man at the notebook was still at prayer but he looked up and our eyes met. To my surprise his forehead unfurrowed and his face split into a beaming smile. I put my hands together and bowed slightly. He put his hand out in benediction and silently gestured that I should meet him the next time.

"Do you know that Sadhu, the one who doesn't speak?" I asked Kumarji at the gates as he struggled into his shoes.

"Which? Oh, him! He's no ordinary Sadhu. Used to be a bureaucrat and a film-maker. Quite high up in Doordarshan. Then he retired and came here. He's highly educated."

4. The sanctum sanctorum

Khir Bhavani, 74° 48' long. 34° 13' lat., an hour's drive north, just off the Srinagar-Leh highway. I found myself returning often, a warm feeling of homecoming suffusing me the moment the car crossed the churning clear waters of the Sind. Few people visit Khir Bhavani but the man selling flowers and incense is always at the gates, greeting me now with marked familiarity, shaking my hand and then touching his heart, "Aap theek hain? Aao chai piyo," he says.

Ghulam Mohammed Ganai looks like a villain with his thick mop of uncombed curls threaded with silver, the scraggly beard, one eye permanently closed, the other dancing behind grimy spectacles. But he's been here all his life, sitting at the Mother's feet, as he says.

Once, after I'd been inside he told me his story. His father had been the temple storekeeper, and after he died Ganai set up his stall outside the temple. It's been seventeen years since.

"Muslims don't come here after eating meat. You're not supposed to. It got so complicated, trying to figure out when I could and couldn't—if I ate at lunch that was it for the day and if I ate at dinner, I couldn't come here in the evening as I usually do—that I turned vegetarian. On Eid this year my family had cooked a sumptuous meal and tried to persuade me to partake of it. And then I thought I'd have to stay away from Her if I did, so I didn't. . ." he explained, grinning lopsidedly.

"How are things here?" I asked

"Quiet now. There weren't many boys who went from here across the border. The few who went were killed. Whosoever picks up the gun has to die," he said sagely. "There were some strange ones though," his voice dropped an octave, "Hubba. Joined the HM. He was a graduate. He'd even studied in Delhi. But he only lasted two years."

We are joined by Umar Butt, the caretaker of the temple for the last 22 years, the same small man whom I saw being bullied by the BSF purohit on my first visit here. He salaams gracefully and squats on the earth next to us.

"And then of course there was Hamid," Ganai continued, "You know Hamid Gadda?"

"Yes."

"Well, Hamid was a dropout, but he loved this place. As a child he used to run away from school, drop his books at the gates— right here— and spend the rest of the day singing bhajans. There used to be an old sadhu who died a few years ago. Hamid was his disciple."

I was intrigued by this place, by the relaxed, generous attitude of the Muslims, not to mention the Pandits, for I know of no other temple in India where there is a Muslim caretaker, where the gates are open to Muslims. Umar Butt, quietly listening all this while, now reads my thoughts, "Hum maante hain," he says emphatically, "We believe in this place. It's not simply that the Hindus believe and we think the idol is stone. No, we truly believe this is Bhagvati's place. We believe it is sacred. There is no cow slaughter in this village. You'll find Muslims coming here and offering milk to the spring just as the Hindus."

"But the Jama'atis, don't they give you a hard time, they're constantly trying to separate pure Islam from what they consider corrupt?"

They both laugh. "The Jama'atis no longer strut around," says Umar Butt with surprising vehemence, "they're so terrified of being picked up by the army for their links with the Hizb that even the most righteous of them declare in writing that they have nothing to do with the organisation."

"And what about the spring?" I ask, aware of the legend that surrounds it.

"The spring is black now," Umar Butt sighs. "Once it was white and sometimes even a rosy pink. The first time I saw the waters turn black was in '84. I heard right after that Indira Gandhi had died and the Sikhs were being butchered in Delhi. Then it became black, pitch black when militancy started, and then Kargil..." he lists the events slowly, carefully, making sure that he hasn't missed anything, "In '95 the waters became white again. Last month, though, they turned black. When things get bad it is reflected in these waters."

The days in Anantnag (literally, limitless spring) are soft as pashmina. The sun warms our skins with the gossamer lightness of shahtoosh. Shafi Chaman is an artist who wears his vocation on his sleeve. *I* am an *Artist* says his bearing, his loping walk, his crooked smile, and people actually defer to him. We swagger down the streets in our pherans ("In the early '90s it was Mast Gul and his cronies with their AKs walking up and down these very streets, my friend"), past the copper shops and bakeries, past the shrine and the mosque. With him I feel we could be Cézanne and Monet. People here have an old-fashioned respect for artists. We drink endless cups of fine Darjeeling tea while Shafi tells me about Ibn Batuta's travels in China as if it happened yesterday and Ibn was a pal. Later, we visit Mattan Nag. This has become ritual for us. Every time I visit Anantnag we must spend an hour or so at the waters of Mattan. Each time I am astounded by the blueness of the water tessellated by the mass of catfish speckled with gold, leaping, seething, moving as one, racing back and forth as we throw the puffed rice here and there, gleaming in the sunlight, glittering. Nishan claps her hands in delight, gurgling and dribbling in her father's arms. Her mother, a Raquel Welch look-alike, is with Jaana, Shafi's mother, circumambulating the spring and then standing respectfully in front of the temple; both women, heads bowed, hands folded, looking like devout Pandit women at prayer. The whole scene is suffused with a noble and sublime indifference to the fact that these are Muslims at a Hindu shrine. These are simply people in love with doing what they have done all their lives.

Water, spring, rock, cave, tree, mountain— all these are honoured, held sacred in Kashmir by Pandit and Muslim alike and imbued with the moving spirit. In truth their differences are on the surface, deeper down they are animists faithfully following the traditions of their common ancestors. In Kashmir you can't take a step without walking into a shrine or temple built along a crevice, under a tree, over a spring. Great islands of peace in these turbulent times. Shafi points to one right near the house, behind the Masjid Sharif of Baba Dawood Khaki. The great Baba's descendent, the Imam of the mosque, leads the way with a huge bunch of keys.

The Sharika Devi Bal spring is tiny, the mandir built over it is the size of a small box room, but it was of great significance to the Pandits of Anantnag. The door swings open with a creak. I peer in. It is desolate, abandoned, a few wan pictures of the Goddess still grace the walls. The spring oozes black filth onto the marble floor. An old rusted pump lies abandoned in one corner.

"Our women come now and then to clean but there isn't much they can do about the water," the Imam says apologetically. "I informed Pyare Lal Handoo when he came here last year, but you know what the government's like."

I approach the spring and look in. Opaque— like looking into a dead man's eyes.

"The waters turned black in the winter of '88-'89 and overflowed. The last time that happened was fifty years ago and then we had the plague which killed thousands, " he continued solemnly.

"And how it overflowed," Shafi recalled, "it ran past my house. The Pandits grew afraid. Some spoke of disaster and wanted to leave right then. It alarmed us all, actually. We all felt something terrible was going to happen."

Name: ***Tika Lal Taploo***. Fathers Name: Pandit Nand Lal Taploo. Born: 6th Oct, 1927. Killed: 14th September,1989. Residence: Chinkral Mohalla, Habba Kadal, Srinagar. Survived by wife (50), sons (24, 21), daughter (27). Name: ***Ajay Kapoor***. Father's Name: Shiva Nath Kapoor. Born: 16.7.1940. Killed: 1.12.1989. Residence: Old Post Office, Sr. Gunj, Srinagar. Survived by wife (47), son (25), daughter (15). Name: ***Sheela Koul*** (Tiku) Husband's Name: ***Pran Nath Tiku***. Born: December 1942. Killed:

31.10.1989. Residence: Dalhasanyar, Srinagar. Name: ***Prem Nath Bhat***. Father's Name: Laxman Ji Bhat. Born: 5.12.1932. Killed: 27.12.1989. Residence: Anantnag. Survived by wife (52), sons (42,38), daughter (31). Name: ***Sarwanand Koul "Premi"*** (Poet) and ***Virendra Koul*** (Son). Father's Name: Gopi Nath Koul. Born: 9.6.1926/ 4.5.1962.Killed: 30.4.1990. Residence: Sofshalli, Anantnag . Survived by wife (60), son (35), daughter (26) Name: ***Bansi Lal Sapru***. Father's Name: Keshav Nath Sapru Born: 30.2.1945 Killed: 24.4.1990. Residence: Gulab Bagh, Srinagar. Survived by wife (37), Sons (16 and 13) Name: ***Radha Krishen Kaw***. Father's Name: Balbhadher Kaw. Born: 18.5.1931. Killed: 24.8.1990. Residence: Kralkhud, Srinagar. Survived by wife (54), mother (75), daughter (35), son (3).Name: ***Ashwani Kumar Garyali***.Father's Name: Shamboo Nath Garyali. Born: 23.4.1965.Killed: 24.6.1990. Residence: Chattabal, Srinagar. Survived by father (70), mother (60), brother (26), sister (22). Name: ***Pushker Nath Razdan***. Father's Name: Tika Lal Razdan. Born: 18.3.1943. Killed: 12.10.1990. Residence: Khonmuha, Pulwama .Survived by wife (43), sons (23,20), daughter (16).Name: ***Makhan Lal Raina***. Father's Name: Gopi Nath Raina. Born: 23.3.1938.Killed: 22.6.1990. Residence: Khanyar, Srinagar. Survived by wife (42), daughter (22), son (20), father (80), mother (68) Name: ***Chand Ji Kher***. Father's Name: Dina Nath Kher. Born: 2.3.1972. Killed: 17.7.1990. Residence: Vessu, Anantnag. Survived by mother (55), sister (35). Name: ***Raj Nath Dhar***. Father's Name: Dina Nath Dhar. Born: 7.8.1931. Killed: 30.6.1990. Residence: Qutub-ub-din pore, Alikadal, Srinagar. Survived by mother (70), sister (40), brother (32). Name: ***Zinda Lal Pandita***. Father's Name: Prakash Ram Pandita. Born: 4.4.1931. Killed: 6.10.1990. Residence: Bagatpora, Handwara. Survived by wife (50), son (30). Name: ***Jagar Nath Pandita***. Father's Name: Ganesh Das Pandita. Born: 17.11.1943. Killed: 7.10.1990. Residence: Bagatpora, Handwara. Survived by mother (62), sons (23 and 20). Name: ***Omkar Nath Wali***. Father's Name: Parmanand Wali. Born: 4.5.1935. Killed: 2.1.1991. Residence: Chak-i-Rajwati, Vessu, Anantnag. Survived by wife (50), son (28), daughters (24 and 22). Name: ***Kanya Lal Peshin***. Father's Name: Kanth Ram Peshin. Born: 4.10.1937. Killed: 18/19.10.1991.

Residence: Pazalpora, Bandipora. Survived by wife (48), sons (24 and 18), daughter (16). Name: *Gopi Nath Raina*. Father's Name: Govind Ram Raina. Born: 1.1.1941. Killed: 7.7.1990. Residence: Manigam, Ganderbal. Survived by wife (45), daughters (28,20,17,15,12). Name: *Ashok Kumar Bazaz*. Father's Name: Ram Joo Bazaz. Born: not known. Killed: not known. Residence: Baghi Sunder Balla Chattabal. Survived by wife and seven daughters (19,16,13,11,7,5,3).

Name: *Pitti Koul*. Husband's Name: Makhan Lal Koul. Born: 1.3.1938. Killed: 7.11.1990. Residence: Mandir Bagh, Srinagar. Survived by husband (53), son (26), daughters (28),mother (70). Name: *Maheshwar Nath Bhat*. Father's Name: Zana Bhat. Born: 20.6.1921. Killed: 15.10.1990. Residence: Hazuri Bagh, Srinagar. Survived by wife (65), son (35), daughters (30,27,24) Name: *Shiban Kishen Koul*. Father's Name: Radha Krishen Koul. Born:13.5.1953. Killed:15/16.7.1990. Residence: Ashmuji, Kulgam, Anantnag. Survived by wife (35), mother (55), son (15), daughter (13). Name: *Girija Kumari Tiku*.Husband's Name: Kanya Lal Tiku. Born: 15.2.1969. Killed: 11.6.1990. Residence: Arigam, Bandipora. Survived by mother (60), husband (25), son and daughter (4 and 2) Name: *Dilip Kumar*. Father's Name: Mohan Lal. Born: 8.7.1962. Killed: 19.5.1990 Residence: Mujamarag, Shopian. Survived by mother (55), brothers (26,18,15).Name: *Manmohan Bachloo*. Father's Name: Janki Nath Bachloo. Born: 5.12.1963. Killed: 18.5.1990. Residence: Qazihama, Baramulla.Survived by Father (67), mother (56), sisters (25,23,19). Name: *Usha Kumari Koul*.Husband's Name: Rathinder Koul. Born: 13.6.1949.Killed: 14.10.1990. Residence: Sehyar, Ali Kadal, Srinagar. Survived by father-in-law (79), mother-in-law (68) son (10) Name: *Veer Ji Bhat*. Father's Name: D.N.Bhat. Born: 31.1.59. Killed: 13.5.1990 Residence: Nagam, Badgam. Survived by wife (30), daughter (5), son (3), father (60), mother (58). Name: *Ashok Kumar*. Father's Name: Basker Nath. Born: 2.5.1963. Killed: 13.5.1990. Residence: Pulwama. Survived by father (55), mother (54), sisters (30 and 24) Name: *Sarla Bhat*. Father's Name: Shamboo Nath Bhat. Born: 30.9.1966. Killed: 18/19.4.1990. Residence: New Qazi Bagh, Anantnag. Survived by father (53), mother (48), brothers (26,18), sister (21). Name:

Surinder Kumar Raina. Father's Name: Jia Lal Raina. Born: 19.3.1967. Killed: 2.5.1990. Residence: Tullamulla, Ganderbal. Survived by sisters (35,21), brothers (27,14) Name: ***K.L. Ganjoo/ Prana Ganjoo (wife)*** Father's Name: N.N. Ganjoo. Born: 4.1.1942/ unknown. Killed: 4.11.1990. Residence: Sopore. Survived by son (6), daughter (8)

Name: ***Surinder Kumar Koul.*** Father's Name: Som Nath Koul. Born: 4.5.1971. Killed: 26.8.1991. Residence: Batagund, Handwara. Survived by father (50), mother (45), brother (30), sister (33). Name: ***Ravinder Kumar Pandita.*** Father's Name: Nanak Chand Pandita. Born: 4.10.1958. Killed: 25.4.1990. Residence: Mattan, Anantnag. Survived by wife (30), mother (60), daughters (4,6,6) Name: ***Bushan Lal Koul.*** Father's Name: Shridhar Koul. Born: 14.6.1948. Killed: 16.5.1990. Residence: Amnoo, Kulagam, Anantnag. Survived by wife (37), son (19) Name: ***D.P. Khazanchi.*** Father's Name: Damodar Khazanchi. Born: 6.10.1939. Killed: 6.10.90. Residence: Kaniya Kadal, Srinagar. Survived by wife (48), son (22), daughter (18). Name: ***Prana Ganjoo.*** Husband's Name: Jawahar Lal Ganjoo. Born: 10.4.1945. Killed: 17.6.1990. Residence: Malapora, Habakadal Srinagar. Survived by son (27), daughters (30,25,19). Name: ***Durga Koul.*** Husband's Name: Badri Nath Koul. Born: 8.10.1934 Killed: 17.6.1990. Residence: Malapora, Habba Kadal, Srinagar. Survived by mother (75) son (30), daughter (28). 2

These are just a few of the names of the Pandits who were killed by the militants between 1989-91. I'd have to add some 900 more for you to get the complete picture. These women and men were not killed in the cross-fire, accidentally, but were systematically and brutally targeted. Many of the women were gang-raped before they were killed. One woman was bisected by a mill saw. The bodies of the men bore marks of torture. Death by strangulation, hanging, amputations, the gouging out of eyes, were not uncommon. Often their bodies were dumped with notes forbidding anyone—on pain of death—to touch them. Nine hundred brutal killings out of a population of around 350,000 Pandits over a period of 24 months is a startling figure. Anyone who says Jagmohan engineered the Pandit exodus is a liar.

April 26, 1990: a press release of the JKLF from Rawalpindi, trying to distance itself from the killings of the Vice-Chancellor of the Kashmir University and his secretary, both Muslims, stated: "The JKLF wants to clarify its position... it might occasionally become necessary to organise operations like kidnapping and execution of hostages, hijacking, etc., the targets should be government officials and collaborators, not sons and daughters of the soil."

But who decides who is a collaborator and who a genuine son or daughter of the soil?

The judge and the executioner together were born in anybody who picked up the AK 47. When the Pandits fled, the sights were set on the Muslim populace. In a grim twist of fate the JKLF suddenly found themselves dislodged and hounded by other Mujahideen groups, hunted in turn like rabbits and killed mercilessly in the warrens of Srinagar's mohallas. Suddenly people were being murdered by shadowy assassins for no apparent reason: a family butchered in their kitchen as they ate dinner; a primary schoolteacher wiped out even as he taught, sitting under a beautiful young chinar; a poet in his eighties, ill and infirm, killed on his death-bed; a university professor dragged out of class, tied to a tree and shot dead... Wandhama, Telwani, Sangrampora, Chittisinghpora... *Senseless violence* is a phrase which takes on new and hitherto unsuspected dimensions in Kashmir.

"No, my name's not Gadda, it's Butt. Ghulam Mohammed Butt. Gadda was a name the security forces gave him." The speaker looked like the quintessential Kashmiri peasant: tall, lean, broad-shouldered, a prayer cap pushed to the back of the head, a waistcoat over the kameez, the shalwar hitched up above the ankles, enormous feet, hands like shovels.

"You see, he eluded them for eleven years. He was very smart, very resourceful. Once, when he'd just become a militant, he was caught in a cordon and search operation. There were so many of them closing in on him so he dived into the water, and swimming underwater he reached the reeds. And there he stayed for seven hours—in that freezing cold water—breathing through a pipe he'd made from the reeds," Ghulam Mohammed said with restrained paternal pride, "That's why they named him Gadda."

Gadda. Hamid Gadda. Hamid the Fish, slippery as an eel.

His house was just a few hundred yards from Khir Bhavani, close enough to persuade Umar Butt, the caretaker, to sneak me past the BSF bunker to meet the family. Gadda's brother was waiting for us in front of the tiny two-storeyed house, nodding a curt greeting. It stood at the edge of the Gangkhai canal, now wide and green, moving slowly between dark banks pitted by the hooves of animals. I had been surprised by the size of the house: a small kitchen below and the room above it that served both as bedroom and living room for the family of six. Obviously, Hamid the Fish didn't make money out of militancy, or if he did he didn't send any home. But that was no reason for any want in hospitality, and soon we were served large glasses of hot milk and plates of biscuits. A few old blankets were quickly pulled out to cover our knees. Cushions were plumped and stuffed between us and the walls. I found myself deeply moved by all the fuss.

Once I had stopped Habla Bano, Gadda's mother, from retiring to the kitchen, she took over from her husband and spoke with remarkable confidence. I was struck by her open, relaxed face. She didn't look like someone who had lost her first-born only a few months earlier. It was only later that I realised he had died so often in her imagination in the last decade, that she had wept so much in the early years, that the actual event so many years later had been a banal formality, and her own response as empty and perhaps even tinged with some relief.

"It was because of the mandir," she said smiling wistfully, "all because of Khir Bhavani." And then she told their story as the shadows lengthened in the courtyard below.

Autumn 1989. Gadda had just finished his dinner. It was harvest time and he'd worked hard in the fields all day, but there was still time enough for a quick visit to the temple. In the lane outside the house he came upon a knot of men, some armed. A few he recognised from a nearby village. They belonged to the Al Umar commandos. When they struck up conversation with him, he realised to his horror that the plan was to blow up the temple.

He tried reasoning with them and when that didn't work, an argument and scuffle followed. Gadda was a big man, capable of taking on the whole bunch. They panicked and ran, leaving behind the gun he had snatched during the scuffle. He didn't know what to do with it so he took it along to the nearest Central Reserve Police Force (CRPF) bunker and handed it over to them. Then he made his way to the temple.

"But they were so angry, these Al Umar thugs," Habla Bano recalled, "that Hamid had to hide from them for days. They came looking for him, threatening all of us. We went to the police, the CRPF for protection but no one helped us. One day when he returned, the Al Umar got to know in no time and they swooped down on us and started dragging Hamid away. My husband wasn't around. I ran behind them crying, falling at their feet, begging them to spare him and take me instead. It was crazy, all these men with guns and me screaming, "Shoot me! Kill me but spare him!" and Hamid struggling against six, seven of them bellowing, "Don't touch her! Kill me, but leave my mother!" The CRPF bunker was so close, just across the canal. They did nothing. There must've been about thirty people watching quietly from their homes. They did nothing. I realised at that moment that we were alone, completely alone in this thing. They took us both but left me behind outside the village."

The ransom was the price of the AK47. When Gadda's father returned he set about selling a kanal of the little land he had. With only 15 of the 40,000 that they had demanded in hand he tried to bargain for his son's life. They released him after the Hizbul Mujahideen, who had been approached by a relative, stepped in and persuaded them to do so.

"But it doesn't end there," said Habla Bano, rising to serve us biscuits, "they came back after a few weeks demanding the rest of the money, threatening us, waving their guns in our faces. We were so scared. Hamid worked as a weaver. He was a master weaver at a loom, an excellent weaver, but he couldn't dream of raising that sum in such a short while. The trips to the police and CRPF yielded no results. It was when Hamid went to the Hizb for help that they struck a deal. They would protect us if Hamid joined up. It was a horrible moment."

Hamid Butt went across the border and trained for six months. Then he crossed over and became Hamid Gadda, code name Bambar Khan. The Hizbul Mujahideen were true to their word and protected the family from the Al Umar commandos, but there was little they could do about the raids of the security forces.

"For eight years the family slept separately, rotating between friends, relatives and neighbours every night, so that if we were picked up or killed the entire family wouldn't be wiped out in a stroke," said Ghulam Mohammed, taking up the tale. "It was so terrible. We used to live downriver. This here used to be a cowshed. But our home was destroyed one night, blasted apart in '96."

"By whom?"

"Who knows. Thank God we weren't there that night."

"It all started because of the temple," Ghulam Mohammed frowned, looking for answers in his upturned palms, "You know, I've devoted my life to it. I'm a karamchari. I clean the temple and don't take a pie for it. I don't know what sins we are paying for. . ."

A long silence settled between us and then Umar Butt, the caretaker, tapped his wrist. "We better leave now," he said worriedly, "we'll all get into trouble. . ."

"Often I'd hear of big militants surrendering," Ghulam Mohammed suddenly said, "and my heart would leap up with the possibility. . . I would send word to Hamid, sometimes even go and see him myself and beg him to surrender. This is a dog's life, I would say to him, for you and for us. Give it up, I would plead. But he was a changed man. Didn't listen.

"Then in '96 during the elections, the renegades picked me up one day and took me to the polling booth. You know how it is during the elections, with the militants doing everything to scare people away and the government forcing the people to vote. Well, these guys were the pro-government Ikhwan. Kuka Parrey's men. They stripped me naked and made me stand in front as a shield saying if Hamid Gadda attacks the booth he'll have to kill his father first. The security forces just stood by and watched the scene. They were twenty, I was alone. Then half way through the polling someone did open fire. Five people were shot. Two killed.

I was lucky," he said rolling up his sleeve to show a dark scar running from his shoulder down the withered bicep to his forearm, "I got away with just this."

"Who. . .?"

"Don't know. . . maybe Hamid's men, maybe someone else. . ." I stared dumbly at him. He wasn't ruling out the possibility of his son pulling the trigger on him.

Umar Butt tugged at my sleeve insistently. "We must go. This is too risky."

I stood up and took my leave, thanking the gracious family. Habla Bano hugged me and showered kisses on my cheeks and forehead. "Come back soon," she said smiling.

Then Ghulam Mohammed took my hand and thanked me. "No, no, thank you, takleef muaaf," I had said, feeling acutely embarrassed. Gadda's sisters stood at the door giggling shyly.

"What's your name?" I asked Gadda's brother as he bade me farewell.

"Fayaz Ahmed Butt."

"What do you do?"

"Nothing now, but I used to be an SPO."

I was shocked. "How were you a Special Police Officer? What about your brother?"

He smiled. "We didn't get along after he became a militant. I didn't want him to become one. Then later when I joined the police he sent messages threatening me," he shook his head. "He once even put out a contract on my head. And then the police would hassle me. Never trusted me. Where's your brother? How should I know, I'd tell them, I hate him. But they didn't believe me and it got too much so I chucked it up."

We looked at each other a long while before I asked, "Well, what would you like to do now?"

His eyes lit up, "Join the police, of course."

5. The gates

He held the blue box up to the light, twirling it slowly as one would a precious jewel, reading: "LOP. . . CHUUU. . . . Phhlowery. . .Orange. . . Pekoe.. Bahh, Bhalo! Wonderful!"

"Happy Diwali, Babaji."

"Oh, aaj ke Kali pujo? Then Happy Diwali to you, too."

I had looked for him all over. He wasn't among his pile of ghee tins in the pavilion and I was starting to worry when I saw a bundle of rags and wooden staff under a chinar. I noticed his feet were covered by a pair of cloth shoes he'd obviously made for himself and those, together with his patchwork gown made him look like an ancient druid. He lay happily in the dappled sunlight, gnarled hands folded across his chest, chewing cud the way very old people tend to do.

"But you better take this back and drink it for me. There's no one here to make it, and I'm too old to do it myself."

I start to insist, calling a BSF jawaan from the kitchen at the back and explaining how to make a decent brew, when the silent meditator appears. The fierce one. We greet each other. He ignores my namaste and embraces me, thumping the wind out of my lungs at the same time. He gesticulates frantically, pulling me behind him back to the Babaji. I give him my notebook and pen so that I can understand him better. *Don't bother about the tea. Take it back. There's no point. He has no* SELF, he writes in English.

I smile, shrugging my shoulders. "My name's Sonia. When your penance, your maun vrat is over, I'd like to talk to you?"

In another month.

The Babaji stirs, opens an eye and says, "Don't talk to him. He's a Pandit. All Pandits are rakshasas, ogres of the highest order."

The man throws back his head and laughs silently. Then he snatches the notebook and writes for a long time before handing it back for me to read.

> My name is SWAMINATRI. I was a press correspondent. Worked for local papers and some foreign papers & lastly UNI. Then I went to the Film and TV Inst. Won international award for my film, 'Never on a Sunday.' Worked for some time in Bombay. Then joined TV, working as ASD News Doordarshan Directorate, Mandi House. I am still a member of the Press Club.
>
> P.S. After retirement facing the odd circumstances here in Kashmir I am now devoted to "Mother".

I look up from the notebook and find him beaming at me. I can't wait to hear the whole story.

"Do you know why there is no peace in Kashmir, Sonia?" Babaji suddenly asks.

"Well, I guess because of intransigent attitudes, no one wants to give an inch." I venture.

"No. The deeper reason?"

I invite him to continue by keeping quiet. I know he's dying to tell me.

"Because this is Kali and Bhairav's place!" he says triumphantly. "Vishnu. Now the places that belong to Vishnu are more or less peaceful, but this belongs to Kali and to Shankar, to Mahakal. There have to be cycles of destruction. Shankarji's dancing the tandav now, and the waters turn black, the Goddess is upset, the waters turn black. But one day, you'll see, the waters will clear. You'll see."

We look instinctively towards the little shrine in the murky waters. There among the yellow and orange marigolds, on the head of the Goddess, perch a pair of exquisite Himalayan bulbuls. I laugh aloud with delight. This is miracle enough, this place: the Gangkhai, this courtyard with the enormous chinars, the clouded spring, the wonderful old men, and now the birds.

"What's the time?" Babaji props himself suddenly on a frail elbow.

"A quarter to one."

He leaps up with amazing alacrity and gathers his things.

"What's wrong, Babaji? Where are you going?"

"I'm late. It started at 12:30"

"What? What's started?" I cry out after the swiftly receding figure dodging behind the trees.

Just then a sudden gust of wind sussurated among the leaves of the great chinars so that the voice that came back was tiny and broken, but I could've sworn it sounded like: "My. . .fav. . . ourite tee. . . veepro. . .gramme. . . Nev. . .ermissit. . ."

6. The path

It is autumn and I'm hovering somewhere between the 9th and

14th centuries, recovering some of Kashmir's rich past in my explorations of ancient sites and still more ancient people—amateur historians, mythologists, anchorites, all. It is truly fascinating and far more engaging than the dreadful accounting of killings and tortures that has occupied me all year. The weather is gorgeous. Brilliant sunshine and a cold that nips pleasurably. The gigantic chinars and poplars are turning to rust and gold. Great flocks of sheep and long-haired goat swarm down from the high pastures, flooding the plains, drowning the highways so that even now, on this road to Ganderbal. . .

Sonia Jabbar is a writer, journalist and peace activist who divides her time between Kashmir, Calcutta and New Delhi.

Originally published in Civil Lines 5, *2001.*

Amira Hass

Missing in action

. . .

The simple room was adorned with a gallery of photographs showing the men of the family. I was in the house of supporters of the Popular Front, once considered the vanguard of Palestinian secularism. The daughter-in-law who entered the room was in an advanced state of pregnancy, held an infant in her arms, and was all of eighteen years old. "Why are there no pictures of women on the wall?" I asked her later. "That's the custom," she said. "It would be a disgrace to show their faces," she explained. "After all, men come to visit, you know."

In my years at Gaza, I almost never wrote about women's inferior position in Palestinian society and its emotional and intellectual consequences. I was hitched to the tireless hunt for breaking news, and the newsmakers were men. The IDF redeployment, Arafat's arrival—these were decidedly male events. The organization heads I interviewed were men; the military and religious leaders, the unionists, the politicians, the economists were almost exclusively men. Even most of the journalists, photographers, sources, and drivers were men. Like a skulk of foxes, we would streak after the male architects of the day's headlines and events. In the pursuit I failed to report on a compelling dynamic: in a patriarchal society such as the Gaza Strip, women's absence from public life becomes a motivational force in itself. Hidden away at home, cut off even from one another, women began to organize themselves; openly, timidly, they had begun to confront their domestic oppression, forcing it into the public and political spheres, bringing it into the light. Feminist developments and expressions had been prominent during the intifada. Women's committees, for example, set up learning centres offering classes in reading and writing and courses in sewing, juice making, and other ways to support a family. Centers like these, coupled with the sudden transformation of many women into household heads while their husbands were in jail, encouraged women to speak out, come forward and make demands of society and the men who dominated it. Unfortunately for me, a woman journalist, I arrived in the Strip at a time when this dynamic was on the wane.

I learned that the distinction between the public and the private domains was carefully observed, even within people's homes. As a guest, I often felt like a *jasusa*, a collaborator, when, with a wave of his hand, a husband or a brother would order the women to make me coffee, or when I, the Isreali guest, joined in a conversation about politics or work while the women were excluded. Or when I sat on the men's side of a length of cloth separating us from the women's area, or when the woman preparing the refreshments would call to her husband to pull himself away from the clouds of cigarette smoke and come get the tray, or when we'd all troop out to visit some interesting people and the women would stay behind to take care of the many children. Every so often, I'd say something about how the men sat around at home during the curfew or when they were unable to work, not lifting a finger while the women did all the household chores.

In Gaza, women's absence from public life is as conspicuous and tangible as their presence at home. As a journalist, I lived most of my life outside, in the world, and realized that I actually knew very few women. Those I knew well, those who had talked to me about their lives, were awake to women's inferior status in Gaza and were part of the effort to remedy it. I would like to believe that their awareness and protest was emblematic, that Palestinian women everywhere were chafing at their constraints, but I had too few such conversations to be able to generalize.

M.H. from the Khan Yunis camp is a determined feminist active in the Popular Front. A thiry-five-year-old mother of four, she lost her job in a kindergarten when it ran out of money to pay her. M.H. grapples with her simultaneous absence and presence in public life. She is clear-headed and vocal about her pain and anger. I once heard a story about a woman who tried to make a match between her engineer son and M.H., a traditional match in which the engaged couple would not meet until their wedding. M.H. was staunchly opposed to arranged marriages but still turned the mother down politely and pleasantly. When the mother refused to give up, M.H. picked up a table, according to her delighted friends, and dropped it at the startled woman's feet. The mother fled and with her all the other potential matchmakers.

At the Islamic University, where M.H. studied biology in 1985, she and her girlfriends organized a Popular Front rally commemorating the massacre at Dir Yassin in 1948. But the Islamic distaste for Communists proved stronger than the national cause and M.H. and her friends were denied permission. The rally went ahead in spite of the university's opposition, and M.H. was eventually expelled.

M.H.

As a child I dreamed of being a fighter like my father and brothers. At ten years old I already had a brother in an Israeli jail, one of the first men to be imprisoned in the Seventies. My father was an officer in the Egyptian police intelligence. When the Israelis took over in 1967, they insisted he continue working in intelligence, but he refused along with eleven other men, preferring to stay at home even though he had no work. Now they are all working for the Palestinian Authority.

So the role models were the men in my family. My mother was shut up inside the house all the time, which might be why I felt I had to resist, to get out, although I didn't really analyze things at the time. I just knew that something was wrong. Whenever my brother went outside, my mother would say I was a girl and had to stay at home. It was always like that, all the way through school. Once I graduated and went to university , it became a little easier, though. But I was the only one of my sisters to behave this way. They said I was strange, aggressive, stubborn. I'd fight with my mother to let me join in the protests, to let me go out in the street with the other kids and demonstrate.

In a way, fighting the occupation led to feminism. It also taught me to not just obey blindly. I watch my sisters obeying orders and I see their lives, which are so difficult. On the other hand, maybe it's easier for them because they don't know what it's like outside, they don't know what they're missing. Still, they're jealous of me sometimes. They ask their husbands why I can make decisions when they're not allowed to. And they ask me why our men make all the decisions. They always tell me that I'm strong but my answer is that we all possess strength.

For example, my sister complains that her husband gives all his wages to his parents. If she needs money she has to get it from them. So my sister is oppressed by her husband and her mother-in-law. Lots of women have to get permission from their in-laws as well as their husbands when they want to visit their families.

Things began to change with the intifada. *During curfews the women instead of the men went out to bring home food. When the soldiers tried to grab at the children, the older women would argue with them, even fight with them. Traditionally women are not allowed to open the door, but during the* intifada *it was the women who opened the door to the soldiers. So our society began to get used to behaviour that had always been considered improper. Also, the men weren't bringing in as much money so the women were encouraged to go out and look for work, to grasp more freedom for themselves.*

And this affected relations in the family. When I was working at the kindergarten, I felt I had more of a role, that I was in a stronger position, I was listened to more. Now I'm not earning anything and my role is weaker. When I want to buy something I have to explain it to S., my husband, because he hands out the money. Now I can't make my own economic decisions and I feel ashamed and angry. S. is relatively okay, but his Middle Eastern way of dealing with things sometimes really irritates me and it makes me rebellious. If we have a decision to make, he always wins because he's the man. When I agreed to marry him, he promised that I could go on studying, that he'd share the chores at home, and that I could carry on being active in the Women's Committee. Now he complains when I'm away from the house and I have to keep reminding him of his promises. Sometimes he apologizes. Still, his attitude is different from that of most men and it's really noticeable. My mother and grandmother told me their husbands always treated them badly and stopped them from doing all kinds of things. Now I understand that my mother was always depressed, especially when she had to live with her husband's parents. They constantly meddled in the way we were brought up.

I began to think about my needs maybe after I got married. Actually, when I thought about myself before that—beyond activism at the university—I realized that I had to get married, the demands of my society made it unavoidable. I wasn't crazy about it—S. asked me three times before I finally agreed at the age of twenty-two, which is considered late.

Most of my friends waited like me, but my sister got married at sixteen. Even now, her husband overrules her on everything. He treats her like a little girl whose only job is to bring children into the world. Getting married so young means the man can remake the woman, actually brainwash her. Sometimes my sister's husband really bullies her and she runs away to our parents.

One time when she was staying at our parents' house, I convinced her not to go back home before our father spoke with her husband. Since our father's signature is on the marriage agreement, all the problems are brought to him. He was angry at her the first time she ran away and sided with her husband, ordering her to go back to him. But when her husband began hitting her, our father took her part. S. and I argued about it. He tried to rationalize the way my brother-in-law behaved, saying that the economic difficulties were making him act badly. This really upset me and we kept arguing until he got fed up and said, "Okay, your sister's not wrong and neither is her husband."

Since Oslo, the atmosphere has changed a little. There's some encouragement for women to work outside the home, but mostly in the towns, not in the refugee camps. Nothing has changed in the family, though. In fact, we've even lost ground. There's no work for men, so they escape the house, the children, and the wife. It's hard for them to deal with the family's demands when they can't even help support the household. At the same time, we women feel that we can't complain or make demands either, given the situation.

Now my one dream is to live in a house by ourselves—me and my husband and the children, without the rest of the family. That's all I want. I suppress any other dreams I might have had. When I let myself think about it I feel terribly sad that I'm satisfied to just dream about a house, not about something really for me. And then I just feel the whole sadness of our society pressing down on me and I can't think about myself.

M.H and I left her house to walk among the tin huts and cinder-block shanties of Khan Yunis camp and she quickly covered her head with a *mandeel*, a scarf. At the university she covered herself up to the eye-balls, she told me. "Here, even if I go out covered with long pants and a long-sleeved blouse, people still call me a *safra*, a barefaced woman disobeying Islamic law, so I certainly can't go without the *mandeel*. I don't really care enough to fight for the right not to wrap up. Actually, it bothers me that people on both sides think it's so important. If the social pressure dies down, then I'll take it off."

. . .

An aside

"You mean, you're Jewish?" the women would say, lowering their voices and swallowing the last syllable. With their limited experience of Israel and Israelis, it was the women of Gaza who tended toward surprise and discomfort when they realized that yes, I was in fact Jewish. Sometimes they would direct the question to my friend or my host, whoever had brought me into their circle. "You mean, she's Jewish?" Their gaze would drop and their tone would falter, confused and uncertain, and the word "Jewish" would come out in a whisper, mostly from good manners, I felt, from a wish not to offend with a probing, delicate question, in much the same way that many Israelis tend to clear their throats and hesitate before saying "Arab."

Early on in Gaza I decided to confront the touchy question head on and told people right away that I was both Israeli and Jewish. Reactions ranged from hushed embarrassment to an open and direct response that dispelled any awkwardness. As it happened, those who rose to the occasion with humour and ease usually turned out to be Popular Front supporters. At one home in Khan Yunis I was sitting with a group of aunts, sisters, and grandmothers shelling peas. "And I thought you were Italian," one aunt said when I told her that I came from Tel Aviv. "Hey!" she called out. "We've got a Jew here!" Then she moved toward me in a self-mocking pantomime of the violent Palestinian and we all laughed. At a vegetable stall in the Faras Market the young man serving me asked the inevitable question. I remember the day was particularly tense—Israeli forces had assassinated an Islamic Jihad man and retaliatory attacks had followed. To make things worse, a bout of cholera had broken out in the Strip, meaning even more restrictions on exporting produce. When I answered the man he grinned and with lavish parody yelled to his friends, "Quick, quick, she's a Jew, bring a knife!"

There were always a few Gazans, though, who seemed to have internalised the Israeli image of the bloodthirsty Palestinian and would warn me never to reveal my identity—for my own safety, they said. (One turned out to be a minor collaborator; another was mentally ill, with the papers to prove it.) To all those who worried for my safety I'd tell about my friend Aouni in Shabura, where I often stayed overnight. "Isn't she scared?" his neighbours once asked. "Why, are we so scary?" he said. I'd also mention that many people who readily and publicly spoke to me in my own language, calling out Hebrew greetings in the markets and refugee camps (and still do, even now, when the IDF soldiers are gone from the streets). "Proof positive that there's nothing to be afraid of in Gaza," said Diab al-Luh, a Fatah leader. "Too bad Israelis don't understand that it's nothing unusual, that if they treat us normally then they'll get a normal response in return."

Skewed perceptions are held on both sides, however. At one of my stays in Aouni's house in Shabura, his children, who were all born during the *intifada*, pointed to the TV screen where UN soldiers were driving around Sarajevo. "Jews, Jews," they cried out. Their mother apologized, explaining that the children say the same thing about Egyptian soldiers as well. Until May 1994, at least, uniforms, guns, death and shooting were all associated with Israelis—Jews—and the occupation. "If you're a Jew," said ten-year-old Yihye, "where's your gun?" and added, "If you get an exit permit, will you take me to see my grandmother?"

The negative associations of the word Jew are not limited to the occupation and expulsion, though. "The Quran teaches us that Jews don't honour their agreements," Hamas people told me more than once in connection with the Oslo agreements. "The Quran teaches us that the Jews are our worst enemy."

Mild versions of the same mistrust and antipathy creep into the language of secular Palestinians, too. Once I promised my awowedly secular friend M.S. to sell my car to him if I had to stop driving it in the Strip. Later I began to regret my promise and backed out of our arrangement. "I made two big mistakes in my life," he said with bitter humour. "The first was being born and the second was making a deal with a Jew." When I told R.S., another friend, about some personal worry, he responded, "May it not fall on your head but on the heads of the Jews," and then laughed immediately when he heard himself using the folksy Palestinian saying (which he doesn't agree with) out of concern for me. R.S. is always careful to point out that the Palestinian confrontation is not with Jews but with Israeli society.

At least until the occupation in 1967, Jews were simply strange and other. R.N. was ten when the IDF briefly occupied the Strip in 1956. He remembers running after every Israeli soldier on the street staring intently at his behind. "What on earth are you doing?" his father asked. "Looking for his tail," the child explained. I've heard similar stories from other Gazans who were taught from Egyptian textbooks and who came to feel pretty silly for believing the information. And despite the present familiarity with Israelis, some anti-Semitic myths persist. M.S. tried to explain to me that Jews are a dominant force in the world because they are wealthy. He was taken aback when I reminded him that these assertions (which appear in the Hamas charter) are in fact drawn from writings published in the decadent West.

Ismail Haniye, a leading Hamas activist, attibuted the anti-Semitic parts of the charter to the Palestinians' bitter experience with Jews since 1947, to a defence of the weak against the strong. From Abu Taher, a Hamas friend, I learnt that "Jews' money" means something plentiful that may be freely wasted. "What do you think this is, Jews' money?" he scolded his son for leaving meat on the plate. Once or twice, when I visited Abu Taher's family I made it a point of bringing fruit or chocolate and mentioned that the gift was Jews' money.

In the end, most reactions to my being Israeli and Jewish simply give more proof of how well Gazans know Israel. "Really?" they say. "You're from Tel Aviv?" then the waiter or policeman or student reels off a string of Tel Aviv garages or restaurants or building sites where he worked, the names of his employers, the one who invited him to a family bar mitzvah, the one who came to his wedding, and the one who did his military service in the Strip.

So many of the feelings Gazans have about the Jews are tempered by personal experience and their knowledge of individuals. Every day I'd be reminded that for more than twenty years the Strip was, in effect, an Israeli bedroom community, and the Gazans know that there are many different Israels: the ultra orthodox world of yeshiva students, the slums of the unemployed where Palestinian workers slept illegally, the haute-bourgeoise suburbs where they swept the streets. And I'd be reminded too that while the women of Gaza were fighting their battles at home, the men were learning what they know of Israel, if not in its stores and factories, then in its jails.

Bring home the POWs

Abu Jamil and Abu Nader liked to sit over a plate of hummus at one of the string of beachfront restaurants that had opened in the last few years. Their restaurant of choice was a favourite of mine too, in spite of the food—it was one of the few places a woman could sit alone without people staring. The seashore offered a rare corner of escape where one could watch the fishing boats set sail for the twelve nautical miles open to Gazan fishermen, and turn one's back on the old Israeli military court building and the police headquarters circled by concrete blocks and ugly reels of barbed wire. And now, after the IDF pullback, the restaurant stayed open past 7:00 P.M. and was blissfully quiet, free of the incessant noise from the police loudspeaker, which had blasted Hebrew songs and soldiers' duty schedules throughout Rimaal and al-Shatti refugee camps.

The entreprenuers had built the restaurant, one of the first along the shore, with a loan from a Palestinian investment and development agency, confident that the chronic shortage of pleasure and relaxation, coupled with the needs of Palestinians returning from exile, young people resuming studies, and ex-prisoners who were picking up the threads of their lives, would make the venture a sure success. On a mound rising up from the shore, the owners had laid tiles for a patio and set up large beach umbrellas; one balmy summer day in 1995 I shared a table with Abu Jamil and Abu Nader. The view had changed: several beachfront hotels had sprung up, the military court had been transformed into a Palestinian fire station, and the old police headquarters, stripped of the concrete and barbed wire, now housed "Arafat's orphans", children whose parents had fallen in the pursuit of the PLO cause and whom the chairman had "adopted."

Abu Nader picked at his hummus while Abu Jamil sipped a bowl of lentil soup. For a long moment Abu Jamil held the spoon in the air as his eyes took on a glazed, contemplative look. "This reminds me of the soup in Ansar," he said suddenly, talking about the mass detention camp that Israel had set up in the Negev desert to deal with the popular uprising. I was taken aback by the nostalgia in his voice, a tone I had heard from other prisoners as well. I remembered the time that Jalal, a taxi driver, had picked me up at the Erez checkpoint. As we drove to Gaza City, we discussed the dangerous rift that had developed between Hamas and the Palestinian Authority. Jalal, a four term detainee and dyed-in-the-wool Fatah man, interruped our talk to point out the new sidewalks (paved with flagstones from Gaza) and praise a park near the Unknown Soldier monument, laid out with palm trees and benches. "Look how nice it is," he said. "*Inshallah*, God willing, there'll be plenty more parks like this." He spoke of Abu Amar—Arafat—with love and reverence and talked of his hopes that all these developments pointed to the emergence of a Palestinian state. Then abruptly, without warning, his tone shifted. "How I miss prison!" he cried. "In prison everything was clear. We knew when to eat, what was right, and what was wrong. We knew who was good and who was bad and when our sentences would be over."

Jalal probably did not know it, but he was heir to a long tradition of post-revolutionary disappointment. His feelings were amplified by Ihab al-Ashqar, a leader in the Unified National Leadership of the *intifada*. "A few days ago," he told me, "I went past the prison. I don't know why, but all of a sudden I remembered the smell of my cell in solitary, the mouldy smell it had, and I missed it. It's strange, missing a jail cell, but those were our best moments, when we really felt we were paying the price for defending other people."

I have since heard many prison memories, often full of pride, nostalgia and even affection, but I am no longer tempted to romanticize the Israeli prison experience. True, most prisoners learnt excellent Hebrew and many acquired English as well: some men finished their high school education and some even registered with the Open University for correspondence courses on such things as anti-Semitism and modern European Jewish history. One seasoned prisoner had earned a reputation throughout the Strip for comforting younger men serving their first sentences. A young prisoner had made his name overnight when he managed to smuggle a dozen transistor radios into the prison tent compound. Rousing as these stories are, I soon learned that they only thinly disguise profound regret and sorrow—for lost time, lost opportunities and years of deprivation.

Once, while waiting to interview a senior member of the Palestinian Authority's security forces, I chatted with the man's bodyguards. "I know Israel very well," one said, "I've been all over its prisons." In the course of some ten years of incarceration, he had been shuttled from one prison to another, seven in all, and the list read like a map of the country: Gaza, Ashkelon, Ramle, Beersheba, Nafha, Tel Mond, and Ayalon. His colleague chimed in, telling me that he had served six years. "Only six?" I asked, without thinking." "What do you mean, only six?" he said. "I remember every day of my life that I lost in prison." A similar lapse occurred when I spoke to Fayez Abu Shamalla, who was one of the prisoners released early under the terms of the Oslo agreements, having served half his eighteen-year sentence. "So you gained nine years," I said, immediately wanting to bite my tongue. "On the contrary," he said, "I lost nine years."

For Palestinians, serving time has played much the same role as the Palmach, the Jewish combat corps of pre-statehood days, did in Israeli society: a gruelling shared rite of passage that forged lifelong bonds among a sizable number of Palestinians. By and large, prison has been a male experience that has accentuated the traditional, religion-based separation of the sexes. At the same time, though, it has enlisted and united entire families in support of their absent kin; indeed it is hard to find a family in the Strip that has not lived through the detention or imprisonment of at least one of its members. Every day I meet someone else who has experienced late night arrest, interrogation by Shabak, detention without trial, or long periods in solitary confinement. Since 1967, 280,000 Gazans have passed through Israeli prisons, detention cells and interrogation rooms; 80,000 during the *intifada*, according to the Association of Veteran Palestinian Fighters and Prisoners. In Gaza ex-prisoners rub shoulders with each other all the time, at every public and private venue. Prison memories, prison gossip, and prison slang crop up in every conversation. In time I came to learn which men had shared a cell, who had gone on hunger strike with whom, which of the prisoners' representatives had abused their powers, who had jumped ahead in the bathroom line, and which men had refused to share their food parcels from home.

For all the talk of jail, however, most ex-prisoners say little about the legacy of trauma, precisely because the experience is so common and widespread, and also because Gazans rarely talk about the emotional aspects of their hardships. Palestinians who have spent years with twelve other men in a tiny cell or a leaky tent in the Ansar detention camp are rarely willing to talk much about the damage to their spirits, taking pride instead in their maturity and fortitude, in the unity of their group. In conversation, they quickly move on to their new lives, saying how pleased they are to be working. Only very few men will acknowledge the disparity between their successful reintegration into public life and their haunted personal lives, their difficult adjustment to a world that went on without them.

"You're not the man I married," Ibrahim Abu Nada's wife told him three days after he was released from jail. "The words were like a knife in my soul," Abu Nada confided, but they alerted him to the crisis among his fellow ex-prisoners and their families. "If there are one thousand prisoners, then there are one thousand wives who have been hurt," Abu Nada said. He spent a year in an Israeli jail; many Gazans have been imprisoned for much longer. Some men yell at their wives, some hit them. Many spend nights with their friends, away from home; their quick tempers are ignited by the children, who find it hard to get along with their fathers. "My son doesn't come to me for money. He goes to his mother, because that's what he did when I was in prison," S. told me with a bitter smile.

. . .

"What makes a good soldier?" I asked Rafat al-Najar, who was released from Ansar shortly before our conversation. Every morning at six the Ansar prisoners would be made to gather in the square near their tents for roll call; they would wait, kneeling on the ground, their bodies bent over their knees, until every prisoner in all the sections and blocks had been accounted for. "A good soldier doesn't deliberately drag out roll call to make it harder for us," Najar said. "A good soldier doesn't point his rifle down our throats; he lowers the barrel." One good soldier pinched cigarettes and coffee from the supply room and threw them into the prisoners' compound when their supplies ran out. The soldier was eventually tried and jailed, but the inmates who were called to testify denied that he had ever done any such thing, Najar recalled fondly.

Some soldiers and prisoners developed friendships, and their stories have become occupation folklore. There is the soldier who wanted an ex-prisoner from Gaza to attend his wedding, but the Strip was under curfew. So the soldier recruited other soldiers, his friends, on a mission. They stole into Gaza in an army jeep, collected the Palestinain friend from his home in the Khan Yunis camp, covered his head with a blanket as they approached the checkpoint. "Where are you going with him?" the checkpoint guards asked, indicating the Palestinian. The soldiers in the jeep said in whispers, "It's okay. We're taking him in for interrogation."

Over time, I heard the same story with slight variations from diverse sources. It had left the realm of historical truth, I believe, and become a symbol of something greater than a friendship between any one soldier and prisoner. The story and the way it spread reveal something about a fantasy and a wish to put aside national enmity. In prison there were opportunities to see the Israeli not as a two-dimensional monster but as a complex human being. This seismic shift required a new approach, not only between individuals, but also politically.

In those jails where Palestinians were locked up together with criminals, that is, Jewish prisoners, they came to have an even more nuanced view. "I like Israeli criminals," my lawyer friend Raji Sourani once declared. "They have style." He waved away my scepticism. "In 1985 I was in Beersheba prison. We were separated from the criminal inmates by a partition between our two wings, but we could hear each other and pass things back and forth. I heard someone calling, asking for a few cigarettes and I threw over a couple of packages. He asked my name, thanked me, and that was that. The next day he said, 'Hey, friend, tell me what you guys need.' I told him: 'Women.' But he persisted. He wanted to know whether we had a radio, and then newspapers and a radio appeared out of nowhere. A week or two later I had an argument with a jailer who really infuriated me and I was about to hit him, a serious offense. The criminal guy called over and calmed me down. The next thing I knew the guard's face had been slashed."

It was this kind of first-hand knowledge of Israelis that began to undermine some Palestinians' belief in liberating all of Palestine through armed struggle. In prison Abu Shamalla discovered what he calls "a people that wants to live". Until then he had thought that Israeli and Palestinian existence were irreconcilable. A.I. began to distinguish between Israeli qualities and flaws: "In Israel, talented people are given the opportunity to develop their abilities. That's how Israel has progressed so far in such a short time. But the Israelis talk about democracy and human rights when they don't respect them. A democratic person treats other people democratically too, even his enemies."

Others like Abu Mustafa reached understanding through the many books they read in prison. "I gained knowledge and came to the conclusion that we needed to do things differently. I hadn't known that Israel had an atomic reactor, for example. I didn't know that Israel had the best weapons in the world. I didn't know that the whole world was helping Israel, even our own Arabs."

Amira Hass lives in Ramallah in the West Bank, where she covers Palestinian affairs for Ha'aretz. *In 1999 she received the international World Press Freedom award in recognition of her work in the Gaza Strip.* Drinking the Sea at Gaza: Days and Nights in a Land Under Siege *(1996) is her first book.*

Excerpted from Amira Hass, Drinking the Sea at Gaza *© Amira Hass. Translation copyright © 1999 by Metropolitan Books. Translated by Elana Wesley and Maxine Kaufman Lacusta.*

Anisa Darwish

Ramallah
October 15, 2000

Dear Ahmad,

It is nearly dark now and I have just drawn the curtain over the window in our bedroom. This curtain is all that shields us from whatever Psagot settlement will throw our way. Psagot is now a military base, complete with tanks stationed on top of the hill, facing us. One wonders if this has not always been the settlement's raison d'etre.

As the sun sets, young men, in ill-fitting (most likely donated), military attire patrol the neighbourhood. They look so vulnerable. They pretend to be fearless and manly, but project a kind of childlike defiance. They could very well be my own children; they can't be older than eighteen or twenty. I cry from weakness.

It is difficult not to be haunted by death in these circumstances. I'm not really worried about myself. I'm 60 now. In Palestine, this is about as old as anybody can expect to live. But I do worry about my son. Life has already taken much away from him. Here, disability is a kind of living death. Mostafa knows about the "other" death as well; his grandmother died three years ago. So now, he looks to me for reassurance time and time again: will we be alright? We're not going to die are we? I do my best, but he will not be reassured. This intense violence has trapped him in a world of fear and I'm helpless to break him free. At times like this, I am only a mother: I curse the war: those cheering the butchery and those sharpening the knife. Arab leadership has turned the "stone" into a symbol of the new Arab awakening. Is the cleansing force that will wipe away all past shame and failures.

Have you noticed the language they used to describe the Uprising? In pro-Uprising interviews, they call for the need to "impregnate" the Uprising so it can "give birth" to honour. This honour will be the new flag of Arab leadership. For without the sacrifice of blood, they ask, how can we wash away a history of defeat and weakness?

I look outside the window onto Satah Marhaba, our neighbourhood. Whoever thought of such a name: (Welcome Plane)? I remember twenty years ago when we built our home here. The area was still undeveloped with only a few houses scattered on top of this beautiful hill. Since then, a mosque has been built, and for a time it seemed that poetry and religion did not make good neighbours. But we found a way of living together. I let my creepers run wild on the fence around the house, and a green barrier has since kept the peace. Now, Israel, like a mad bull, is kicking up clouds of horror as it charges at our homes. Every night, the people in our neighbourhood and in every other "contact zone" go to bed unsure if they will live to see daybreak.

In the darkness, I see my parents. Father looks on sternly as if to say, "This will come to nothing". Mother, Mariam, as serene as her namesake, Mary, seems more optimistic. Maybe there is a chance for peace, she seems to say. Maybe Palestine will rediscover itself as the land of wheat and wine and prayer. I see the forced, slow trek of the first Palestinian migration of '48, when terror-struck people fled their homes and villages. I see our second hijra: the treacherous journey East across the River Jordan after the defeat of '67. My family crossed the River back in a hasty, but equally perilous return. All the cease-fires, agreements and handshakes that follow suddenly become like a whirlwind that draws me in and I'm left tearful and completely drained.

Do you know what really saddens me? It's that all my papers and books are in one place and if that room is hit, all those words, all that passion that inhabits me will be blown away. How can life be so cruel!

Ahmad, if Sharm al- Sheikh falls, pray for us, for Psagot is "heavy" with its weapons and we are the welcoming plane.

Much love,
Anisa

Ramallah
December 4, 2000

Dear Ahmad,

Life in "contact zones" is becoming harder and harder. The shelling has muted most sounds of life. The place feels like an abandoned film-set: activity, hustle and bustle have been replaced by a ghostly stillness.

Families in "contact zones", too old or too young to throw stones, sit the night out in a dreary, "safe" corner somewhere, while shelling is followed by shooting, then more shelling. At least those able to shoot or throw stones feel empowered to resist, despite their efforts being met by death or injury. We can only keep our heads down and wait for the storm to pass, while TV screens flicker images of more dead, more funerals, more leaders telling us of the nerve of our blood-thirsty enemy. Some have despaired of ever feeling safe again. Some have despaired of a resolution.

You can't believe what a nightmare it is trying to get from one town to another. Until a few days ago, we managed to get from Ramallah to Jerusalem using rough, dirt "roads" through fields. The Israeli army has now blocked even these improvised passageways with mountains of soil. Access to other West Bank towns, like Nablus, is more dangerous. To avoid being turned back by military road-blocks, people are taking the Israeli bypass roads. The normal journey of 40 miles, from Ramallah to Nablus, now takes two and a half hours. More worrying than the difficulties of getting from town to town is the danger from settler attacks on these roads. Settlers lurk, waiting to ambush unlucky Palestinian travellers. You can imagine the effect all this is having on the Palestinian economy, let alone the other aspects of life.

There has been uprooting of trees by the Israeli army near all the contact zones. They claim there is a "danger" that Palestinians could use these trees as cover when throwing stones at Israeli soldiers. Hundreds of ancient olive trees and orange trees have been cut down. This year, people went olive picking despite the risk of attacks from settlers and the army. This should have been the best olive harvest for years. But now, the Israeli army will not even allow people to transport their jars of olive oil. It is tragic that after all that hard work, people are unable to sell or properly store their harvest. For many, this was a long-awaited income which they are now denied. Day-labourers who used to work in Israel have been hardest hit by Israeli measures. As the West Bank and Gaza are closed off, labourers are unable to get work. Lack of work means that thousands of families are without food. These are the hardest of times.

I should tell you the rumours about ammunition smuggling. Apparently, some Israelis are smuggling in bullets for Palestinians. But the irony is they will only sell us a small amount. In rare, happy moments, Palestinians joke that the smugglers are keeping to the Oslo Peace Accords which limit the amount of ammunition Palestinian policemen are allowed to have. The other joke is the talk of a Palestinian resistance that will match that of Hisb Allah in Southern Lebanon! We could never be on par with Hisb Allah, with no support from a strong Arab state and no freedom of movement.

People are worried that plans are underway for some kind of settlement that will neither guarantee us a homeland, nor the security we now crave. It seems very unlikely, given the present situation, that we will be offered anything other than a mock version of an independent state. Israel is obviously the stronger military force, and we seem wrapped up in dreams and fantasies. As long as brute force is allowed to rule and as long as we, like Cinderella, continue to wait for the fairy godmother with the magic wand, others will continue to draw our maps for us.

I am so pleased you telephoned this morning and your letter was a bonus. We are parched for contact with the outside world. Your words help me forget all this pain for a while. They take me back to the good old days and the things we used to talk about. Think of us.

Much love,
Anisa

Ramallah
December 28, 2000

Dear Ahmad,

It's Eid today, the first Eid in this Intifada. And it's only daybreak, but the sound of group prayer has already travelled the short distance from the mosque to my window. "Allaho Akbar, Allaho Akbar" arrives with a mixture of the worldly and the spiritual: continual and rhythmical, it is the music of the faithful ritual. But "Allaho Akbar" also comes low-pitched and strained. It is almost like the lunar calendar had caught these men off-guard and here they find themselves, celebrating, while still pressing on fresh bullet wounds to contain the pain.

The neighbourhood children are up. One or two are even already dressed in their Eid best and are strutting around, chewing sweets: perhaps some things never change after all. I, as all women, will get up to cook and to stay brewing Eid coffee: bitter by custom. You know I still cannot work out why after so many generations, we do not even consider drinking sweet coffee instead. And how did this tradition start in the first place? Do you think we drink bitter coffee to commemorate hijra, to remind ourselves of flight, this essential element of Palestinian identity?

Well, the first to migrate of my children, Ashraf my son, has not remembered to ring, or is it that Eid hasn't happened yet in the US. I wonder if there is still time for Eid in that postmodern space. Hala, my daughter, has just rung. Maybe women experience hijra differently, maybe there is something about the experience of femininity that can better equip the self to find some anchor. Either that or she still remembers Eid because her hijra has only just started and Palestine is still a home to which she could return. Mostafa, as you know, is still in his "philosophical" mood. Horror has taken its toll on him, left him uninterested in speech. And so he sits muted, watching Eid go by.

Ahmad. I've just come back from a short visit to the Palestinian soldiers stationed near the house. They are part of what is now termed, "the national guard" set up to protect citizens who live in "contact zones". I put on the traditional dress, some make-up (and even high-heeled shoes!) to mark this as a special event. One of the soldiers needed to help me step inside the hastily assembled "room" they live in. "Khala(aunt) Anisa", they all shouted in surprise and greeting as I stepped in. In that moment, all the cynicism that I am burdened by, the cynicism of all writers, just disappeared. As we sat on the floor of that obviously poor but clean and tidy room, I felt so proud of these young men who had nothing to offer but their Palestinianness. For a brief time, I felt at peace with myself and this cruel world. Back home, I cried hot tears for them, for us all.

In the respite that Eid provided, we sand-bagged another window. If this is peace, Ahmad, let us not consider what war will bring.

Much love,
Anisa

Ramallah
January 1, 2001

Dear Ahmad,

Last night marked the passing of another year. Today is the anniversary of the founding ("launch" as it is known) of Fatah. Ramallah is such a sight with large numbers of people, many brandishing guns, crowding all public spaces. It's a strange, sad scene of celebration: what a tight space this is for a large dream! On TV, Palestinian officials are doing what officials usually do, saying, without enthusiasm, what officials usually say. The whole scene is one of boredom and frustration.

A friend telephoned late last night to wish us a happy new year. He then asked in a shy voice if the shells that shook his house a few moments ago landed near us. It was difficult to know as the noise seemed to come from all directions. This is everyone's concealed horror, that if shells hit your neighbour's house this time, your turn is next.

Bulldozers on the Star of David settlement on the hill facing us from the East were busy all day yesterday, digging and erecting more guard posts fitted with even larger searchlights, beaming at us now 24 hours a day. We've been busy ourselves today, sand-bagging the windows in the downstairs flat, which we now call "the shelter".

You know, I can hardly remember a time when we felt anything other than fear, when we were happy or when this tight feeling in my chest felt unusual, something that would pass. This cycle of recurrent nightmare has coloured everything black. A new category of "being" needs to be invented to describe Palestinian life where all beginnings are aborted, where there is more presence of death in life, where any respite is bordered by flight. Is there still meaning when all life is a narrative of martyrdom?

Ahmad, do you remember the "good old days" when the only electric lights in town were the lamp-posts on the road, when writers used to suffer the gestation of ideas under the light of oil lamps? The image haunts me. Was it the last chapter of the history they wrote?

I will not write more. I think I have over-burdened you and you have your own narrative to write. But perhaps fate is kinder in Oslo and vision is less constrained. Perhaps you have some hope of "resisting" your "Palestinianness" and existing outside this dark text.

Much love,
Anisa

Ramallah
May 1, 2001

Dear Ahmad,

I am so happy you faxed today. In fact, the fax machine is the only object left in this empty space that used to be my office. My books had to "emigrate" after last night's shelling from Psagot settlement. The room wasn't very badly damaged. A bullet pierced through one of the windows, tore the curtain, bounced against the wall and splintered. This is the seventh bullet to do this over the past few weeks and we've become experts at unravelling bullet behaviour! I was worried, though, that the next bullet will be one too many before the whole room goes up in a blaze. So, I'm writing from my books' makeshift home downstairs. I'm still looking for a safe place for other personal things I keep in the office: an old scarf that belonged to my mother, that I draped over one of the walls, a rosary and a very old rug. I kept all these in an attempt to "counter modernity" and to keep faith with the past. I feel I've left a whole world behind. Objects apart, how could one transport laughter or anguish or all the words one has said, the history of a place, as it were, that you know lingers unseen, like scent?

The fifty-third anniversary of the Al-Nakba or War of 1948 is in a couple of weeks. With a group of other writers, I attended a meeting today organized by the Ministry of Information. Representatives of the media and civil organisations were also invited. The meeting was part of a consultation about how best to commemorate this catastrophe. Cynics would say there is no need to remember an event when there are live reminders of it every day. In fact you could say the Israeli "celebrations" have already started with last night's shelling. My daughter, who is visiting from the UK where she now lives, discovered that she wasn't as brave as she thought. She huddled in a "safe" corner and struggled not to shake with fear. This is nothing like the terror of the occupation she grew up with. Then, if you took shelter in your home, you had a chance of not being harmed. This aggression is naked and unashamed and will find you no matter where you hide. But here is an anecdote to cheer you up. As we switched on TV to the local station (as we normally do when shelling commences to get information about what is happening), there I was on the screen in an old recorded interview about my poetry! We were stunned as the station provided minute-by-minute accounts about the shelling outside, in subtitles! You could say this surreal event is representative of how Palestinians now live. We are determined to live a normal life even when we know that at best, this is a form of heroic defeat.

As far as the political situation is concerned, we do not know where we are anymore. We hear talk of a return to negotiations, but the shelling continues. It is clear you can no longer trust the Israelis, nor it seems can they trust us. Within this uncertainty, it is impossible to imagine what tomorrow will bring: an Intifada that will continue for many years? A regional war? Do we have any chance to win a war? You look at young Palestinain faces and you see old people, defiant perhaps, but prematurely aged all the same. Nearly eight months of siege, poverty, unemployment and an undeclared war have left visible marks on this nation.

Ahmad, a voice from a "normal" "out there" is like a cool breeze in a hot, dusty desert. Keep writing and think of us.

Anisa

Letter to Hala

March 28, 2002

My dearest Hala,

Two days of desert storms have covered everything with sand. The skies are dark with atoms of sand still suspended in the air. This has been the best the skies could do in place of spring rain. Witness to so much pain, they seem to have dried up, leaving the earth thirsty and sore.

As the sun sets, I am gripped by foreboding. Something feels wrong, dangerous. I know it is only a feeling, but I still look around trying to locate a source. I am almost faint with what seems like an irrational fear when the phone rings: the Israeli army is advancing on Ramallah. Suddenly alert, I rush to remove the glass panes from the windows and check our "emergency" list: candles, bread, jugs of water, medicine. As I hurry, I recall images of the Second World War from documentaries I had seen on TV: the earth shaking with the weight of marching troops, so much death, blood, devastation and skies dark with the smoke of debris and suffering.

We huddle in a corner of the house as the tanks and armoured personnel carriers thunder past like beasts hungry for human flesh. What protection can the light of a candle, or even the wall of a house offer against such armoury?

We switch on to the local TV news channel to find out what is happening. We mute the sound so we can hear as much as possible about what is going on in our neighbourhood. We watch in silence as our story, the story of all of Palestine, begins to unfold before us. The images are too surreal to be real: are we awake or dreaming? We watch as our lives turn into a kind of silent drama, as TV cameras travel from street to street. We see tanks demolishing, with apparent ease, the walls of homes. We see armoured personnel carriers throwing up masses of soldiers into the darkness. Infiltrators, tools of death, they occupy schools and people's living rooms and use the rooftops of homes and the minarets of mosques as sniping points. Shells light up the night sky, smoke billows from buildings. This is the law of the jungle; all that is beautiful and sacred is being violated.

I turn from the TV screen to my son's face, distorted with fear, and to my own dishevelled appearance. My mind wanders to an image from another war that has never left me, that of a mother looking in horror at the body of her child, raped by soldiers in an old church. I realise in this moment there is nothing I can do to protect my son should harm come our way. I could appeal, call for help. But what appeal will be of use when injured people are left on the streets for dogs to pick through, when people are hunted down and shot for the crime of wanting to live in safety in their own homes.

The world watches too, and is silent, as history and all that is sacred, mosque, church and Wailing Wall, explode with the body of a teenage girl into a million pieces. It seems the world has decided that some crimes can go unpunished, or is this the process of "democracy" in a new millennium, redrawing the map of the world?

I fear no hope is left for the younger generation, let alone for people like us, your father and I, in our sixties, or for Mostafa, who has suffered 42 years of disability.

It is unlikely that dawn will break up this darkness for a while yet. We love you, dearest Hala. Try not to worry.

Your mother

Anisa Darwish is a Palestinian female poet and writer whose life and writings are marked by experiences of displacement and war. Born in 1940 in the village of Malha in Jerusalem, Anisa's family emigrated to Jordan during the war of 1948. She was educated in Jordan and returned to Ramallah/Palestine in 1960 with her husband and family. With the start of the war in 1967 she and her family again sought refuge in Jordan, leaving behind their home and possessions. Within a year they returned to Ramallah and she has lived there ever since.

Anisa published her first book, a collection of poems in classical Arabic, in 1991. Since then she has seven other collections, two of which are in the Palestinian Arabic dialect. She has also published her autobiography, two collections of experimental prose writings and a Journal of the Al-Aqsa Uprising. *Some of her work has been translated into English and Hebrew. Recent translations appear in* Bitter Oleander *Literary Quarterly, Spring 2002. Anisa is a member of the Palestinian Writers' Union.*

Excerpted from Tinatol Waja, Diary of the Al-Aqsa Intifada, *Translated by Hala Edwards.*

Lena doesn't live here anymore

Since 1967, 6,000 Palestinian houses have been destroyed, rendering some 30,000 Palestinians homeless. The Israeli government claims that these homes were built illegally, and justifies its demolition of them. This is hypocritical: in three decades of occupation, Israel has issued virtually no building permits to Palestinians, while construction in the Israeli settlements has gone on and on—in blatant defiance of the fourth Geneva convention on human rights. It is the settlements that are patently illegal, not the Palestinian homes, built only to accommodate their growing families.

Bat Shalom helped initiate the "Israeli Committee Against Home Demolitions", a coalition of Israeli peace and human rights organizations, to educate and advocate vigorously on this subject.

Yesterday was a day I won't ever forget. Neither will Salim and Arabiyeh Shawamreh or their six children. We had planned a joint Israeli-Palestinian protest against home demolitions. The idea was to set up a tent on the site of a demolition, a tent that would serve several purposes: protest, solidarity, documentation, and compassionate listening to the family members. We planned to move this tent from site to site, wherever the Israeli army used its bulldozers. Yesterday's inauguration of the tent was planned for opposite the so-called "civil administration" headquarters—the nerve center of Israel's control of the occupied territories—those who actually do the dirty work of demolishing people's homes and other acts of oppression.

Our bus from Jerusalem held activists from several peace movements—Bat Shalom, Rabbis for Human Rights, Gush Shalom, and Peace Now. We are all partners in a coalition called the Israeli Committee Against Home Demolitions, and our demonstration was to be held jointly with the Palestinian Land Defense General Committee.

Through the bus microphone, I listened to Meir Margalit

explain the action and sketch one chilling scenario. "If the soldiers try to prevent us from holding the demonstration, proceed in an orderly manner to the planned alternative site. There must not be violence on our side, but if the army engages in violence, do not separate from the Palestinians. The army will be more brutal to the Palestinians if the soldiers manage to separate us."

It was a sobering thought as we drove across the Green Line and toward the protest tent. Suddenly a call came across a mobile phone and Meir took the mike again. "We have just had word that a demolition is taking place at this very moment not far from here." It's a rare occurrence to catch a demolition in progress, no less with a group of peace activists; most demolitions take place with virtually no warning, and hence no time to protest.

With no further discussion, we turned toward Anata on the edge of Jerusalem, a town composed almost entirely of Palestinian refugees who had lived in the Old City of Jerusalem and fled in 1967. They thought they had found refuge in Anata.

After driving the narrow unpaved streets of Anata for what seemed an interminable time, we finally located the area and the bus parked as close as possible. We still had to walk 10 minutes down narrow, zig-zagging dirt roads between crowded homes until we came to the outskirts of Anata. There we practically ran toward the edge of the hill and looked below—a beautiful home set into the pastoral valley with one of its walls now crumpled into rubble by a roaring bulldozer; a family and neighbors sobbing nearby; and a unit of Israeli soldiers preventing anyone else from approaching the scene.

The scene was horrific. We surged down the hill in our small group until the soldiers blocked our progress with their guns and bodies. There were scuffles trying to get past them, but more soldiers joined the barricade. M.K. Naomi Chazan who was with us demanded to see the order proclaiming this a "closed military zone", as the soldiers claimed, and after several long minutes the officer complied. Who knows if the order was genuine or invented at the last minute. But the guns were real.

So there we stood on the side of the hill and watched with an unbearable sense of helplessness as the "civil" administration's bulldozer took the house apart wall by wall. He drove through the front garden with a profusion of flowers and a lemon tree and slammed the front door as if he were God Almighty. Backing away, he slammed again until the entire front was shattered and dangling from metal rods. Then he came from every side, slamming and crashing his shovel against the walls. Finally he lifted off the roof, barely suspended, and sent it crashing below. When that was done, he went around the back of the house and crashed through all the fruit trees, including a small olive stand. He saw a water tank on a platform and knocked that over, the tank tumbling down and a cascade of water drenching the trees now uprooted and broken. He saw two more tanks nearby and knocked those over as well. I have never seen anyone in the Middle East deliberately waste so much water. Then he noticed a shack in the corner of the yard and he churned over to that, his cleated treads grinding and squealing over the rubble he had to climb over. The shack was an easy swipe for his shovel, and we were surprised to see two doves fly out, one white and one black, frightened out of their wits. They flapped their wings briefly and landed not far from their former home.

All the while, a crowd of Palestinian neighbors and young men were gathering behind us on the mountain crest, cat-calling and jeering. From our Israeli group, many engaged the soldiers in challenges: "How can you sleep at night?" "Is this what is meant by defending Israel?" "Don't you understand the immorality of this action?" and the like. Every single soldier, from the high commander to the lowest GI responded the same way: "This is legal; we're only following orders." One woman tried to yell at the bulldozer driver every time there was a lull in the din. But nothing we could think to say stopped the roar of devastation. By then I had managed to move down past the soldiers and was with the family outside their former home. One woman was sobbing and I put my arms around her. When I began to cry too, she put her arms around me. A weeping girl joined us and we both encircled her with our arms. I later learned that this was 14-year-old Lena and this house had once been hers.

Then suddenly, gunshots rang out. Some of the young Palestinian men had begun throwing stones—from a very great distance, I note—and Israeli soldiers retaliated by opening fire and running up the hill after them.

The soldiers were shooting as they ran, setting off their guns like the wild west. I saw the commander and told him that this was illegal, a clear violation of the "open fire regulations" of the Israeli army, which stipulate that a soldier's life be in danger before he opens fire. I demanded repeatedly that he tell the soldiers to stop. The commander shrugged and didn't bother answering. After 10 minutes or so, the shooting stopped.

Amazingly, no "stray" bullets had hit any of our group, although the Palestinians, as usual, were not as lucky. A man approached the crowd of neighbors, said a few words, and instantly two women let out piercing shrieks and tore up the hill, running at top speed. The son of one of them had been hit by a bullet. I don't know his condition. Already in the hospital was Arabiyeh, the mother of the family, who had been violently struck by soldiers when she tried to prevent them from destroying her home.

By then there was nothing to do but sift through the rubble. I picked through the rocks and talked to Jeff Halper, who is organizing the program to "adopt" Palestinian families whose homes are slated for demolition. Jeff had sat in the living room of this home last week, now a pile of jagged concrete slabs, hearing Salim and Arabiyeh talk about the problem of Palestinians not being issued construction permits. "Just last night," Salim had told Jeff during the demolition, "friends and family had sat in this home watching the World Cup soccer game." Now there are six children without TV, toys, books, diapers, bottles, or a place to lay their heads. Instead, they remain with the trauma of the Israeli bulldozer turning their home and security into a bottomless pit of hatred for this Occupation and the people who carry it out.

For the first time, I noticed the scenery around us. On a nearby mountain—not a distant one, mind you—were the classrooms and amphitheater of the Mount Scopus campus of Hebrew University. Had they looked out their classroom window, the students studying ethics and justice could have had a clear view of the scene of brute power and the trampling of this family's lives. And surrounding everything, on mountains and hilltops to our left, right, and center, were the bright orange rooftops of the settler homes in the Occupied Territories. The settlers have no problem whatsoever in getting construction permits. And no one would dare uproot their olive trees, waste their water, harm their homes, or turn their children out into the streets. A lot of us picked up olive branches from the yard as we walked back to the buses. Most of the branches, like mine, were crushed by the treads of power run amuck.

Well, it's almost over, this long, sad story, but it must not end here.

Our group, the same people and more I hope, will be going back next Friday to begin rebuilding this home. This is a new tradition of non-violent resistance that began a few weeks ago, and is gaining momentum. The Palestinians rebuild, the Israeli army demolishes, and they rebuild again.

As one of the neighbors said, "We'll see who lasts longer."

Gila Svirsky has been a member of Women in Black since its founding in 1988. She is co-founder of the Coalition of Women for a Just Peace, which brings together nine Israeli women's peace organizations, and has staged a number of dramatic acts of resistance to the Occupation. Svirsky has been executive director of Bat Shalom and chairperson of B'Tselem, two leading peace and human rights organizations. For six years she served as director in Israel of the New Israel Fund, a foundation that works to strengthen democracy in Israel. This year (late 2002), Gila Svirsky and Sumaya Farhat-Naser, a Palestinian woman, will jointly be awarded two major prizes in acknowledgement of their efforts for peace: the Hermann-Kesten-Medaille, awarded by the P.E.N. Association of Writers in Germany, and the Solidarity Prize of the City and State of Bremen.

7
Women Against War

Statement

September 12, 2001

WOMEN IN BLACK

In the aftermath of the terrible attack on New York and Washington on September 11, we urgently call on those with responsibility and authority, in our national governments and international institutions, to step back from war.

Our hearts go out to those people who have lost family and friends, and our deep sympathy to those injured. Those who perpetrated the violence must be brought to justice under international law. But we strongly believe the urge to vengeance must be resisted. A war waged by the US and its allies will cause the death of many innocent people, will destabilize many governments and societies, and its long-term effects on relations between countries and regions of the world will be disastrous.

Terrorism cannot be defeated by such means. We have to ask why so many people around the world have felt mixed feelings in response to the suffering of the US. While poverty and hunger, injustice and exploitation, are experienced by so many, and the policies of the rich countries are seen as contributing to them, genuine despair will sometimes turn to desperation, and will fuel terrorism.

We urge all political and military authorities, national and international, to turn away from strategies of war and combine their efforts in seeking strategies for an inclusive, just and equal global society. Without that, we will never see peace.

Women in Black: London; Edinburgh, Scotland; New York; Mendocino, California; San Franscisco, California; Toronto, Canada; Seville, Spain (Mujeres de Negro); Madrid, Spain (Mujeres de Negro); Bologna, Italy (Donne in Nero)

WLUML, *Women Living Under Muslim Laws, France*

Women for Peace, Switzerland and the group from Basle, Switzerland
Grupos de Mujeres, Zaragoza, Spain
Peace Group, Denmark
Inizjamed (Mediterranean Cultural Initiative), Malta
Sabrang Communications, Mumbai, India

Statement

Barbara Lee

In the US House of Representatives Barbara Lee was a minority of one, voting against giving the President power for military attacks. She is an African-American Congresswoman from California. Below is the text of her statement of September 14, 2001.

Mr. Speaker, I rise today with a heavy heart, one that is filled with sorrow for the families and loved ones who were killed and injured in New York, Virginia, and Pennsylvania. Only the most foolish or the most callous would not understand the grief that has gripped the American people and millions across the world.

This unspeakable attack on the United Sates has forced me to rely on my moral compass, my conscience, and my God for direction. September 11 changed the world. Our deepest fears now haunt us. Yet I am convinced that military action will not prevent further acts of international terrorism against the United States.

I know that this Use-of-Force Resolution will pass, although we all know that the President can wage a war even without this Resolution. However difficult this vote may be, some of us must urge the use of restraint. There must be some of us who say, let's step back for a moment and think through the implications of our actions today—let us more fully understand its consequences.

We are not dealing with a conventional war. We cannot respond in a conventional manner. I do not want to see this spiral out of control. This crisis involves issues of national security, foreign policy, public safety, intelligence gathering, economics, and murder. Our response must be equally multi-faceted.

We must not rush to judgment. Far too many innocent people have already died. Our country is in mourning. If we rush to launch a counter-attack, we run too great a risk that women, children, and other non-combatants will be caught in the crossfire.

Nor can we let our justified anger over these outrageous acts by vicious murderers inflame prejudice against all Arab Americans, Muslims, Southeast Asians, or any other people because of their race, religion, or ethnicity.

Finally, we must be careful not to embark on an open-ended war with neither an exit strategy nor a focused target. We cannot repeat past mistakes.

In 1964, Congress gave President Lyndon Johnson the power to "take all necessary measures" to repel attacks and prevent further aggression. In so doing, this House abandoned its own constitutional responsibilities and launched our country into years of undeclared war in Vietnam.

At that time, Senator Wayne Morse, one of two lonely votes against the Tonkin Gulf Resolution, declared: "I believe that history will record that we have made a grave mistake in subverting and circumventing the Constitution of the United States. I believe that within the next century, future generations will look with dismay and great disappointment upon a Congress which is now about to make such a historic mistake."

Senator Morse was correct, and I fear we make the same mistake today. And I fear the consequences.

I have agonized over this vote. But I came to grips with it in the very painful yet beautiful memorial service today at the National Cathedral. As a member of the clergy so eloquently said, "As we act, let us not become the evil that we deplore."

Barbara Lee was first elected to the House of Representatives for the Ninth District of California in a 1998 special election. She came to Washington after serving in the California State Assembly 1990–96 and the California State Senate 1996–98. Throughout her political career Congresswoman Barbara Lee has sought to bring her training as a social worker to bear on the problems and challenges that confront the nation and the world. She has worked to build bipartisan coalitions to provide for the basic and inter-related needs of all people: health care, housing, education, jobs, and the quest to create liveable communities in a peaceful world.

Urgent appeal

September 17, 2001

VIOLENCE AGAINST WOMEN IN WAR NETWORK, JAPAN

A call for global solidarity against global war

We categorically reject the retaliation war of the United States against the terrorist attack and we demand a peaceful solution. We demand:

1. The United States government should call off the preparation for the retaliation war against the international terrorist attack.
2. The Japanese government should not cooperate with the United States military policy.
3. The United Nations should establish International Criminal Tribunal to prosecute and punish the perpetrators of the terrorist attack.
4. The racist attacks against Arab people should be stopped.
5. A just and co-existent world should be created in order to eliminate the root causes of terrorism.

We, VAWW-NET Japan and our friends have addressed the issue of Japan's war crimes committed in the 20th century. Our objective is to create a violence-free 21st century. We are deeply shocked at the terrorist attack that occurred in the first year of the new century, and we are frightened by the United States government call for the retaliation war.

We express our profound condolence for thousands of loss of lives and share grief of those who have lost their loved ones. This attack may be an unprecedented tragedy in American history in which so many Americans perished in a single day. What the tragedy implies, however, is that security policy of the world's largest military might did not protect their citizens. The center of its economy and the military power were so vulnerably destroyed. Yet, even before the perpetrators are identified, President Bush called it "acts of war", and announced the military attack in revenge and vowed the United States will win this war of "good versus evil," and "civilization versus barbarism." We express our uncompromising rejection to the retribution by force.

This terrorist attack is an international crime, not a war. This carnage is a crime against humanity. The crime needs to be brought to justice at the International Criminal Tribunal which the United Nations should establish: the perpetrators and the accomplices need to be prosecuted and punished through due process according to international law. However, President Bush declared that the United States and its allies would destroy not only terrorist groups but also the states which aid and harbor the terrorist groups, ignoring the role of the UN. A budget of 40 billion dollars is now allocated for the military strategy. Isn't this act of President Bush a violation of international law? It is a renunciation of democracy and the rule of law—the very pride of the United States. We oppose this belief of the United States leaders—violence against violence. Violence does not eradicate terrorism. Violence only produces more violence. The history has proven it. Peaceful means is the only way to end the cycle of violence.

The United States media fans the emotion of the public towards the direction of the Third World War as the public opinion overwhelmingly supports the use of force. We wonder whether the United States citizens who support the retaliation ever thought of the reasons why they were targeted. The victims of this tragedy are the victims of the mistaken foreign policies of their own government. The victims include a number of people from other nations. We recall the millions of deaths of not only other Asian people, but also of Japanese citizens caused in the Japanese war of aggression in the last century.

People of the world remember that the United States has killed thousands of thousands more people in the world—in the Vietnam War, in the Gulf War, by aiding the dictatorships in South America and in Asia, by bombing Sudan and former Yugoslavia, and in supporting the Israeli government who continues occupation of the land of Palestine. In the present time, it is the United States which propels globalization that has caused enormous economic disparities between wealthy and poor nations, environmental destruction, and armed conflicts. The United States government rejects international cooperation on such issues as global warming, nuclear non-proliferation, establishing International Criminal Court, and the UN World Conference against Racism. Peoples in the world feel outrage and even hatred against the United States. We also recall that the United States itself has provided terrorist groups with weapons. These are the causes of this terrorist attack. Without addressing these root causes, terrorist attacks would never be eliminated. It would remain "the weapon of the weak."

A woman from an Asian nation has written to us: "I wonder if Americans know how devastating a war is." She suffered the war waged in her own land. If one feels enraged at the loss of thousands of Americans, would not she/he think of the possible loss of lives of women and children in such nations as Afghanistan? Those people would be killed in the war that the United States is about to initiate. Should not these deaths be prevented? The military attack against Afghanistan will certainly cause more deaths among 4 million people who have already suffered from hunger caused by the United States economic sanctions. We are also concerned about violence against women in the case when the ground troops are deployed.

As Americans were plunged into sorrow, these people would experience the same. Is it true that the victims of the terrorist attack would want such cruel revenge? Is it true that their souls may rest in peace by another tragedy? We do not believe that hatred nationalism is what they want. The lives in the non-western world need to be protected as much as the lives in the western world need to be protected. This belief lies in the heart of democracy and in the principle of human rights—the "civilization" that the United States values.

We have heard that people of Arabic origins in the Unites States are now facing vicious racist violence. We demand such violence be stopped immediately. At the same time, we are encouraged by receiving "other voices," many statements against war from United States citizens of conscience. We want to act in solidarity with those who courageously pursue peace in the midst of patriotic warlike chauvinism. NATO nations' support of the United States military attack is, we perceive, an expression of repressive means against peoples in the South such as Muslims. The NATO support of the United States government is a refusal of the reflection on their past of imposing colonialism. It denies the efforts to reform unjust North-South inequality that exists today. We hope civil society in the West takes action for peace, not the use of force.

As Japanese citizens, we are deeply concerned about the Japanese government's support of the United States government. The Koizumi administration already decided to modify the Self Defense Forces Law in order to protect the United States military bases located in Japan. It already talks about establishing the emergency preparation system and deployment of Self Defense Forces to keep public order. Right wing nationalists abuse this tragedy to implement the Guidelines for US-Japan Defense Cooperation system to cooperate the United States military action. This is a major step to turning Japan into a nation capable of waging war. We are apprehensive that violence against women may worsen in Okinawa where the United States military bases are heavily located and the function of which will be intensified. We, again, express our strongest rejection to proceeding on the road to militarization and to cooperating war. We shall not cooperate any military action to kill. We steadfastly stand for the principle of our peace constitution.

We must prevent a global war by any means. It will be a global war of the "North"—the United States, Europe and Japan—against the "South." These nations of the "North" have promoted globalization that has caused a rising of fundamentalism and nationalism worldwide. People in the "South" especially suffer from these effects of globalization, and they resist globalization. We appeal to citizens of the world including United States citizens of conscience to unite and oppose the globalization of war by our "globalization" of solidarity. Our deep belief firmly stands in the philosophy of non-violence that denies all forms of violence. We ask women all over the world to work together to create a 21st century of peace, not to repeat the century of war.

Yayori Matsui
Chairperson of VAWW-NET Japan

Statement

September 21, 2001

WOMEN LIVING UNDER MUSLIM LAWS (WLUML)

In search of justice, human rights, and a just peace

The network Women Living Under Muslim Laws wishes to extend its deepest condolences to the aggrieved, their families, and the people of America following the crimes against humanity that were committed on September 11, 2001. Our sorrow is particularly heartfelt because many of those linked through the WLUML network have directly experienced terror and the devastation that goes with it, and also because of our links of solidarity with allies in the women 's movements and other progressive people in the US.

We know that indiscriminate violence and terrorism by state and non-state actors is a global phenomenon. We are particularly aware of the human cost of terrorism and war, frequently perpetrated in the name of religion or belief systems. However, we regard all of these as assaults on the principle of respect for civilian life.

Vengeance is not justice

We urge the US and their allies not to pursue fruitless retaliation with military force. The world must focus on transparent investigation and bring the perpetrators to justice under the principles of international law through an appropriate forum such as an International Criminal Court (ICC). Violence cannot eradicate terrorism. Many people in our communities are deeply distressed by these events but many are at the same time also angered by the poverty and deprivation, injustice and exploitation they experience; they are also angered by domestic and foreign policies that they perceive to be hypocritical. All of this can fuel extreme and violent attitudes. Ending terrorism requires addressing the roots of global inequality.

Misguided retaliation?

It is WLUML 's experience that terrorism in the name of Islam is a transnational force. Politico-religious movements across the world are reinforcing each other through funding, military training, educational exchanges, joint international lobbying, etc. The profound impact on women can be seen, for example, through restrictions on access to education and limitations imposed on freedom of movement as well as changes in family laws that severely curtail women 's legal rights. And yet the current focus of retaliation is against one person and one country. If the US is talking about taking action against "those harboring terrorists " it should consider that the US and the UK have both become safe havens for those who openly advocate violence against those who do not share their opinions. For example, Anouar Haddam, a leader of the Algerian Islamic Salvation Front, is currently seeking asylum in the US and numerous politico-religious extremists are operating out of the UK. Human rights concepts such as freedom of expression have been misused by some international human rights organisations as well as manipulated by governments and co-opted by politico-religious extremists, thereby giving unwarranted space and credibility to such views. Also Saudi Arabia has been bankrolling extremist *madrassahs* in Pakistan where many Taliban supporters are being trained. It should be remembered that bin Laden and the Taliban emerged in the context of Cold War confrontation and the vacuum of its aftermath. Global reaction should not be determined by US political and economic interests alone. We are concerned that legitimate grief is being exploited as a cover for increased military spending—weapons that are aimed mainly at civilian populations. Such military action will cause further suffering to civilians elsewhere. After twenty years of war, Afghanistan is already destroyed while the intended "targets" have escaped. Furthermore, bin Laden and the Taliban are not in Afghanistan. The consequences of demonising "the other" have already increased, resulting in violent attacks on innocent individuals. Talk of "crusades" is buying into the agenda of the perpetrators, at the risk of world war. Already the situation has given public exposure to previously unheard-of fringe groups. And already there have been moves towards sweeping restrictions on civil liberties under the guise of this crisis. In those countries which will bear the brunt of any military action, the space for alternative positions will vanish. People may find themselves forced to make choices which they had no say in formulating. Any military action will destabilise an already unstable and nuclearised region. Women in Muslim countries and communities, in particular, may suffer the direct impact of militarisation and a potential backlash from politico-religious movements.

Signed by 270 women living under Muslim laws.

Women Living Under Muslim Laws (WLUML) was formed during the years 1984–85. It is an international network that provides information, solidarity and support for all women whose lives are shaped, conditioned or governed by laws and customs said to derive from Islam. The Network aims to increase the autonomy of women by supporting the local struggles of women from within Muslim countries and communities and linking them with feminist and progressive groups at large; facilitating interaction, exchanges and contacts, and providing information as well as a channel of communication.

Letter from Rigoberta Menchu to President George Bush*

September 23, 2001

Mr George Bush
President of the United States
Washington DC
USA

Esteemed Mr President:

In the first place, I want to express solidarity and condolences to all of your people regarding Tuesday, September 11th. After hearing about the painful events that occurred in your country, I would also like to share my indignation and condemn the threats inherent to those terrorist acts.

During the past few days I have been paying attention to the development of events and trying to the best of my knowledge to respond to the aforementioned events with reflection, not obsession; with sanity, not anger; seeking to search for peace, not revenge. I have called upon the conscience of all the people of the world, the media, eminent personalities with whom I share an ethical obligation to peace, and the heads of state and of international organizations, so that wisdom illuminates our acts.

Nevertheless, Mr President, upon listening to your address to Congress last night I was not able to repress a sensation of fear at the message expressed through your words.

You call on your nation to prepare itself for "a long campaign like we have never seen before." You call on your military to save the nation's pride, marching to a war that attempts to unite all nations of the world.

* *English translation by Beth Baltimore*

In the name of progress, pluralism, tolerance, and liberty, you do not leave any option for those of us who do benefit from having the good fortune of liberty and the fruits of civilization that you want to defend for your nation, and those of us who never sided with terrorism since we were its victims. There are no options for us who are proud expressions of other civilizations, who live day by day with the hope of converting discrimination and pillaging to achieving recognition and respect, who carry in our souls the painful genocide perpetrated against our peoples, us who, in short, are tired of providing the victims for other nation's wars. We cannot share the arrogance of your infallibility nor the single path down which you wish to push us when you affirm that "All nations in all regions should make a decision now: either you are with us or with the terrorists."

At the beginning of this year, I called upon the men and women of the planet to share a Code of Ethics for a Millennium of Peace, demanding that: there will be no peace if there is no justice.

> There will be no justice if there is no equity.
> There will be no equity if there is no development.
> There will be no development if there is no democracy.
> There will be no democracy if there is no respect for the identity and the dignity of peoples and cultures.

In today's world, all of these values and practices are very scarce; nonetheless, the unequal manner in which they are distributed only feeds impotence, hopelessness, and hate. The role of your country in the actual world order is far from being neutral. Last night we were hoping for a prudent, reflexive, self-critical message, but what we heard was an unacceptable threat. I share with you that "the course of the conflict is unknown," but when the belief is that "its result is certain," the only assurance that invades me is that of a new and gigantic futile sacrifice, that of a new colossal lie.

Before you order the assaults, I would like to invite you to think about a different world leadership. A leadership in which you do not need to anguish, but to convince; in which the human species can demonstrate that in the last thousand years we have overcome the sense of "an eye for an eye" that is considered justice by the barbarians that submerged humanity in the medieval dark ages. A leadership in which there will be no need for new crusades to learn to respect those who uphold a different idea of God and God's creations; a sense of justice in which we can share the fruits of progress and take better care of the resources that still remain on the planet, and that no child lack bread or schooling.

With a thread of hope, yours truly,
Rigoberta Menchú Tum

Recipient of the Nobel Peace Prize, Emissary of Good Will of the Culture of Peace.

Rigoberta Menchu Tum was born in 1959 at Chimel, a small Guatemalan village located in Quiche. Witnessing the discrimination and exploitation of the indigenous people, she decided to follow the labour of her father, who was a peasant leader. In 1980, when terror was stretching over her country, she went to Mexico into exile to denounce the atrocities committed in Guatemala and to defend the indigenous cause. In 1992 the Nobel Committee awarded her the Nobel Peace Prize. One year later the Rigoberta Menchu Tum Foundation was born. The institution, whose mission is to bolster the recognition of indigenous peoples' rights and identity, promote respect for human rights through justice and fight against impunity, support a Culture of Peace and contribute to self-managed initiatives, has offices in Guatemala and Mexico City. Rigoberta Menchu now lives in Mexico City due to the reign of terror that still prevails in Guatemala. Among her publications are I, Rigoberta Menchu *(1984) and* A Girl from Chimel.

Statement

October 1, 2001

DIVERSE WOMEN FOR DIVERSITY

We, women of diversity committed to a peaceful world, celebrate our differences. From our differences come our strengths. We come from all the continents, different faiths, cultures and races and are united in our vision of peace and justice in the world today. We want to leave a more peaceful and just world for our children and for the generations to come. We celebrate and uphold cultural diversity. We will defend all forms of diversity and resist all forms of monoculture, fundamentalism and violence from which intolerance and hatred arise.

The tragedy on September 11 has shown us another face of terror.

We join in the pain of all people who have faced the terror of those who do not value the sanctity of human life. We especially abhor the use of human beings themselves as weapons. In this regard the terror of September 11 cannot be viewed as a lone event. Many acts of such terror have been inflicted on the peoples of this earth. The sacredness and dignity of human life and the right to peaceful existence and justice have been destroyed through the fundamentalism of imperialistic globalisation and religious fundamentalism.

Among the many tools of terror in the modern world are:

- economic sanctions that lead to starvation and disease epidemics;
- biotechnologies that threaten the roots of life;
- monocultures that destroy social and biological diversity;
- degradation of the environmnet for monetary gain;
- widespread application of pesticides that lead to deformities and death;
- pollution of soils, water and eco-systems at large;

- the pursuit of profit by global corporations at the expense of sustainable livlihoods, cultural identities, and the right of people to basic necessities of life, including corporate monopolies on water, seeds, food and medicine;
- patriarchy, racism, casteism which negates and violates the majority of the world.

Given the extent of such structural terror in the world it is perhaps surprising that direct terrorist attacks, like that of September 11, are not more common. If we want to end terrorism we must pay attention to all sources of injustice that widen the gap between rich and poor, men and women, nature and humans and create the hopelessness that can lead to terrorism. We stand with those who are working to remove the structural causes of injustice.

Women, children, the differently-abled and the aged are the worst victims of this reign of terror:

- the terror of not having water to drink and food to eat;
- the terror of water and food contamination;
- the terror of losing home, homeland, family and community and becoming a refugee;
- the terror of persistent poverty that leads to the sale of life and body organs;
- the terror of being forced into prostitution as a means of survival;
- the terror of living in communities where drug abuse has become a way of life;
- the terror of losing our children to a culture of violence and to all kinds of conflicts and wars;
- the terror of domestic and other violence against girls and women;
- the terror of living in a society where basic human rights for women are not respected.

We women of diversity pledge ourselves to work against terrorism in all its forms and to work positively towards a world free of war, and call on all nations to boycott pacts of aggression. We invite all women of the world to join us in stopping governments from rushing into a mindless global war. Together we will find peaceful, creative and non-violent ways to end terrorism in all its forms.

We ask all people of the world to stand with us in defending and celebrating diversity, peace and hope.

Signed by 40 women from the five continents of the world, in New Delhi.

Diverse Women for Diversity is a Southern initiative to build an international coalition of women to respond to globalization and its impact by creating diverse solutions at the local level, and a common defence at the global level.

Statement

October 2001

BAT SHALOM

Dear Bat Shalom friends and allies,
Individuals and organizations around the world have been asking for ways to show their support for Israeli women's peace initiatives. We are grateful for the support and concern you have expressed, and now ask you to raise your voices, loud and strong and in great numbers. Please sign (by replying with your name and address at the top of the message) the following petition. Print it out and collect signatures and mail them to Bat Shalom. Help us to ensure that our women's voices are heard by sending a donation that will allow us to publish the petition, in Hebrew and Arabic, in as many places as we can. Let us talk! Let us act!

Let the women talk! Let the women act!

We know that two peoples CAN live in this land. WE know that our children deserve a life of dignity and peace. We do not want our children to be killed, nor do we want them to be killers. We must stop this madness. We must stop the use of brute force.

Let the women talk! Let the women act!

Let Palestinian and Israeli women lead the way. It was Israeli women who changed public opinion about the terrible and pointless war in Lebanon. It was Palestinian women who were courageous enough to engage in joint peace initiatives with Israelis. We the women can find an end to this cycle of violence as well.

Let the women talk! Let the women act!

The men tell us not to be scared. They all tell us to be strong. We are scared, and we want them to be scared too. We do not want to be "strong". We don't want them to think that they are strong enough to make the other nation disappear or go down in defeat and disgrace. We want each and every person to have the right to live in peace and dignity.

We want to share the resources of this land, its water, its vines, and its holy places. Jerusalem can be shared; this whole area can be shared between two independent and equal nations. Israel should not rule the lives of Palestinians. Neither Palestine nor Israel should believe that peace can be won through violence and force.

Let the women talk! Let the women act!

Palestinian and Israeli women have been talking for years about their future here. Tens of thousands of women from around the world have been supporting our vision of making peace. These have been quiet efforts thus far. Now is the time to raise our voices and insist on being heard.

Let the women talk! Let the women act!

Let the women try to make sense where men did not. We are launching an international initiative to stop the violence immediately. We are insisting that all negotiating teams include at least 50% women—in the Palestinian and Israeli leadership, in the UN teams, among representatives of all the governments involved in attempts to resolve this conflict.

The women will talk—they will not shoot.

There are too many men with too many egos involved in burning this piece of land. Let the women talk—we can bring peace.

Let the international community form a group of women from all around the world to become the Women's Peace Corps—an international mediating body of women who will listen, facilitate, help us save ourselves.

Let the women talk! Let the women act!

Bring the women in. The men have not done a good job here.

They talk of a security based in might. We know that security means being good neighbors.

Without forgetting the wrongs of the past, nor the unequal distribution of power, we will focus on how to LIVE here in peace. We do not want the next generation of children to wear uniforms, to go to war. We want them to know self-determination and dignity, without the need to fight for them.

Let the women talk! Let the women act!

We feel the pain, we are outraged, we are scared. Before it is too late—let the women talk.

Bat Shalom is a feminist peace organization working toward a just peace between Israel and its Arab neighbors. Bat Shalom, together with The Jerusalem Center for Women, a Palestinian women's peace organization, comprise The Jerusalem Link.

Statement

October 2001

NATIONAL COALITION OF 100 BLACK WOMEN

We, the National Coalition of 100 Black Women, an organization of African-American women dedicated to advocacy that assembled in Philadelphia, PA, in commemoration of our 20th anniversary, hereby issue this resolution.

Expressing our sympathy with the tragic loss of life on September 11, 2001.

Declaring our hope that the perpetrators will be brought to justice.

Being ever mindful of the historic erosion of civil liberties by our government in communities of color, both here and abroad.

Acknowledging the persistent practice of linking race to crime suspicion as evidenced in the internment of Japanese Americans during World War II, the categorization of civil rights activities as threats to national security and, more recently, racial profiling of African-Americans and other people of color.

Recalling our contributions as African-American women to the struggle for equity, peace, and liberation.

Recognizing the dangers of patriarchy that all women face, and that armed conflict disproportionately affects women and children; affirming the importance of women's voices from all classes in establishing a multinational, multiracial, and multiethnic dialogue toward global justice.

Celebrating the courageous stance of Congresswoman Barbara Lee in being the only representative not to abandon constitutive responsibility in refusing to authorize an open-ended war with neither an "exit strategy or a focused target."

Recognizing the Congressional Black Caucus' role as the voice of the African-American constituency in addressing the particular consequences of this war both in terms of loss of civil liberties and loss of critical resources for education, enforcement of civil rights, and other important social programs.

We therefore resolve to:

1. Commend Congresswoman Barbara Lee of the 9th congressional district for her courageous stand and steadfast commitment to democratic values.
2. Abhor the terrorism to which she has been subjected because she exercised her constitutional responsibility.
3. Encourage African-American women to adopt a race/gender/class analysis on all programs and proposals connected to the recent crisis.

We demand that the Congressional Black Caucus resist all efforts to undermine the civil liberties that have been so critical to our survival as a people and to their very presence as elected representatives.

We stand in solidarity with Afghan women and women throughout the world whose very violent survival hinges upon a nonviolent solution to global conflict.

Adopted Saturday, October 6, 2001

Statement

October 2001

TRANSNATIONAL FEMINISTS

Transnational feminist practices against war

As feminist theorists of transnational and post-modern cultural formations, we believe that it is crucial to seek non-violent solutions to conflicts at every level of society, from the global, regional, and national arenas to the ordinary locales of everyday life. We offer the following response to the events of September 11 and its aftermath:

First and foremost, we need to analyze the thoroughly gendered and racialized effects of nationalism, and to identify what kinds of inclusions and exclusions are being enacted in the name of patriotism. Recalling the histories of various nationalisms helps us to identify tacit assumptions about gender, race, nation, and class that once again play a central role in mobilizations for war. We see that instead of a necessary historical, material, and geopolitical analysis of 9/11, the emerging nationalist discourses consist of misleading and highly sentimentalized narratives that, among other things, reinscribe compulsory heterosexuality and the rigidly dichotomized gender roles upon which it is based. A number of icons constitute the ideal types in the drama of nationalist domesticity that we see displayed in the mainstream media. These include the masculine citizen-soldier, the patriotic wife and mother, the bread-winning father who is head of household, and the properly reproductive family. We also observe how this drama is racialized. Most media representations in the US have focused exclusively on losses suffered by white, middle-class heterosexual families even though those who died or were injured include many people of different races, classes, sexualities, and religions and of at least 90 different nationalities. Thus, an analysis that elucidates the repressive effects of nationalist discourses is necessary for building a world that fosters peace as well as social and economic justice.

Second, a transnational feminist response views the impact of war and internal repression in a larger context of global histories of displacement, forced migrations, and expulsions. We oppose the US and European sponsorship of regimes responsible for coerced displacements and we note how patterns of immigration, exile, and forced flight are closely linked to gender oppression and to the legacies of colonialism and structured economic dependency. Indeed, history shows us that women, as primary caretakers of families, suffer enormously under circumstances of colonization, civil unrest, and coerced migration. Taking this history into account, we critique solutions to the contemporary crisis that rely on a colonial, Manichean model whereby "advanced capitalist freedom and liberty" is venerated over "backward extremist Islamic barbarism." Furthermore, we draw upon insights from post-colonial studies and critical political economy to trace the dynamics of European and US neocolonialism during the Cold War and post-Cold War periods. Thus questions about the gendered distribution of wealth and resources are key to our analytical approach. Neo-liberal economic development schemes create problems that impact women in profound and devastating ways in both the "developing regions" as well as the "developed world." So while middle-class Euro-American women in the United States are held up as the most liberated on earth even while they are being encouraged to stand dutifully by their husbands, fathers, and children, women in developing regions of the world are depicted as abject, backward, and oppressed by their men. One of the important elements missing from this picture is the fact that many women in Afghanistan are starving and faced with violence and harm on a daily basis not only due to the Taliban regime but also due in large part to a long history of European colonialism and conflict in the region. The Bush administration's decision to drop bombs at one moment and, in the next, care packages of food that are in every way inadequate to the needs of the population, offers a grim image of how pathetic this discourse of "civilization" and "rescue" is within the violence of war. We see here a token and uncaring response to a situation to which the US has contributed for at least 20 years, a situation that is about gaining strategic influence in the region and about the extraction of natural resources, not the least of which is oil.

Third, we want to comment on the extent to which domestic civil repression is intrinsically linked to the violence of war. Thus the effects of the current conflict will be played out in the US and its border zones through the augmentation of border patrolling and policing, as well as in the use of military and defense technologies and other practices that will further subordinate communities (especially non-white groups) in the US. Such state violence has many gendered implications. These include the emergence of patriarchal/masculinst cultural nationalisms whereby women's perspectives are degraded or wholly excluded to create new version of cultural "traditions." And, for many immigrant women, other devastating effects of state repression include increased incidents of unreported domestic violence, public hostility, and social isolation. In practical terms, policing authorities charged with guaranteeing national security are likely to have little sympathy for the undocumented immigrant woman who is fleeing a violent intimate relationship, unless her assailant fits the profile of an "Islamic fundamentalist." Thus we need an analysis and strategy against the "domestication" of the violence of war that has emerged in these last few weeks and whose effects will be felt in disparate and dispersed ways.

Fourth, we call for an analysis of the stereotypes and tropes that are being mobilized in the current crisis. These tropes support, sustain, and are enabled by a modernist logic of warfare that seeks to consolidate the sovereign (and often unilateral) power of the First World nation-state. When President Bush proclaims that "terrorist" networks must be destroyed, we ask what this term means to people and how it is being used to legitimate a large-scale military offensive. The term is being used to demonize practices that go against US national interests and it permits a kind of "dragnet" effect at home and abroad which legitimates the suppression of dissent. We also want to inquire into constructions of "terrorism" that continue to target non-native or "foreign" opposition movements while cloaking its own practices of terror in euphemisms such as "foreign aid." Deconstructing the trope of "terrorism" must include a sustained critique of the immense resources spent by the US in training "counter-terrorists" and "anti-Communist" forces who then, under other historical circumstances, become enemies rather than allies, as in the now famous case of Osama bin Laden. We are concerned about the ways in which the "war against terrorism" can be used to silence and repress insurgent movements across the globe. We also emphasize how racism operates in the naming of "terrorism." When the "terrorists" are people of color, all other people of color are vulnerable to a scapegoating backlash. Yet when white supremacist Timothy McVeigh bombed the Murrah federal building in Oklahoma City, killing 168 men, women, and children, no one declared open season to hunt down white men, or even white militia members. The production of a new racial category, "anyone who looks like a Muslim," in which targets of racism include Muslims, Arabs, Sikhs, and any other people with olive or brown skin, exposes the arbitrary and politically constructed character of new and old racial categories in the US. It also reveals the inadequacy of US multiculturalism to resist the hegemonic relationship between being "white" and "American." Finally, the short memory of the media suppresses any mention of the Euro-American anti-capitalist and anti-imperialist "terrorist" groups of the 1970s and 1980s. A critical attention to the idioms of the present war mobilization compels us to deconstruct other politically loaded tropes, including security, liberty, freedom, truth, civil rights, Islamic fundamentalism, women under the Taliban, the flag, and "America."

Fifth, we recognize the gendered and ethnocentric history of sentimentality, grief, and melancholy that have been mobilized in the new war effort. We do not intend to disparage or dismiss the sadness and deep emotions raised by the events of 9-11 and its aftermath. But we do think it is important to point out that there has been a massive deployment of therapeutic discourses that ask people to understand the impact of the events of September 11 and their aftermath solely as "trauma." Such discourses leave other analytical, historical, and critical frameworks unexplored. Focusing only on the personal or narrowly defined psychological dimension of the attacks and the ensuing war obscures the complex nexus of history and geopolitics that has brought about these events. We are not suggesting that specific forms of therapy are not useful. But the culture industry of "trauma" leads to a mystification of history, politics and cultural critique. Furthermore, therapeutic discourse tends to reinforce individualist interpretations of globally significant events and it does so in an ethnocentric manner. Seeking relief through a psycho-therapeutic apparatus may be a common practice among Euro-American upper- and middle-class people in the United States, but it should not be assumed to be universally appealing or an effective way to counter experiences of civil repression and war among people of other classes, ethnicities, and cultural backgrounds. Signs of the current trauma discourse's ethnocentricity come through in media depictions staged within the therapeutic framework that tend to afford great meaning, significance, and sympathy to those who lost friends and family members in the attacks on the World Trade Center and the Pentagon. By contrast, people who have lost loved ones as a consequence of US foreign policy elsewhere are not depicted as sufferers of trauma or injustice. In fact, they are seldom seen on camera at all. Similarly, makeshift centers in universities around the US were set up in the immediate wake of 9-11 to help college students cope with the psychological effects of the attacks. They tended to assume that 9-11 marked the first time Americans experienced vulnerability, overlooking not only the recent events of the Oklahoma City federal building bombing, but moreover erasing the personal experiences of many immigrants and US people of color for whom "America" has been a site of potential or realized violence for all of their lives.

Sixth, our transnational feminist response involves a detailed critical analysis of the role of the media especially in depictions that include colonial tropes and binary oppositions in which the Islam/Muslim/non-West is represented as "uncivilized" or "barbaric." We note the absence or co-optation of Muslim women as "victims" of violence or of "Islamic barbarism." We note as well the use of those groups of women seen as "white" or "western," both as "rescuers" of non-western women but also as evidence of the so-called "civilizing" efforts of Europe and North America. We see these discursive formations as a result not only of colonialism's discursive and knowledge-producing legacies, but also of the technologies and industrial practices that produce contemporary global media, and transnational financing of culture industries. We seek especially to analyze the participation of women in these industries as well as the co-optation of feminist approaches and interests in the attack on a broad range of Islamic cultural and religious institutions, not just "Islamicist/extremist" groups. Thus we point out as a caution that any counter or resistance media would need to have a firm grasp of these histories and repertoires of practice or risk reproducing them anew.

Seventh, we call for a deeper understanding of the nature of capitalism and globalization as it generates transnational movements of all kinds. Thus, we seek to counter oppressive transnational movements, both from the "West" as well as the "non-West," with alternative movements that counter war and the continued production of global inequalities. We note in particular that religious and ethnic fundamentalisms have emerged across the world within which the repression of women and establishment of rigidly dichotomized gender roles are used both as a form of power and to establish a collectivity. Such fundamentalisms have been a cause of concern for feminist groups not only in the Islamic world but also in the US. Feminist and other scholars have noted that these movements have become transnational through the work of nation-state and non-governmental organizations, with dire consequences for all those who question rigid gender dichotomies. Since these movements are transnational, we question the notion of isolated and autonomous nation-states in the face of numerous examples of transnational and global practices and formations. The recent displays of national coherence and international solidarity (based on 19th and 20th century constructions of international relations), cannot mask the strains and contradictions that give rise to the current crisis. Thus, we need an analysis of the numerous ways in which transnational networks and entities both limit and at the same time enable resistance and oppression. That is, the complex political terrain traversed by transnational networks as diverse as al-Qai'da and the Red Cross must be understood as productive of new identities and practices as well as of new kinds of political repression. Transnational media has roots in pernicious corporate practices yet it also enables diverse and contradictory modes of information, entertainment, and communication. Feminist analyses of these complex and often contradictory transnational phenomena are called for.

In closing, we want to make it very clear that we oppose the US and British military mobilization and bombing that is underway in Afghanistan and that may very well expand further into the West, Central, and South Asian regions. We are responding to a crisis in which war, as described by the George W. Bush administration, will be a covert, diversified, and protracted process. At this moment we call for a resistance to nationalist terms and we argue against the further intensification of US military intervention abroad. We refuse to utilize the binaries of civilization vs. barbarism, modernity vs. tradition, and West vs. East. We also call for an end to the racist scapegoating and profiling that accompanies the stepped-up violations of civil liberties within the territorial boundaries of the US. We urge feminists to refuse the call to war in the name of vanquishing a so-called "traditional patriarchal fundamentalism," since we understand that such fundamentalisms are supported by many nation-states. We are also aware of the failures of nation-states and the global economic powers such as the IMF and the World Bank to address the poverty and misery across the world and the role of such failures in the emergence of fundamentalisms everywhere. Nationalist and international mobilization for war cannot go forward in our name or under the sign of "concern for women." In fact, terror roams the world in many guises and is perpetrated under the sign of many different nations and agents. It is our contention that violence and terror are ubiquitous and need to be addressed through multiple strategies, as much within the "domestic" politics of the US as elsewhere. It is only through developing new strategies and approaches based on some of these suggestions that we can bring an end to the violence of the current moment.

Paola Bacchetta, Tina Campt, Caren Kaplan, Inderpal Grewal, Minoo Moallem, Jennifer Terry.

Transnational Feminists. The authors of this statement are faculty members at varous univversities around the USA. They share interests in transnational culture, postcolonial and ethnic studies, and contemporary politics of gender and sexuality.

Statement

TWELVE POINTS: STOP THE WAR, REBUILD A JUST SOCIETY IN AFGHANISTAN AND SUPPORT WOMEN'S HUMAN RIGHTS

These Twelve Points were developed in exchanges among several women's human rights activists in New York, Asia and Latin America following the September 11 terrorist attacks in the United States. They are intended to suggest alternatives to military action and the cycle of violence, destruction and death. Please use these suggestions in whatever way you find helpful.

The rapidly escalating cycle of violence and retaliation in Afghanistan and many other countries requires a response led by the United Nations and carried out in accordance with international law. A United Nations- led response offers the best hope for assuring justice for the victims of the September 11 attacks and the people of Afghanistan. The women of Afghanistan, long subjected to brutal repression by the Taliban regime, must now be assured a central role in determining the future of their country. The international community must provide the political and economic support necessary to secure a future in which women and all other sectors of Afghani society can fully exercise their human rights. We therefore urge all governments to support and implement the following:

STOP MILITARY ACTION BY THE UNITED STATES AND ITS ALLIES AND ENSURE HUMANITARIAN ASSISTANCE

1. The United States and its allies must immediately halt all military action in Afghanistan. The UN Security Council should explicitly reject any claim that the right of self-defense authorizes further military action by the United States and its allies in Afghanistan and should itself take the necessary

measures to restore international peace and security as outlined below.

2. The United States and its allies should not carry out any military attacks in other states. The United Nations Security Council must explicitly reject any claim that the right of self-defense authorizes further military action with regard to other states and other organizations.
3. The international community must take urgent steps to:
   a) ensure sufficient humanitarian assistance to civilians in Afghanistan and Afghan refugees in neighboring countries, including health care, shelter and food and involve Afghan women's organizations in the delivery of such assistance; and
   b) protect Afghan civilians and refugees, especially women, from violations of their rights.
4. Military, political and economic support for the Taliban or the Northern Alliance from any State or other external source must be halted immediately in order not to prolong the conflict.
5. The UN must take the lead in peace-making, peace-keeping and peace-building in Afghanistan. Among the key elements that should be considered in developing a UN-led response are:
   - brokering ceasefire and peace agreements
   - promoting the broadest possible participation of civil society in peace negotiations, with specific measures for women's equal access and participation;
   - ensuring disarmament and demobilization of all combatants;
   - clearing landmines throughout the country;
   - maintaining peace and security;
   - preventing and responding to human rights violations;
   - stopping arms and drug trafficking; and
   - overseeing reconstruction.

The UN and the authorities of troop-contributing nations must ensure that any UN forces act in full conformity with international human rights and humanitarian law. In particular, the UN and national authorities must take effective measures to prevent and respond to violations against women by UN forces or other actors.

SUPPORT THE REBUILDING OF A JUST SOCIETY IN AFGHANISTAN AND ENSURE JUSTICE FOR THE AFGHAN PEOPLE

6. Peace-building processes should be undertaken at the earliest possible time, with the goals of restoring the rule of law, building sustainable democratic structures representative of all sectors of society, and promoting a just social and economic order in Afghanistan. Steps to achieve these goals include:
   - provision of the necessary political and economic support by UN Member States and regional organizations;
   - promotion of the broadest possible participation of civil society in reconstruction, with specific measures for women's equal access and participation;
   - effective guarantees of the right of Afghan refugees to return under conditions of safety and security;
   - measures to protect the human rights of internally displaced persons;
   - rejection of any attempts by the United States, the United Kingdom, Russia, Pakistan, Iran, or any other government or external sectarian groups to interfere in the processes of reconstruction; and
   - the requirement that decision-making about the use of Afghanistan's natural resources be carried out only when sustainable democratic political and economic structures are in place and the participation of civil society in such decision-making is guaranteed.
7. During post-war reconstruction in Afghanistan, an ad hoc tribunal or other processes compatible with international law must be established to ensure justice for the people of Afghanistan for violations suffered in the past.
8. Specific steps must be taken to secure the full participation of Afghan women and Afghan women's organizations in all stages of peace negotiation and post-war reconstruction, including any transitional government and all processes of justice.

REDRESS THE CRIMES AGAINST HUMANITY COMMITTED ON SEPTEMBER 11 AND ADOPT ANTI TERRORISM STRATEGIES CONSISTENT WITH HUMAN RIGHTS

9. The perpetrators of the crimes of September 11 should be brought to justice using international law and procedures, through their prosecution for crimes against humanity by an ad hoc international tribunal or by an individual State acting in accordance with international law, including fair trial guarantees.
10. Future efforts to prevent and punish terrorism must comply with international law, including all efforts by individual States and the international community as a whole. Among the basic principles that should guide those efforts are the following:
    - Anti-terrorism campaigns must not be used as a means of restricting human rights;
    - The prevention and punishment of terrorism should be carried out under international criminal law and, where applicable, the Statute of the International Criminal Court and international human rights guarantees;
    - All States, and in particular the United States, must ratify the Statute of the International Criminal Court;
    - All States should ratify international treaties against terrorism and cooperate fully in their implementation, including the 1999 International Convention for the Suppression of the Financing of Terrorism; and
    - All States must ratify and implement international human rights treaties, and fulfill their duty under human rights law to prevent and respond to human rights violations committed by private individuals, groups or organizations, or other non-state actors, including extremist groups under their jurisdiction that commit violations in their own territory or other States.
11. Strategies to prevent future terrorist acts should address the root causes of political and religious extremisms. Among those causes are economic policies that create the conditions of poverty and inequality in which terrorist and extremist

groups can find support for their activities and domestic and foreign policies that authorize or condone human rights violations. As a part of anti-terrorism strategies:

- The policies of individual states and the international community should be aimed at alleviating the inequalities in and among States that have been linked to the dominance of free-market policies and trade regimes that favor highly developed countries;
- All States should adopt economic policies that promote the realization of all human rights and the just and equal distribution of economic benefits at the national level and among all States;
- All regional and international organizations for economic cooperation, trade or finance, and their individual member States, should adopt policies that aim at the just and equal distribution of economic benefits among all States and among all groups within national societies; and
- All States should adopt national policies that aim at the full realization of human rights for all sectors of society, including access to health care, housing, education, food, water, and sanitation, without discrimination based on race, sex, ethnicity, class, religion, social or national origin, political or other opinion, language, disability, citizenship, sexual orientation, age, occupation, or other status.

12. In many societies around the world, the politicized use of religion by extremists takes the form of restrictions on women's right to participation in public life, denials of their economic and social rights, and violence and repression in private life. These violations and the extremist beliefs that are advanced to justify them must be addressed by individual States and the international community as threats to the human rights of all persons and to sustainable open societies.

Presented with signatures to US and United Nations officials on October 30, 2001.

Statement

DELHI WOMEN'S PETITION

Women oppose war

"As a woman I have no country. As a woman my country is the whole world."

With most of the world, we the undersigned women's organisations, condemn both the tragic events of September 11 and the war unleashed by the US on the people of Afghanistan as deplorable acts of terrorism. We condemn the slaughter of thousands of Afghans, the destruction of cities, the bombing of hospitals and old people's homes, and most of all the trauma, horror and suffering caused by this war to ostensibly avenge the crimes committed by Osama bin Laden and the Taliban. Victimising thousands of poor ordinary people who have already suffered 23 years of the destruction and devastation of war in no way can wipe out the roots of terrorism.

It is common knowledge that the terrorist groups the US is trying to eliminate were its own creation. In addition, the US has trained, supported, and supplied with arms various groups, invasions, and dictators all over the world. The millions killed in Korea, Vietnam and Cambodia, in Israel's invasion of Lebanon, the 200,000 Iraqis killed in Operation Desert Storm, the thousands of Palestinians who have died fighting Israel's occupation of the West Bank, the millions who died in Yugoslavia, Somalia, Haiti, Chile, Nicaragua, El Salvador, the Dominican Republic, Panama—are all victims of such state terrorism. Nor has the US been alone in this, for in Afghanistan, if the killing squads were financed by the US, the Russian occupation too was responsible for colossal death and destruction.

And it is well known, too, that wherever fundamentalism has taken root, women are among its first victims. In Afghanistan, after the Taliban came back to power with CIA support, it unleashed a reign of terror whose first victims were its own people, particularly women. It closed down girls' schools, dismissed women from government jobs, and enforced Shariat laws under which women deemed to be "immoral" are stoned to death, and widows assumed to be guilty of being adulterous are buried alive.

Oppose religious fundamentalism across the globe

Religious fundamentalism and military aggression are two sides of patriarchy, that aim to seek control and wield power over women and other oppressed sections. The struggle for abortion rights by women in the US and other parts of the western world is a struggle against such fundamentalist governments and policies. The denial of education to women in Afghanistan, acid-throwing attacks on young women to impose the burkha in Kashmir, the attacks by the Hindu Right in India on films depicting lesbian love or the travails of widowhood, are all part of the same orchestrated campaign of religious fundamentalists to terrorise and control women. The women's movement opposes the forces of religious fundamentalism whether they are from the US or Afghanistan or from India or Pakistan because fundamentalist forces in essence trample upon all democratic and women's rights and seek to reverse the gains made by women's liberation movements.

War is patriarchy

We see the violence, death and destruction caused by wars as an extension of the violence we confront daily within the family, in the community, and by the state. We have seen the aftermath of war and related crimes; thousands of women have lived through the burden of bearing the "honour" of the community and nation in war after war. Bruised minds and battered bodies: that is all war achieves. In 1992, more than 20,000 women and girls were raped in the Balkans followed by 15,700 in Rwanda. The disruption of normal life in military situations adds additional burdens and dangers to women's continuing responsibility for subsistence and household provisioning. The militarisation of our societies has made brutalisation a way of life. War films, war toys and video games, and daily violence in films and on television have created a militaristic chauvinistic macho culture. For women, this means an increase in violence within the home and by the "custodians of law." As women, we are deeply concerned about the increased regional hostility, fanning of communal hatred and violence, and the deepening of inequality and prejudices being caused by this war.

The politics of militarisation

The increasing communalisation of politics can lead to more violence and war in both India and Pakistan. In the name of 'security,' the state is already becoming more repressive and intolerant of dissent in both these countries. National security is being used as an excuse for both Pakistan and India to increase their levels of militarisation. National and religious chauvinism built on mutual hostility becomes the binding force to maintain the nation state. It becomes possible, even commendable, to kill, humiliate, maim and threaten citizens of another country, religious or ethnic group, or nationality in the name of preserving the unity of one's own country. The existence of any manufacturing base for armament production in India creates a demand for more and more wars and lays the material basis for Indian dominance in the South Asian region. In the 1980s, India's defence expenditure shot up from Rs. 4, 329 cores to Rs. 14, 500 crores in 1989-90. It is Rs. 66,382 crores (2000-2001) today, which is more than what the central government spends on health, education, women and child "welfare" and other social services put together!! This is also 89% higher than the entire country's expenditure on primary education!! The doubling of the defence expenditure in just the last 5 years in India, the biggest ever increase since independence, shows the priorities of our warmongers in a country in which people continue to die of starvation.

The global arms export market is valued at 54.2 billion dollars of which US controls 50% while Britain and France together control 30%. Russia, China, Germany, Israel, South Africa, Belgium etc., control the rest. Only because weapons of war and huge military machines exist everywhere does genocide/war take place. If organised violence, terror, genocide, wars have to end, the military establishment and also the monstrously big police and toruring apparatuses have to be abolished from the face of this earth. But can one hear even faintly about any such measures from the US and other big powers or any states anywhere?

Whose freedom, whose justice, whose democracy ?

While claiming to fight for freedom, justice and democracy, the USA is itself behaving in the most unjust and undemocratic manner. Their President has the audacity to threaten the world at large with the words, "If you are not with us, you are against us." No nation, organization or individual has the freedom to even express a contrary opinion, let alone act on it. The USA seeks to avenge the tragic loss of 5,000 lives through bombing Afghanistan. But if the rest of the world were to live by the same logic, then who shall we destroy for the 16,000 who perished at the hands of the US multinational, Union Carbide, in Bhopal, the 500,000 Iraqi children who died due to US sanctions, the thousands killed in Vietnam by the US military. . . .? Even after victory was already assured for the US in the 2nd World War they dropped the horrific nuclear bombs on the people of Hiroshima and Nagasaki to demonstrate their awesome killing power to the world. Generations bear the torture and the scars of such irreparable damage. And yet, if this were a concern about peace and democracy, it should start by destroying its own monstrous stockpile of nuclear, chemical and biological weapons. All peace loving people will welcome such a move. But in spite of tens of millions of people around the world, especially in western Europe, demanding total nuclear disarmament, the US and other nuclear countries have turned a deaf ear to this. Western powers and the US have used every violent means to keep their stranglehold over all resources of the world, particularly oil. Often they have used the weapon of economic blockade to starve people to death, to strangulate them economically. This is almost like a permanent class war waged by the rich and the powerful against the poor and the powerless. Hundreds of millions died and are dying in just over five decades after the 2nd WW due to hunger, disease, wars, genocide, violence and due to the poisoning of the biosphere and ecological disasters. Large sections of the media everywhere are of course part of the apparatus to manufacture and force consent for the war in the name of democracy, to spread misinformation, to wage campaigns for the rulers, to whip up war hysteria, rabid nationalism, and hatred of the 'OTHER'. To speak the truth is to invite the wrath of the local global rulers.

We believe that armed conflict can never be, and will never be, a substitute for dialogue. The failure to pursue democratic dialogue is to betray the aspirations of millions, to jeopardise the future and to put into question the very existence of democratic institutions and mechanisms. If we want to end terrorism we need to address all the structured sources of injustices that are increasingly widening the gap between the rich and the poor, men and women, nature and humans and create the pauperization and hopelessness that leads to terrorism. The women's movement seeks to challenge the structures of oppression that people all over face daily:

- the fear of domestic violence within the home
- persistent poverty and the desperation it leads to such as the sale of body and life organs
- the loss of our children to a culture of violence and to all kinds of conflicts and wars
- the loss of jobs, home, homeland, family and community and becoming a refugee
- the invisibility and violation that comes along with being lesbian, gay, bisexual and transgendered in a predominantly homophobic and patriarchal society
- the fear of enforced prostitution as a means of survival
- the fear of living in a society where rape, molestation, female infanticide, widow burning and witch hunting are daily realities
- the authoritarianism of having our voices silenced whenever we dare to protest

THIS IS NOT OUR WAR. WE REJECT IT UNEQUIVOCALLY. WE DO NOT BELIEVE IN THIS WAR FOR IT SNATCHES AWAY FROM US THE MOST BASIC RIGHT: THE RIGHT TO LIVE.

We represent forces that are engaged in struggles and processes based on respect for human life, on yearnings, desires, and dreams for a pluralistic peaceful egalitarian world. We raise our voice for peace and freedom against repression, war, terrorism, and pogromist politics to make the world a better place to live in. We are protesting against this war along with thousands and thousands from the US, Britain, France, Germany, Pakistan, Indonesia, Nigeria, Indonesia, Korea, Japan and India.

FOR LOVE PEACE FREEDOM EGALITARIAN VALUES AGAINST DEATH, TERROR AND WAR!!!

Ankur, Action India, Caleri, Forum Against Sexual Harassment (D.U.), Jagori, Kali for Women, Saheli, Sangini, Stree Adhikar Sangathan

Statement

WORLDWIDE SISTERHOOD AGAINST TERRORISM AND WAR

Not in our name

We women who are Muslims, Christians, Jews, Hindus, Buddhists, Sikhs, Jains and women of many beliefs from the countries that lost lives in the terror of September 11th, unite on these principles:

We will not support the bombing or US invasion of Afghanistan, for it would only punish suffering people, and increase the hatred on which terrorists feed. No military action has ever ended terrorism.

We stand with our sisters in Afghanistan who are suffering and dying under the gender apartheid and sexual terrorism of the Taliban. The world has endangered itself by failing to heed their pleas. We must help them build a democracy that includes women.

We believe the mass murders of September 11 were crimes against humanity that must be prosecuted. All terrorists must be brought to justice. We pledge to judge people by their acts, not the group into which they were born. We will boycott financial institutions that refuse to disclose the flow of funds to terrorists. We will target and expose political leaders who refuse to require disclosure.

To stop the spiral of terror and vengeance, we believe there must be an act as positive as the terrorist act was negative.

Signed by Alice Walker, Gloria Steinem, Jane Fonda, Robin Morgan, Noeleen Heyzer and many others.